Writing with Consequence

What Writing Does in the Disciplines

Howard Tinberg
Bristol Community College

New York San Francisco Boston
London Toronto Sydney Tokyo Singapore Madrid
Mexico City Munich Paris Cape Town Hong Kong Montreal

UNIVERSITY OF CHICHESTER

Senior Vice President/Publisher: Joe Opiela
Acquisitions Editor: Susan Kunchandy
Development Editor: Leslie Taggart
Executive Marketing Manager: Ann Stypuloski
Senior Supplements Editor: Donna Campion
Production Manager: Charles Annis
Project Coordination, Text Design, and
    Electronic Page Makeup: Pre-Press Company, Inc.
Cover Design Manager: John Callahan
Cover Designer: Laura Shaw
Cover Illustration: Bryan Friel, Courtesy of the Stock Illustration
    Source
Manufacturing Manager: Roy Pickering
Printer and Binder: Courier Corporation
Cover Printer: Lehigh Press, Inc.

For permission to use copyrighted material, grateful acknowledgment is made to the copyright holders on pp. 339–340, which are hereby made part of this copyright page.

Library of Congress Cataloging-in-Publication Data

Tinberg, Howard B., 1953–
    Writing with consequence : what writing does in the
disciplines / Howard Tinberg.
    p. cm.
    Includes index.
    ISBN 0-321-02674-8
    1. English language--Rhetoric. 2. Interdisciplinary approach in
education. 3. Academic writing. I. Title.

    PE1408 .T55 2002
    808'.042--dc21   2002070218

Please visit our website at http://www.ablongman.com

ISBN 0-321-02674-8

2 3 4 5 6 7 8 9 10—CRW—05 04 03

808.
042
TIN

For Leah, Miriam, and Toni

·

BRIEF CONTENTS

Detailed Contents ix

Preface. xix

Chapter 1 Writing as Knowing-in-Action 1

Chapter 2 Inquiry: Framing a Question 37

Chapter 3 Scholarship: What Has Been Done Before? 71

Chapter 4 Research: Gathering New Data 139

Chapter 5 Reflection: What Does It All Mean? 205

Chapter 6 Presentation: What to Write? For Whom?
Why? 253

Chapter 7 Action: Drafting, Revising, Editing,
and Distributing Writing 293

Credits. 339

Index 341

CONTENTS

Preface . . . . *xix*

Chapter 1
Writing as Knowing-in-Action .1

   Writing with Consequence 2

   Writing as a Way of Knowing 3

   How We Know What We Know 5

      Participating in Knowledge Communities 6

      The Nature of the Curriculum: Knowledge as
      Distributed into Disciplines 7

   Identifying Six Ways of Knowing 8

      Inquiry: Framing a Question 9

      Scholarship: What Has Been Done Before? 11

      Research: Gathering New Data 12

      Reflection: What Does It All Mean? 14

      Presentation: What to Write? For Whom? Why? 16

      Action: Drafting, Revising, Editing, and Distributing
      Writing 18

   Knowing-in-Action Across the Disciplines 20

      Psychology: "Libidinal Types"/*Sigmund Freud* 21

      Linguistics: "Words and Children"/*S.I. Hayakawa* 20

      Management: "Let Us Entertain You"/
      Mariwyn Evans 22

   EXPLORING GENRE IN THE EXTRA-
   CURRICULUM 23

Casey Martin and the Americans with Disabilities
Act of 1990   24

The Boy Scouts of America   33

Genres in the Public Domain   35

Chapter 2

Inquiry: Framing a Question 37

Asking Interesting Questions   38

Getting Started to Write: An Inquiry-based
Process   40

Taking Stock: Determining What You Already
Know about Your Subject   40

Working with What You Know   43

Mapping and Listing   43

Discovering Detail: Asking Who? What? Where? When?
Why? How?   45

Freewriting   47

Reading to Generate Ideas   49

Education: "The New Counterculture"/
Margaret Talbot   49

Biology: "On Societies as Organisms"/
Lewis Thomas   51

What Do You Need to Know?   54

When Others Ask the Questions   56

Responding to Writing Prompts: A Checklist   58

Responding to Discipline-Specific Writing Prompts:
A Checklist   59

DISCIPLINARY PERSPECTIVE: HISTORY AS
INQUIRY   60

Thinking Like a Historian: An Interview with a
Teacher of History   61

Case Study: Ana Prepares to Engage in a Critical
Inquiry of Columbus   63

Ana's Background   64

Reading the Assignment   64

Organizing the Inquiry   65

FRAMING INQUIRY IN THE EXTRA-CURRICULUM:
MEMOIRS   67

What a Memoir Is and What It Is Not   67

Limiting Your Subject: Knowing How to Ask the
Right Questions   68

Discovering Critical Questions about Which to Write:
A Checklist   69

Chapter 3
Scholarship: What Has Been Done Before? 71

Relying on the Works and Voices of Others   72

Selecting Primary and Secondary Sources   72

Taking Reflective Notes: A Dialectical Notebook   75

Summarizing to Understand Sources   77

Understanding the Format   78

Genetics: "Viable offspring derived from fetal and
adult mammalian cells"/I. Wilmut et al.   79

Understanding Specialized Language in a Reading   88

Understanding the Contours of the Argument   89

Semantics: "Words and Children"/S.I. Hayakawa   89

Biology: "Imagine That!"/Steven Pinker   93

How to Summarize: A Checklist   94

Evaluating Source Material   98

Evaluating the Credibility of a Source: A Checklist   99

Evaluating the Credibility of a Source on the Web:
A Checklist   100

Writing with Sources   100

Referring to Key Works   102

Summarizing for Readers   103

Paraphrasing Specific Passages   105

Quoting Word for Word from Sources   106

When and How to Quote Sources: A Checklist   108

Integrating Your Ideas and Source Material   109

Citing Your Sources   111

Modern Language Association (MLA)   112

American Psychological Association (APA)   113

The Council of Science Editors (CSE)   114

Bibliographical Indexes in the Disciplines   116

Humanities   116

Social Sciences   118

Natural Sciences   118

Business   120

DISCIPLINARY PERSPECTIVE: SCHOLARSHIP AND AUTHORITY IN BIOLOGY   120

Working as a Biologist: An Interview with a Teacher of Biology   121

Case Study: Referencing Sources in Biology   123

A Student Writes about Her Research   124

"Protecting the Nation's Water Supply"/*Kristin Leutwyler*   126

SCHOLARSHIP IN THE EXTRA-CURRICULUM: THE ADVOCACY PAMPHLET   129

Producing an Action-Based Advocacy Pamphlet: A Checklist   136

Chapter 4
Research: Gathering New Data 139

What Is Research?   140

Research Instruments   145

The Interview   145

Conducting an Interview: A Checklist   147

Types of Surveys   149

Preparing a Survey: A Checklist   150

Designing a Survey   151

The Observational Notebook   152

Designing a Case Study: A Checklist   155

The Case Study   156

Evaluating Research Methods   156

"Student Participation in a Discussion-Oriented On-line Course: A Case Study"/*Dawn M. Poole*   157

DISCIPLINARY PERSPECTIVE: DOING RESEARCH IN PSYCHOLOGY   176

Making Knowledge: An Interview with a Teacher of Psychology   176

Case Study: Robyn's Research on Birth Order and Personality   179

Robyn's Background   179

Preparing the Research Paper   180

Format   180

Moving from the Individual Case to the Larger
Situation   181

Being Comfortable with the Language and Methods of
the Discipline   182

Essay: "Nature and Nurture: Does Birth Order Shape
Personality?"   185

**CONDUCTING RESEARCH IN THE
EXTRA-CURRICULUM: ORAL HISTORY   196**

Choosing a Worthwhile Topic   197

Researching the Historical Record   197

Creating a Time Line   198

Interviewing   199

Locating Informants and Arranging the Interview   199

Obtaining Informed Consent   199

Taping and Transcribing the Interview   200

Asking the Right Questions   200

Writing Up and Analyzing Your Findings:
A Checklist   201

The Power of Oral History   201

Chapter 5
Reflection: What Does It All Mean? **205**

Seeing the Big Picture   206

**The Difference Between Deductive and Inductive
Reasoning   207**

Laying the Groundwork for Reflection: Questions
to Ask   208

**Knowing When the Evidence Is
Good Enough   210**

Discerning the Shape of the Evidence:
Questions to Ask   211

Drawing Inferences   212

Drawing Inferences: A Checklist   214

**DISCIPLINARY PERSPECTIVE: REFLECTIVE PRAC-
TICE IN EDUCATION   216**

An Interview with a Teacher of Education   216

Case Study: Reflecting on a Tutoring Session   219

Lynne's Background   219

The Assignment   220

Making Sense of the Tutoring Session   222

Essay: "Anatomy of a Tutoring Session"   224

Beyond the Midwife: Making "Real World"
Connections   241

**REFLECTIVE WRITING IN THE EXTRA-CURRICULUM:
THE ELECTRONIC BULLETIN BOARD   244**

Effective Communication on Listservs and Bullentin
Boards: A Checklist   250

Chapter 6
Presentation: What to Write? For Whom? Why? 253

**Understanding Genre, Audience, and
Purpose   254**

The Dictates of Genre   257

Considering Genre: A Checklist   262

Thinking about Academic Genres   262

Components of an Abstract: A Checklist   263

The Abstract   263

The Critical Annotated Bibliography   265

The Essay Exam   266

The Survey of Literature   270

The Argument   271

English Language: "Metaphorical Thinking"/
Daniel Kies   272

Working with an Audience   277

    Considering Your Audience: A Checklist   279

Writing with Purpose   280

    Considering Your Purpose: A Checklist   281

**DISCIPLINARY PERSPECTIVE: THINKING ABOUT
GENRE IN NURSING   282**

An Interview with a Teacher of Nursing   282

Case Study: Mapping Patient Care   285

    Matching Audience with Purpose:
    The Case of Derek   285

    Understanding the Genre of the
    Care Plan   286

**PRESENTATION IN THE EXTRA-CURRICULUM:
WRITING A PRESS RELEASE   290**

Chapter 7
**Action: Drafting, Revising, Editing, and Distributing
Writing 293**

Writing as Production   294

Drafting   294

    An Overview of the Process   294

    Beginning Well: Five Examples   297

    Building Connections   299

    Beginning a Draft: A Checklist   299

    Ending Well   302

    Preparing for Closure: A Checklist   303

Focusing Your Draft   306

    Constructing an Outline   307

Distilling a Draft into an Abstract   309

Sharing Your Writing with Others   311

Sharing Your Writing: The Writer's Role   311

Sharing Your Writing: The Reader's Role   312

Revising   313

An Overview of the Process   313

Restructuring and Reconnecting   314

Editing   316

Error and Writerly Intention   318

Distribution   318

Preparing a Reflective Portfolio   318

Composing a Reflective Cover Letter: A Checklist   319

Preparing a Paper for Distribution   322

DISCIPLINARY PERSPECTIVE: COMPOSING AND DISTRIBUTING A PAPER IN ENGLISH STUDIES 323

An Interview with a Teacher of Composition   323

Case Study: Revision as Meaning Making   328

Kathy's Background   328

The Draft   328

Confusing Revising with Editing   329

Thinking Structurally   330

Revising: A Checklist   331

REVISION IN THE EXTRA-CURRICULUM: PEER REVIEW   333

Credits   339

Index   341

PREFACE

To the Instructor

This textbook provides writing instruction with a special focus: enabling students to write with consequence, and to do so not only in traditionally academic forms, such as the essay or lab report, but also in forms available outside the classroom, such as the brochure or the oral history. The premise of this book is that writing takes shape and acquires consequence by students' demonstrating not merely a set of skills but also an ability to engage in diverse ways of knowing. Employing a model of writing that is epistemological as well as rhetorical, *Writing with Consequence* identifies and is organized by six ways of knowing that experienced writers exhibit in college and beyond:

Inquiry:	Framing a question or posing a problem to write about
Scholarship:	Surveying the literature on your subject
Research:	Gathering new data
Reflection:	Finding significance in your data
Presentation:	Understanding genre, audience, and purpose
Action:	Drafting, revising, editing, and distributing writing

This text presents writing as essentially knowing-in-action. In other words, in acquiring these ways of knowing and continuing to work through them, students will eventually grow to *inhabit* these ways, or, to put it more simply, they will begin to think and act like writers.

Features

Writing with Consequence assumes an incremental model of learning. As students move from chapter to chapter, they will build on what they've learned. They are asked to write a great deal (short pieces and extended writing) as they move through the text, but only at the end will they have truly completed the journey and be ready to enact what they've learned. I want to emphasize, however, that students have ample opportunity to write longer pieces throughout the text.

Each chapter contains a disciplinary casebook (in history, biology, psychology, education, nursing, and English), including an interview of a practitioner in the field and a case study of a student working in the discipline. Models of professional and student writing in the disciplines are included throughout the book.

Each chapter provides opportunities to explore genres in what has been called the "extra-curriculum," in other words, those areas outside the classroom where writing plays a vital part. After deliberate and explicit discussions of the conventions of the genre (including a review of models), students are asked to try their hand composing a memoir, an advocacy pamphlet or brochure (desktop-produced), an oral history, an electronic bulletin board posting, a press release, and a review of a peer's writing.

The writing that students are asked to do in this textbook will help prepare them to write both for the various courses that they will take in college and for the writing opportunities that await them during all the years ahead (as well as for the demands of their current workplace as they attend college). Rather than assume that writing for college and writing for the work beyond college are dramatically different, this book encourages students to create links between the world of school and the world of work. I think you and your students will be excited to learn of ways to establish that link. For example, students will learn that doing research while in school can be an opportunity to engage in a genuine process of discovery, both for them and you. They are invited to design their own surveys, engage in their own observations, and collect artifacts from the past. They are even encouraged to apply for grants expressly created to encourage the publication of student research.

Engaging in such research has in large part become possible for the nonspecialist through the power of the Internet. For the first time, students can join professional historians in studying documents online (such as the records of slave trades or of the maintenance of Nazi death camps). They can also access thousands of scholarly journals through a dazzling array of electronic databases, many of which are described in this text. Online and digital technologies have indeed meant greater access than ever before to the means by which knowledge is made.

But access carries with it a responsibility, a responsibility to weigh and sift the remarkable amount of information available. In this text, students will be shown how to reflect on the quality of information that comes their way, and to do so with an understanding of the stakes involved. In fact, this text insists that concepts and theoretical statements be grounded. In this text, it is not enough simply to say that students must use a certain format when setting up a bibliography or citing their sources within their writing. They are also asked to think of the reasons why it is important to do so—to think, in other words, of how knowledge is built, brick by brick, citation by citation. In this light, the need to avoid plagiarism, for example, becomes easier to understand. Knowledge cannot be built on quicksand or with smoke and mirrors.

I need to emphasize that all the writing samples, interviews, and case studies represent my attempt to make authentic all the claims made in this text. In other words, the samples collected here are offered not as models of perfection but as models of process and progress. I wanted very much to capture the sense of what it means to do the work, what it means, for example, for a teacher of biology to work with novice students in an introductory course, or for a first year student to write effectively in a literature course. Perhaps more than anything else students will, through the interviews, gain some comfort in knowing that even teachers have struggled and continue to struggle to achieve expertise. And I hope as well that students will be stimulated and engaged as they discover exciting and innovative research done by other students. Perhaps then they will be convinced that their own work can also have genuine consequence.

An Instructors Manual is also available to adopters of this edition.

Acknowledgments

I would like to thank all the students who have graciously allowed me to reprint their works in this book: Lynn Arruda, Lynne Bernier, Kathleen Feeney, Shawn Lecomte, Patricia Nadeau, Ana Pacheco, Susan Plaud, Derek Poitras, Nancy Trautz, and R. Robyn Worthington. I am particularly indebted to the following colleagues who graciously agreed to be interviewed for this text: John Bennett, Chris Gilbert, Richard Miller, Rosalee Seymour, Maureen Sowa, and Ronald Weisberger. Thanks go, too, to the instructors listed below who reviewed the manuscript as it evolved. Their ideas were pragmatic and insightful.

Anne Beaufort, *American University*

Diana Boehm, *Saginaw Valley State University*

Gloria Dumler, *Bakersfield College*

Lynée Lewis Gaillet, *Georgia State University*

Babs Gordon, *Arizona State University*

Lila Harper, *Central Washington University*

M. Todd Harper, *Kennesaw State University*

Mary Ellen Hartje, *Angelo State University*

Koren Kessler, *North Carolina State University*

Michael T. Lueker, *Our Lady of the Lake University-San Antonio*

Lisa J. McClure, *Southern Illinois University, Carbondale*

Kerri K. Morris, *University of Alaska*

Mary Kay Mulvaney, *University of Illinois, Chicago*

Joan Mullin, *University of Toledo*

Emmanuel S. Nelson, *SUNY-Cortland*

Tim Peeples, *Elon College*

Chelsea Rathburn, *University of Arkansas*

Jeanette Riley, *University of New Mexico*

Connie Rothwell, *University of North Carolina, Charlotte*

David R. Russell, *Iowa State University*

John Allen Shearer, Jr., *Geneva College*

Stephanie Vanderslice, *University of Central Arkansas*

Terry Myers Zawacki, *George Mason University*

Finally, I would like to acknowledge the able work of my editor, Leslie Taggart, whose insights were invaluable.

Howard Tinberg

Writing with Consequence

Chapter 1

Writing as Knowing-in-Action

Writing with Consequence

Can the writing that you do as a student have consequence outside the classroom? Can your writing make a difference to your town? To the world? Can it produce some kind of public good? At the heart of this textbook is a firm belief that, yes, student writing can have public and civic consequence.

Invitations to write towards public consequence abound. You might be asked to write and design an advocacy pamphlet to promote the services of a literacy center. Perhaps the task is reporting your research on the quality of your community's drinking water, or, in the field of human services, you could find yourself designing a questionnaire whose purpose is to determine an agency's effectiveness in meeting the needs of its clients. In your management course you could be devising a marketing plan for a business that you intend to pursue or are currently engaged in. Invitations to write are available within a variety of disciplines and subject areas, and in each of them your response matters.

Just as writing opportunities are not limited to the classroom, writing instruction does not always occur in school or college settings. Writing and reading groups—both in and out of school settings—are currently popular places for writers to receive constructive feedback on their work and for readers to share reactions to books (your local bookstore likely hosts "book clubs," as do Oprah and National Public Radio). Recent scholarship reveals that significant "extracurricular" literacy instruction has existed for a long time; the workplace has in the past served as a virtual classroom, where working men and women received training in reading and writing. In an earlier century, women's clubs were instituted for the exact purpose of endowing literacy among working women.

However, the writing that you do in college will likely originate in a teacher's assignment. A second, and very significant, premise of this textbook is, therefore, that writing done in school or college settings is *disciplinary*. It is bound by the conventions of writing and ways of knowing that help define a particular discipline. What does it mean to do thinking and writing that will meet the requirements and expectations of those in a particular field? How can you effectively communicate your knowledge? This textbook tries to provide some answers. Its instruction is made more relevant as we follow interviews of teachers in a variety of subject areas and examine case studies of students as they try to gain a foothold in a specific discipline.

Writing as a Way of Knowing

Writing well is a complex activity. When we sit down to write, we must worry not only about saying what we want to say accurately and authoritatively but about doing it clearly and in a language and tone appropriate to our subject and readers. In order to write effectively, we should work to be true to our own intentions (what we feel needs to said) but should also consider what our readers need to know.

All of it matters—from the overall structure and logic of the writing to the placement of commas and apostrophes. And yet when writing instruction occurs, whether in elementary or secondary schools, colleges, universities, adult literacy centers or work sites, much energy is expended in separating *form* (the grammar, for example) from *content* (the ideas themselves). A good deal of time may be spent on developing strategies for generating ideas and structuring them logically and considerably less time on matters of grammar. Or the reverse may be true, with much more time spent on grammar and punctuation, or different conventions of formats (like the memo or the academic essay), than on the reasons for writing in the first place—on purpose and content. We wonder, where should we devote most of our energy as writers—to the form or to the content?

Our goal in this text is to move beyond such simplistic either/or thinking. Instead we ask, What if we imagine writing—with all of its varied requirements, from stating an important and relevant point to making certain that subjects and verbs agree—as "knowing-in-action"? The phrase comes from the work of Donald Schoën, an educational theorist who believes that professionals are defined, in part, by their ability to absorb a body of knowledge and enact it in just the appropriate moments and ways. For some that process is intuitive and not truly understood by practitioners. But for others— and Schoën includes the most accomplished professionals among them—such "knowing-in-action" has been reflected upon and understood and can be reliably called upon again and again. Teachers, for example, operate intuitively when, discovering that a question put to their students elicits very little response, they begin to reformulate the question to produce a more useful reaction.

What if we regard writing itself as not so much a product of skills as an activity that requires certain ways of knowing? So instead of thinking of writing as a matter of mechanical practice (the more we do it, the better we become at it) or memorization of rules (effective writing comes from internalizing grammar maxims), we might envision writing as the enacting of certain kinds of knowledge. In other words, writing well is dependent on *knowing how* to write well—on a self-awareness of what it takes to do the job and on conscious decision-making. For example, a writer's inability to compose a clear thesis statement may be less a function of not understanding the definition of a thesis and more a lack of understanding of how to ask a meaningful and relevant question. Or a confusedly written lab report may reflect as much ignorance of the genre of the lab report (or of the methods of lab research) as a breakdown in language.

All writing is done in response to particular questions posed in particular situations. Our ability to respond well to a writing assignment or situation depends on how successfully we've mastered some of the tools specific to the subject at hand. For example, when a teacher asks students to write an essay on the irony demonstrated in a short story, certain kinds of knowledge are assumed. Students need to know exactly what constitutes an academic essay as well as strategies for composing one. But they need also to understand the concept of irony in a work of literature and be able to read that work in the light of such understanding. In other words, the processes of thinking and writing are interconnected.

How We Know What We Know

In large part due to the groundbreaking work of feminist psychologists (like Carol Gilligan, Mary Belenky, Blythe Clinchy, Nancy Goldberger, and Jill Tarule), our understanding of how we come to know the world has, in the last two decades, grown by quantum leaps. Rather than see knowledge as a mere product—as a concrete, objectively rendered fact—feminist researchers proposed the view that the perspective from which facts are seen actively affects what we know to be true. Until we understand the nature of our own perspective, we will not, with confidence, understand the phenomena around us. Rather than focus simply on *what* we know, these researchers have directed our attention to *how* we know. And rather than assume that there is one way of knowing, they have taught us that there are multiple ways of knowing. For example, we may learn through *received knowledge,* that is, from reading or listening to authorities outside ourselves, or we may know through a more *personal knowledge,* from, say, intuition or feelings. An example of "received knowledge" would be your awareness that the Declaration of Independence was signed in 1776, whereas "personal knowledge" might focus on what independence means to you. Although we are used to considering feelings as somehow separate from a way of knowing (and from reasoning), we now have come to see that feelings are themselves a way of grasping the world, a way of thinking, as it were.

Psychologists use the term "metacognition" to describe "thinking about thinking." Your ability to recognize ways of knowing allows you to break down the learning process and to acquire a critical awareness about how and what you learn. And then you can select and use appropriate knowledge areas in your work. For example, knowledge of the genre in which you are expected to write, say, a lab report, gives you greater control over the demands of the writing itself (knowing, for example, the difference between the "methods" section of your report and the "results" section). Learning doesn't happen in a vacuum. Within a school setting, it occurs as part of the rules and conventions of particular subject areas or disciplines.

Participating in Knowledge Communities

One of the enduring contributions of the researchers mentioned above is the realization that ways of knowing are connected to the norms of particular knowledge communities. This means that the thinking emphasized in a history course may be different from what is highlighted in a marketing course. In a history course, you might be expected to draw upon kinds of knowledge regularly stressed in the discipline, such as making inferences as to cause and effect or making connections between the life of individuals and the spirit of the age in which they lived. In contrast, your work in a marketing course might call upon knowledge of consumer practices or retail strategies. This is just one distinction that can be made between the two disciplines. There are also differences in the procedures that each depends on (for example, how to conduct an oral history or how to design a marketing plan). And, obviously, there is a whole body of written authority known to practitioners and scholars in each field. Furthermore, each discipline has its own specialized terminology.

What does all this mean for your own writing? Does a clear understanding of how to conduct market research, for example, necessarily produce a clear and effective marketing plan? Perhaps not. But you would be hard pressed to write an effective plan without such knowledge. Your growing attentiveness to the varied ways of knowing called upon by particular writing assignments produces an enhanced awareness to all facets of your writing in that subject area. Of course, the same may be said about the curriculum itself: the more self-consciously aware you are about what each discipline is asking for, the more likely you are to work effectively in that field.

The Nature of the Curriculum: Knowledge as Distributed into Disciplines

As you take course after course, it will become obvious to you that knowledge is distributed over a wide range of subject areas or disciplines. The curriculum, or the group of subjects offered by your college, is likely organized by departments or programs, each of which contains a discipline or group of disciplines. The division of knowledge into separate groupings actually began in Western civilization with ancient Greece, and the *triad* (or *trivium,* as it was called) of rhetoric, poetics, and natural philosophy. In modern times we have organized knowledge into the broad categories of the humanities, social sciences, and the natural sciences. The formation of disciplines that make up college curricula goes back to the nineteenth century, with the beginning of the modern university system in Germany. State-owned German universities at that time could decide on its own curriculum and could, and, in fact, did, become not simply places where knowledge is transmitted but where knowledge is actively made—primarily through innovative research.

The humanities, which would include subjects such as literature, history, music, and the arts, traditionally have taken as their concern the creative products that express the human condition. Social sciences, of which psychology and sociology are examples, attempt to describe the various social relationships that serve to define our species. And, finally, the natural sciences, such as chemistry, biology, and physics, try to determine the operations of nature itself.

Today a college or university is as likely to offer courses in the technical, business, and allied health fields as it is the classically defined disciplines. The technical area might include subjects such as mechanical engineering (the study of materials and their mechanical properties) or aquaculture (the management of coastal and marine resources), while the business division might provide training in networked systems (such as Novell) or retail management. Allied health offerings might include nursing, dental hygiene, and occupational therapy—as well as an increasing number of subspecialties.

Each of the academic classifications, together with the disciplines that comprise them, represents an attempt by human beings to make sense of themselves and their environment. Each category, broad or narrow, is a construction only; men and women, rather than some higher authority, have drawn these lines. Because of this, such classifications can and do undergo reexamination and change. In recent times, for example, we have seen the emergence of interdisciplinary study. Scholars and experts have collaborated across disciplinary lines to create new fields of study. The field of brain research, for example, includes practitioners and experts from disciplines as wide ranging as neural science, linguistics, and psychology.

Identifying Six Ways of Knowing

Of course, if each discipline were completely different in its practices and expectations, there would be little justification for the existence of an academic institution or college curricula as they stand. Nor would there be any reasonable hope of being able to gain an understanding of any of the courses that you would typically take in your college career. As a practical matter, there is an overlap in the kind of work that disciplines do, and that overlap will allow you to transfer knowledge from one area to another. With varying emphases, all disciplines draw upon the following kinds of knowledge:

- **Inquiry:** Framing a question
- **Scholarship:** What has been done before?
- **Research:** Gathering new data
- **Reflection:** What does it all mean?
- **Presentation:** What to write? For whom? Why?
- **Action:** Drafting, revising, editing, and distributing writing

These six aspects of exploring, building, and sharing knowledge are the backbone of this book. Each of the following chapters will focus on one of them. Here, we begin with a look at what each part of the process involves.

Inquiry: Framing a Question

This is the first, crucial step: framing a question for research, study, and writing. Knowing how to pose a question will pave the way for discovery and guide our research, making clear the distinction between what we know now and what we need to know. Sometimes initial questions will lead to more profound questions or problems. The point here is that a question provides a purpose and rationale for our work, as well as a necessary limitation.

The kinds of questions for writing and research asked in various disciplines vary. Although each specific discipline frames different content as matter for inquiry, the following disciplines can stand as examples for the broader disciplinary areas given in parentheses.

Inquiry in the Disciplines

- **Literature (a field in the study of humanities):** Students of literature frame questions in relation to a written text, asking

  What meanings are being expressed by the text?

  What assumptions and expectations am I (or another reader) bringing to it?

- **Biology (the natural sciences):** Students of biology start by asserting a *hypothesis*, a prediction of a phenomenon occurring in nature, whose usefulness is then tested against observable experience. Questions take shape during the testing process:

  To what extent was the hypothesis a predictor of observed events in the laboratory?

  What variations, if any, occurred?

- **Psychology (a social science):** Students of psychology project a view of behavior, as expressed in an individual or a defined group or type. Questions that come to be asked include

  Does the observable behavior match the projected behavior?

  Does the behavior of the individual stand in for the behavior of a group?

- **Management (business):** Management operates from either the micro or macro level—which are best defined, respectively, as looking narrowly at a problem or adopting a global approach. Questions include

  How does the layout of a retail establishment contribute to customer satisfaction?

  What strategy needs to be employed in order to market a product successfully?

▓ **Nursing (allied health):** Nurses ask questions in large part from the empirical data given them—in other words, what they observe in their patients' condition. Such questions derive also from an accepted list of nursing diagnoses, a standard body of knowledge known to all in the profession and tested against experience. For example:

To what extent is the patient's oxygenation affected by her observed condition?

Scholarship: What Has Been Done Before?

One way to think of writing is to see it as a continuous conversation among members of a knowledgeable community (the "received knowledge" mentioned on page 5). Our own work builds on and is indebted to the work of others. Another way to look at such communication of knowledge is that it establishes our own credibility within a field or subject area and grants us access to the disciplinary and community conversation. A scholarly knowledge requires a whole range of activities and subsets of knowledge: knowing the locations of sources, knowing the differences in quality and relevance among those sources, knowing the differences between primary and secondary sources. Using sources in turn involves procedural knowledge about taking notes on reading, as well as summarizing, paraphrasing, quoting, and synthesizing source material. In this regard, it is a mistake to consider the learning of citation formats—the standard rules among knowledge communities for indicating where writers have found source materials—as a matter of simply memorizing examples and rules. Even more important than rules are the rationales for using them: In addition to the ethical obligation that we have to credit the work of others, we need to see writing and research as knowledge-making, adding to the work of those who have come before us, or displacing that work in some way.

Scholarship in the Disciplines

- **Literature:** Students of literature initially demonstrate their scholarship by *explicating* the text, that is, offering a close reading of the poem or short story about which they are writing. Advanced study requires, additionally, consulting the works of scholars and critics who have written about the text.

- **Biology:** Students of biology are expected to reference previously done experimental studies that have laid the groundwork for their own work. That work may replicate previous studies or build upon them.

- **Psychology:** Students of psychology survey the available literature on their subject, referencing both experimental and scholarly work, both primary and secondary sources.

- **Management:** As in the traditional disciplines, students of management have access to both primary and secondary sources. Students may consult case studies and marketing plans of particular companies as well as scholarly work done in the field.

- **Nursing:** As a profession, nursing has, in recent years, accumulated considerable resources, through scholarly work and through on-site patient care.

Research: Gathering New Data

Writing that has consequence adds to what we already know. It reflects research (in the sense of making new meaning and discovering truths through the process of seeking and seeking again) and study. In the academic community, writing may qualify or even rebut someone else's ideas or findings, or it may be so distinctive that it departs from prevailing beliefs. Such acts depend on the writers' knowledge of research methods, which is different from a knowledge of previous scholarship and varies considerably from discipline to discipline and community to community.

A key component of writing in a discipline is knowing the methods of collecting and interpreting data within that discipline; this includes knowledge of the various tools in a biology lab and the statistical formulas for determining demographic detail in a moment of history. But lest we think of research as purely procedural knowledge—how to work with a Bunsen burner or use a particular software program—we need to remember that it consists of personal knowledge as well. The experiences each of us brings to the research effort is inevitably a part of that research. Such personal experiences may be worthy of our research and study in their own right.

Much writing in the sciences currently discusses the connection between the personal and the procedural, between the subjective and the seemingly objective truths in the lab and in the natural world. Writing that aims to get at such connected knowledge may consist of field journals, in which researchers write down what they observe in the field (or in the sky) and offer their own personal reactions to what they have observed.

Research in the Disciplines

- **Literature:** How is knowledge acquired in literary studies? In recent years, literary scholars have enlarged their view of how a work of literature conveys meaning. More and more researchers study the historical circumstances during which a poem or short story was produced. In addition, scholars have increasingly included readers' responses as part of a text's meaning. In the past, scholars might have confined their research to the text itself (the so-called New Criticism of the 1940s and 1950s) or applied to the literary text an ideological or psychological framework (Marxist or psychoanalytical, for example).

- **Biology**: Research in biology proceeds by building on the work of others who have come before. The key principle is replication: how effectively can a study be reproduced under the conditions prescribed by the study under consideration? Recent studies, influenced by feminist scholarship, have included the impact of the observer on lab experimentation.

- **Psychology**: To what extent, ask psychologists, is a study of individual behavior reflective of group or social behavior? And how can social groupings predict individual behavior? Knowledge is made through the making of such connections.

- **Management:** Surveys, focus groups, and market analysis are all used in management to determine the conditions of the market and enhance a company's or organization's profitability. Data collection has of late also included less traditional concerns, such as ethical and environmental research.

- **Nursing**: Data collection, achieved through the charting of patient care, is at the heart of the health professions. The making of knowledge occurs through the rigorous diagnosis of ongoing patient conditions.

Reflection: What Does It All Mean?

Personal reactions to observed phenomenon pave the way to more thoroughgoing reflection on the meaning and importance of data. The ability to reflect—to stand back and gauge the significance of our data or to see their implications or inferences—is a crucial component of knowledge-in-action. Reflection requires that we be strong, critical readers of the texts we use or of the phenomena we have observed, asking questions like these:

> What implications may we draw from the particular data that we have gathered?

How do our sources (or experimental results) compare with one another for consistency, reliability, and credibility?

Among the evidence gathered, what might serve as the most useful to bolster our argument or thesis?

What is the least useful and most flawed evidence?

To promote active reflection, thinkers in diverse fields of study may use *reading logs* (an informal set of reactions to readings), *observational notebooks* (a record of observed phenomena), and *dialectical notebooks* (two-column response notebooks) to track sources, evaluate evidence, and think about the significance of what they have observed.

Reflection in the Disciplines

- **Literature:** To promote reflection, students of literature might ask the following:

  What were my assumptions about the work before starting to read?

  In what way did the text surprise me?

  After additional reading and discussion, what do I see now that I didn't see earlier?

- **Biology:** Students of biology might well ask

  What meaningful patterns, if any, can I see in my data?

  How do those patterns match up with my predictive hypothesis?

  What are the implications of any differences between the two?

- **Psychology:** As in biology, reflection in psychology relies in part on making sense of experimental data, given the hypothesis tested against that data. But psychology may also ask us to tease out the implications of a case study for a broader population:

How, we need to ask, does this individualized study predict the behavior of a distinguishable group?

- **Management:** Reflection in the management area requires looking both forward and backward.

  How are we best able to predict a company's output, based on the data collected?

  How successful has a company been in producing and promoting its goods?

- **Nursing:** Consistent and effective patient care depends on the caregiver's ability to discern the relationship between a condition's symptom and cause.

  Now that the symptoms have been noted, what connections can be made among them?

  What diagnosis can be produced to account for those symptoms?

  What interventions can appropriately be provided as treatment?

Presentation: What to Write? For Whom? Why?

If our goal is to report what we have learned through inquiry, scholarship, research, and reflection in writing, we need to pay attention—early in the learning and reporting process—to the *genre* or form in which our findings will be presented, the audience to whom they will be presented, and our purpose for disseminating this information in the first place. Our decision as to genre—which we may think of as the kind of writing we are asked to do, and its format— affects the content of our writing in dramatic ways. For example, if we are writing a brochure, the amount of space available on the six panels will effectively limit the amount of text that can be included. This limitation will shape the content we provide.

Considerations of audience may also affect decisions as to the kind of information that we offer, the kinds we omit, and the language and tone that we adopt. And our very reasons for writing in the first place naturally shape what we say and how we say it. If our purpose is to denounce the exportation of U.S. labor abroad, we will select materials that illustrate the adverse consequences of such a policy on national and individual interests (again, within the constraints of genre and in consideration of our audience).

Presentation in the Disciplines

- **Literature:** Literary study would seem to require the use of only one genre, the academic essay, but, in fact, other forms are available, such as the reader's log, the annotated bibliography, and the book review. We might ask about genre

  To what degree should an annotated bibliography critique or evaluate a source, rather than merely summarize?

- **Biology:** Work in biology typically relies on the lab report, but may also require reading a published, scientific paper. It's important to ask

  What are the rules and expectations governing each kind of writing?

  What, for example, occurs in the "methods" section of a lab report?

- **Psychology:** A variety of genres is used in psychology, including the case study, the qualitatively designed and measured experiment, and the scientific article. Each genre suggests different questions. If we are writing a case study, we might ask

  What level of detail is required?

▪ **Management:** Knowing answers to questions such as the following requires familiarity with the various genres employed in the management area.

What are the contours and components of an effective marketing plan?

How can a market survey be designed to meet the needs of the client?

▪ **Nursing:** As in other fields, knowledge of genres is essential in the health professions:

How can nurses communicate a patient's condition effectively to fellow caregivers?

What, specifically, is demanded when composing a care trajectory or mapping of patient care?

Action: Drafting, Revising, Editing, and Distributing Writing

Finally, we sit down to write up our findings and disseminate them, whether to our teachers, our peers, our supervisors, or to other communities with whom we wish to share our work. Implementing what we know in writing requires an understanding of the *composing process*. For example, we need to know the difference between a draft and a finished product (knowing the right moment at which to "send off" our writing), and we need to know the difference between revision and editing (knowing how to distinguish between large and small writing matters and when to attend to them).

Experienced writers possess a conscious awareness of their composing practices—evidence of the metacognitive skills mentioned earlier. In other words, they are able to monitor themselves as they write and rewrite; they are fully conscious of the strategies that will enable them to produce the meaning that they desire, and of the kinds of questions that will guide them to that point. The process does not occur in isolation, however. For example, writers must attend to the conventions of the genre in which they are writing, the needs of their reader(s), and, of course, the amount of time available for writing. It is worth noting that in some settings writing is by necessity done—and done effectively—within very short time frames, such as in the case of nurses reporting care in patients' records. But what connects such writing with writing done over considerably longer stretches of time is a keen awareness of the writing scene: of genre, audience, and purpose.

Action: Implementing Knowledge in the Disciplines

* **Literature:** Since writing about literature is in reaction to a particular text (short story or poem or play), the writing must reference the text in a clear and meaningful way. But, beyond that obvious fact, the writing must undergo a thorough consideration of all that we have discussed to this point:

  What is my question? To what extent have I answered it?

  What support have I brought to bear in answering it?

  How significant are the implications that I have drawn?

  What are the expectations as to genre and audience?

* **Biology:** Since biology operates in reference to observable phenomena in a lab or natural setting, distribution of the writing should involve critical questions such as

  What is my hypothesis going into the experiment?

  To what extent has that hypothesis predicted the data obtained?

  What, if any, adjustments need to be made to that hypothesis?

  Is this experiment replicable?

▓ **Psychology:** Prior to distribution, work in psychology—in addition to considerations of genre and audience—should attempt to assess the hypothesis in the light of the evidence presented.

Does the writing draw out the implications of the study, especially if the study focuses on a narrow population?

▓ **Management:** Leaving aside the question of whether all the elements of such a plan are in place, distribution of the plan hinges on the "fit" between the action intended and the organization's product or purpose.

Does its marketing plan thoroughly match a company's mission and organizational structure?

▓ **Nursing:** In the health professions, effective documentation translates into effective patient care. Key among the questions that nurses need to ask when preparing to distribute such documentation is

To what extent will consistent and appropriate care be provided by colleagues who read care maps and other forms of record keeping?

Knowing-in-Action Across the Disciplines

Now that we have identified the various ways of knowing that distinguish writing and thinking across the disciplines, let's take a look at those ways of knowing in action. How are they expressed in actual writing?

Linguistics
From "Words and Children"

by S. I. Hayakawa

Children are newcomers to the language. Learning a language isn't just learning words; rules of the language are learned at the same time. Prove this? Very simple. Little children use a past tense like "I runned all the way to the park and I swimmed in the pool." "Runned" and "swimmed" are words they did not hear. They made them up by analogy from other past tenses they had heard. This means that they learned not only the vocabulary, they learned the rule for making the past tense—except that the English language doesn't follow its own rules. And when the child proves himself to be more logical than the English language, we take it out on the child—which is nonsense. Children's language should be listened to with great attentiveness and respect.

In a single paragraph, the semanticist Hayakawa has employed a variety of ways of knowing. He has a clear subject for inquiry: how the rules of language are "learned." He draws upon observations of phenomena that he has done in the past (studies of children's use of language). Significantly, Hayakawa makes the provocative claim that communication occurs regardless of any breaking of the "rules" of conventional English. He supports that claim by drawing inferences from the ways children consistently employ language (becoming more consistent than even English will allow). Hayakawa masters the genre in which he is writing (the mainstream essay, aimed at a lay audience but nonetheless engaged in semantics). And, finally, he has composed a piece that through clarity of language and commonplace observation makes its point effectively.

Psychology
From "Libidinal Types"

by Sigmund Freud

Observation teaches us that in individual human beings the general features of humanity are embodied in almost infinite variety. If we follow the promptings of a legitimate desire to distinguish particular types in this multiplicity, we must begin by selecting the characteristics to look for and the points of view to bear in mind in making our differentiation. For this purpose physical qualities will be no less useful than mental; it will be most valuable of all if we can make our classification on the basis of a regularly occurring combination of physical and mental characteristics. [. . .]

> Now we can distinguish three main libidinal types, . . . the
> *erotic*, the *narcissistic*, and the *obsessional* type.

Although his sources are unstated, Freud is drawing
upon an immense range of scholarly and empirical work
having to do with how the human species can be differentiated and upon his own observational studies of people. He
wants to determine the extent to which human beings can
be differentiated in ways other than the merely physical, or,
more precisely, a combination of the physical and mental.
His research is presented in the form of classification or
type (*erotic*, *narcissistic*, and *obsessional*). He chooses to
present his findings as a finite taxonomy or classification, a
kind of grid in words. You could think of a taxonomy as a
system of organizing materials, perhaps like the system you
might use on your computer desktop: all e-mails go under
"general correspondence" and downloaded songs go under
"my music."

Management
From "Let Us Entertain You"

by Mariwyn Evans

A 1996 survey of 11 malls sponsored by ICSC [International
Council of Shopping Centers] concluded movie patrons did have a
positive impact on mall sales. An article in the Spring 1997
Research Review stated that approximately 60 percent of movie patrons shopped in a mall during a visit to the theatre. Patrons that
did shop spent an average of $20 on non-food items (compared to
$56 for the average shopper) and spent approximately 30 minutes
shopping. While these sums are not large, the article does point out
that much of this income is added revenue.

The editor of a consumer journal and observer of consumer trends, Mariwyn Evans inquires as to the role of entertainment in luring shoppers to malls. She presents herself as a scholarly member of her field by referencing and
quoting from journals in that field. Her referencing of prior
studies indicates an awareness of audience (fellow students

of the consumer scene) and genre (an article in a specialized journal). And she has published her findings for others to consider.

Let's see if we can apply some of these concepts.

Grounding the Theory

1. Describe the kinds of writing (whether in college or high school) that you have done in a wide range of courses, from the humanities, social sciences, natural or lab sciences, technical, business, or allied health fields. How are they different? How are they similar?

2. Using course descriptions in your college catalog, explore a discipline that interests you. Read the descriptions of at least five of the courses offered by a particular department. Can you determine (or make educated guesses about) the types of questions, the methods of inquiry and research, and the genres of presentation typically used in the discipline?

3. We have said that writing is "knowing-in-action." You are probably competent in at least one other activity (for example, a sport, a craft, a job) that could be considered "knowing-in-action." Think of such an activity. What do you know about it? How do you know it?

Exploring Genre in the Extra-Curriculum

When we think of writing done in school, the essay will likely come to mind. But if we extend our reach beyond the classroom and consider the writing done in what has been called by scholars the "extra-curriculum," we quickly realize that there are more forms of writing currently practiced than the academic essay. In the public domain, writing takes on a variety of forms, each of which is governed by certain rules and expectations. The profile of a movie star in a popular magazine, a legislative act of Congress, and a political pamphlet: all follow distinctly different formats. Yet, as a piece of writing, each draws from one or more of the ways of knowing that we have identified: inquiry or the desire for discovery, for example, or the actual making of new knowledge, as well as familiarity with genre and audience.

As is the case with all of the following chapters, each focussed on one way of knowing, this one concludes with examples of published writing. After reading each, you have an opportunity to examine its form and content.

Casey Martin and the Americans with Disabilities Act of 1990

Here is a news account from the Associated Press on the matter of Casey Martin vs. the Professional Golfer's Association. Martin, a disabled golfer, petitioned the U.S. Supreme Court for the right to use a golf cart during matches.

High court says golfer Casey Martin has right to use cart

WASHINGTON (AP) Disabled golfer Casey Martin has a legal right to ride in a golf cart between shots at PGA Tour events, the Supreme Court said Tuesday.

In a 7–2 ruling with implications for other pro sports, the justices ruled that a federal disability-bias law requires the pro golf tour to waive its requirement that players walk the course during tournaments. That rule is not fundamental to the game of golf, the court said.

In the majority opinion, Justice John Paul Stevens said Congress intended for an organization like the PGA Tour to give consideration to disabled golfers.

Lawmakers intended that such organizations "carefully weigh the purpose, as well as the letter" of its rules before rejecting requests of disabled golfers out of hand.

Justice Antonin Scalia wrote the dissent, joined by fellow conservative Justice Clarence Thomas.

"In my view today's opinion exercises a benevolent compassion that the law does not place it within our power to impose," he said.

The 1990 Americans with Disabilities Act bans discrimination against the disabled in public accommodations, including golf courses and entertainment sites. The law requires "reasonable modifications" for disabled people unless such changes would fundamentally alter the place or event.

That law applies to professional sports events when they are held at places of public accommodation, the justices said.

The decision upholds a lower court ruling that ordered the PGA Tour to let Martin use a cart. The lower court said using a cart would not give him an unfair advantage over his competitors.

Martin has a circulatory disorder in his right leg called Klippel-Trenaunay-Weber Syndrome that makes it painful for him to walk long distances. He sued the PGA Tour in 1997, saying the ADA—enacted in 1990—gave him a right to use a cart during tour events.

Martin was a teammate of Tiger Woods at Stanford University, and the two used to room together on road trips. Woods has said that Martin sometimes would be in so much pain that he couldn't get up to use the bathroom.

Jack Nicklaus and Arnold Palmer have spoken against allowing any player to use a cart in elite competition to accommodate a disability. They have said that using a cart would give Martin an advantage and take away a basic part of the game: the ability to walk an 18-hole course.

The San Francisco-based 9th U.S. Circuit Court of Appeals ruled for Martin in March 2000. But the next day a Chicago-based federal appeals court ruled against Indiana golfer Ford Olinger, who sued the U.S. Golf Association for the right to use a cart in U.S. Open qualifying. The appeals court said a cart would change the nature of competition.

Among those supporting the PGA Tour in friend-of-the-court briefs were the Ladies Professional Golf Association and the men's pro tennis organization, the ATP Tour.

A timeline of Casey Martin's lawsuit against the PGA Tour:

Nov. 26, 1997—Martin files a lawsuit in federal court in Oregon against the PGA Tour for the right to ride a cart in competition.

Dec. 1, 1997—U.S. Magistrate Thomas Coffin in Oregon grants Martin an injunction that allows him to use a cart during the PGA Tour's qualifying tournament.

Dec. 9, 1997—Martin ties for 46th at the qualifying tournament, giving him exemption on the second-tier Nike Tour (now the Buy.com Tour).

Jan. 11, 1998—Martin closes with a 69 to win the Nike Lakeland Classic by one stroke over Steve Lamontagne.

Feb. 11, 1998—After a six-day trial, U.S. Magistrate Thomas Coffin rules in favor of Martin, saying the PGA Tour failed to show how waiving its walking-only rule for Martin would fundamentally alter competition. Tour says it will appeal.

June 9, 1998—Despite a double bogey on the final hole, Martin qualifies for the U.S. Open in the second hole of a playoff.

June 21, 1998—After becoming the first player to ride a cart in U.S. Open history, Martin ties for 23rd at The Olympic Club in San Francisco with a four-day score of 291, one stroke behind Tiger Woods.

July 2, 1998—Martin makes his debut on the PGA Tour by taking a sponsor's exemption to the Greater Hartford Open. He misses the cut by five strokes.

Nov. 8, 1998—Fails to reach the final stage of the PGA Tour qualifying tournament, but Lakeland victory allows him to retain his card on the Nike Tour.

Oct. 25, 1999—Finishes 14th on the Nike Tour money list and earns full exempt status on the PGA Tour for the 2000 season.

Jan. 19, 2000—Becomes the first PGA Tour member to use a cart in competition, shooting a 4-under 68 in the first round of the Bob Hope Classic. He wound up missing the cut by three strokes.

March 6, 2000—Ninth U.S. Circuit Court of Appeals in San Francisco upholds lower court ruling that allows Martin to use a cart.

July 5, 2000—PGA Tour appeals the decision to U.S. Supreme Court.

Sept. 26, 2000—Supreme Court agrees to hear PGA Tour appeal.

Nov. 5, 2000—Needing to finish second in the final tournament of the year to keep his PGA Tour card, Martin ties for

60th in the Southern Farm Bureau Classic and ends the season 179th on the money list.

Dec. 4, 2000—On the final day of qualifying tournament, Martin finishes one stroke short of regaining his PGA Tour card. He gets full status on the Buy.com Tour.

Jan. 17, 2001—Supreme Court hears oral arguments.

May 29, 2001—Supreme Court rules Martin has legal right to ride in a cart between shots at PGA Tour events.

Margasak, Larry. Associated Press, May 29, 2001.

If the writer were composing a fictional narrative, a piece of fiction instead of a news story, she would be guilty of putting the cart before the horse: in this case, revealing to us that the U.S. Supreme Court has found in the favor of Mr. Martin. But the genre of a journalistic story requires that the court's judgment be the "lead" of the story, with the details to follow.

Taking a Closer Look

1. What question does the article seek to answer? Do you think this question would be an appropriate one to try to answer in a college essay? Why or why not?

2. What means of surveying and presenting the available information does the writer use? Is this use effective? Why or why not?

3. What types of sources of information might the writer may have used in composing this news article?

4. What does the form of the writing—the lead, the very short paragraphs, the level of vocabulary—suggest about the likely audience for the story?

5. How are you the same and/or different from the intended audience?

As contrast to the news account, consider the American with Disabilities Act of 1990 itself as an example of writing in the extra-curriculum (the full text is available at http://www.usdoj.gov/crt/ada/pubs/ada.txt). The document provides a detailed table of contents.

Americans with Disabilities Act of 1990

SECTION 1. SHORT TITLE; TABLE OF CONTENTS.
   (a) Short Title.—This Act may be cited as the "Americans with Disabilities Act of 1990".
   (b) Table of Contents.—The table of contents is as follows:
   Sec. 1. Short title; table of contents.
   Sec. 2. Findings and purposes.
   Sec. 3. Definitions.

TITLE I—EMPLOYMENT
   Sec. 101. Definitions.
   Sec. 102. Discrimination.
   Sec. 103. Defenses.
   Sec. 104. Illegal use of drugs and alcohol.
   Sec. 105. Posting notices.
   Sec. 106. Regulations.
   Sec. 107. Enforcement.
   Sec. 108. Effective date.

TITLE II—PUBLIC SERVICES

Subtitle A—Prohibition Against Discrimination and Other Generally Applicable Provisions
   Sec. 201. Definition.
   Sec. 202. Discrimination.
   Sec. 203. Enforcement.
   Sec. 204. Regulations.
   Sec. 205. Effective date.

Subtitle B—Actions Applicable to Public Transportation Provided by Public Entities Considered Discriminatory

Part I—Public Transportation Other Than by Aircraft or Certain Rail Operations
   Sec. 221. Definitions.
   Sec. 222. Public entities operating fixed route systems.
   Sec. 223. Paratransit as a complement to fixed route service.

Sec. 224. Public entity operating a demand responsive system.
Sec. 225. Temporary relief where lifts are unavailable.
Sec. 226. New facilities.
Sec. 227. Alterations of existing facilities.
Sec. 228. Public transportation programs and activities in existing facilities and one car per train rule.
Sec. 229. Regulations.
Sec. 230. Interim accessibility requirements.
Sec. 231. Effective date.
Part II—Public Transportation by Intercity and Commuter Rail
Sec. 241. Definitions.
Sec. 242. Intercity and commuter rail actions considered discriminatory.
Sec. 243. Conformance of accessibility standards.
Sec. 244. Regulations.
Sec. 245. Interim accessibility requirements.
Sec. 246. Effective date.

TITLE III—PUBLIC ACCOMMODATIONS AND SERVICES
OPERATED BY PRIVATE ENTITIES
Sec. 301. Definitions.
Sec. 302. Prohibition of discrimination by public accommodations.
Sec. 303. New construction and alterations in public accommodations and commercial facilities.
Sec. 304. Prohibition of discrimination in specified public transportation services provided by private entities.
Sec. 305. Study.
Sec. 306. Regulations.
Sec. 307. Exemptions for private clubs and religious organizations.
Sec. 308. Enforcement.
Sec. 301. Examinations and courses.
Sec. 302. Effective date.

TITLE IV—TELECOMMUNICATIONS
Sec. 401. Telecommunications relay services for hearing-impaired and speech-impaired individuals.
Sec. 402. Closed-captioning of public service announcements.

TITLE V—MISCELLANEOUS PROVISIONS
Sec. 501. Construction.
Sec. 502. State immunity.
Sec. 503. Prohibition against retaliation and coercion.

Sec. 504. Regulations by the Architectural and Transportation Barriers Compliance Board.
Sec. 505. Attorney's fees.
Sec. 506. Technical assistance.
Sec. 507. Federal wilderness areas.
Sec. 508. Transvestites.
Sec. 509. Coverage of Congress and the agencies of the legislative branch.
Sec. 510. Illegal use of drugs.
Sec. 511. Definitions.
Sec. 512. Amendments to the Rehabilitation Act.
Sec. 513. Alternative means of dispute resolution.
Sec. 514. Severability.

SEC. 2. FINDINGS AND PURPOSES.
  (a) Findings.—The Congress finds that—
      (1) some 43,000,000 Americans have one or more physical or mental disabilities, and this number is increasing as the population as a whole is growing older;
      (2) historically, society has tended to isolate and segregate individuals with disabilities, and, despite some improvements, such forms of discrimination against individuals with disabilities continue to be a serious and pervasive social problem;
      (3) discrimination against individuals with disabilities persists in such critical areas of employment, housing, public accommodations, education, transportation, communication, recreation, institutionalization, health services, voting, and access to public services;
      (4) unlike individuals who have experienced discrimination on the basis of race, color, sex, national origin, religion, or age, individuals who have experienced discrimination on the basis of disability have often had no legal recourse to redress such discrimination;
      (5) individuals with disabilities continually encounter various forms of discrimination, including outright intentional exclusion, the discriminatory effects of architectural, transportation, and communication barriers, overprotective rules and policies, failure to make modifications to existing facilities and practices, exclusionary qualification standards and criteria, segregation, and relegation to lesser services, programs, activities, benefits, jobs, or other opportunities;
      (6) census data, national polls, and other studies have documented that people with disabilities, as a group, occupy an

inferior status in our society, and are severely disadvantaged socially, vocationally, economically, and educationally;

(7) individuals with disabilities are a discrete and insular minority who have been faced with restrictions and limitations, subjected to a history of purposeful unequal treatment, and relegated to a position of political powerlessness in our society, based on characteristics that are beyond the control of such individuals and resulting from stereotypic assumptions not truly indicative of the individual ability of such individuals to participate in, and contribute to, society;

(8) the Nation's proper goals regarding individuals with disabilities are to assure equality of opportunity, full participation, independent living, and economic self-sufficiency for such individuals; and

(9) the continuing existence of unfair and unnecessary discrimination and prejudice denies people with disabilities the opportunity to compete on an equal basis and to pursue those opportunities for which our free society is justifiably famous, and costs the United States billions of dollars in unnecessary expenses resulting from dependency and nonproductivity.

(b) Purpose.—It is the purpose of this Act—

(1) to provide a clear and comprehensive national mandate for the elimination of discrimination against individuals with disabilities;

(2) to provide clear, strong, consistent, enforceable standards addressing discrimination against individuals with disabilities;

(3) to ensure that the Federal Government plays a central role in enforcing the standards established in this Act on behalf of individuals with disabilities; and

(4) to invoke the sweep of congressional authority, including the power to enforce the fourteenth amendment and to regulate commerce, in order to address the major areas of discrimination faced day-to-day by people with disabilities.

SEC. 3. DEFINITIONS.

As used in this Act: . . .

(2) Disability.—The term "disability" means, with respect to an individual—

(A) a physical or mental impairment that substantially limits one or more of the major life activities of such individual;

(B) a record of such an impairment; or

(C) being regarded as having such an impairment.

Given the public and political nature of the document, the framers of the Act needed to present a rationale for such wide-sweeping legislation and offer carefully stated definitions before embarking on the actual changes recommended by the bill. Fully aware of the profound implications of the ADA, the sponsors make a carefully prepared case for the revolutionary accommodations suggested.

Taking a Closer Look

1. What questions does the Act seek to answer? Do you think these questions would be appropriate ones to try to answer in a college essay? Why or why not?

2. What differences do you notice between the two parts of Section 2, "Findings" and "Purposes"?

3. Does Casey Martin's inability to walk the entire 18 holes of a golf course seem to fit the definition of "Disability" given in Section 3? Why or why not?

4. What does the form of the writing—the outline format, the numbered sections, the formal language, the vocabulary level—suggest is the major purpose of the document? Why do you think so?

5. Do you find the Act easy or difficult to read? What aspects of the writing make it so?

6. *Web Follow-up.* Following up on the Casey Martin matter, go to the Web site of the Professional Golfer's Association, the public face of the PGA on the Internet. Locate the PGA's mission statement. Describe what you think a mission statement is supposed to do. What is its purpose in this case? Who is its intended audience? Does that audience include Casey Martin?

The Boy Scouts of America

In response to a U.S. Supreme Court decision that it need not reinstate a member who is openly gay, the Boy Scouts of America produced a statement as part of its official press release (which can be found at http://www.bsa.scouting.org/press/000628/index.html)

NEWS RELEASE, June 28, 2000

Boy Scouts of America Sustained by United States Supreme Court

We are very pleased with the U.S. Supreme Court's decision in the Dale case. This decision affirms our standing as a private association with the right to set its own standards for membership and leadership.

This decision allows us to continue our mission of providing character-building experiences for young people, which has been our chartered purpose since our founding.

For more than 20 years, the Boy Scouts of America has defended its membership standards. We went to the highest court in the land, the U.S. Supreme Court, in order to do so. The Boy Scouts of America, as a private organization, must have the right to establish its own standards of membership if it is to continue to instill the values of the Scout Oath and Law in boys. Thanks to our legal victories, our standards of membership have been sustained.

We believe an avowed homosexual is not a role model for the values espoused in the Scout Oath and Law.

Boy Scouting makes no effort to discover the sexual orientation of any person. Scouting's message is compromised when prospective leaders present themselves as role models inconsistent with Boy Scouting's understanding of the Scout Oath and Law.

Scouting's record of inclusion is impressive by any standard. However, we do ask all of our members to do their best to live the Scout Oath and Law. Today, boys from every ethnic, religious, and economic background in suburbs, farms, and cities know and respect each other as they participate in our program.

We thank the parents, volunteers and friends of Scouting who have supported us in this case and others. We respect other people's right to hold differing opinions and ask that they respect ours.

In a support brief filed by three of Scouting's largest chartered organizations, they addressed why Scouting has been so effective for 90 years: "Scouting's program for character development is effective precisely because it teaches through both precept and concrete examples of its adult leaders. . . . Scoutmasters exist not only to espouse the ideals of Scouting, but more importantly to live and embody them; they are the role models of the Scouting movement."

The Boy Scouts of America

Taking a Closer Look

1. This is a news release. How is this genre different from the others that you have studied so far (the journalistic reportage, the legislative act, and the institutional mission statement)?

2. How does a consideration of audience factor into the writing of such a piece?

3. To what extent do scholarship and research play a part?

4. From what you've learned, compose guidelines for designing an effective news release. Discuss the headline, the opening statement, the type of language used, and any other matters that seem important.

5. Try your hand at composing a news release. You might recount an award given to a member of your community, publicize an important event that is about to happen locally, or make an announcement about an organization you are a part of.

6. *Web Follow-up.* As we have seen, institutions use public forms of writing to promote their services, resources, and philosophies. Sometimes communities and corporations publish the rules for admittance or employment. Research the eligibility rules of the Boy Scouts (you can do so by accessing http://www.boyscouts.com/index2.htm). As a piece of public writing, how would you

characterize the documents that you see? In other words, what is their function? Who is the intended audience? To what extent are scholarship, research, and reflection components?

Genres in the Public Domain

Collect as many different genres of writing as you from home, work, place of worship, and any other community group to which you belong. Name each genre represented (newsletter, press release, celebrity profile, and so on). Analyze a sampling of three of the pieces in light of the various ways of knowing that we have discussed. Here are some questions to consider:

Taking a Closer Look

---

1. What question is the writing attempting to answer?
2. What level of detail does the writing provide as support?
3. What new or surprising information is offered?
4. How is the piece formatted or organized?
5. Who is the intended audience?

Chapter 2

Inquiry: Framing a Question

Asking Interesting Questions

The writing you do will be as interesting as the questions you
start out with. The power of your writing is directly related
to the quality of the question(s) you address: If you are writing about something that moves you, or something you want
to know more about, your writing will have impact. At the
heart of writing is the idea of *inquiry*—of asking important
questions in order to get at equally important answers. Inquiry guides our writing in all disciplines, from scientific to
literary. Indeed, the word *essay* comes from a French word
meaning trial or attempt or test; we ask, we explore, we attempt to explain.

How do you arrive at the key questions? Do you need to
know a certain amount of information before you can even
ask the right questions? In the humanities, the act of phrasing
a question is usually tied to the act of reading a text, whether
that text is a poem or a piece of archival research (a journal or
town register, or even a cultural event or a set of behaviors).
Imagine that you've learned from visiting a town's records
that between the years of 1943 and 1949 incidence of infant
mortality peaked (in contrast with a similar period a decade
before). You might be led to ask, What factors, environmental
or biological, could have produced such an effect? When
studying literature, questions emerge as we react to the written text. The writing becomes a reaction to what has been
read. For example, his reading of Joseph Conrad's novel
Heart of Darkness (and other works that represent Africa in
similar ways) prompted the Nigerian writer Chinua Achebe
to produce his influential essay "An Image of Africa: Racism
in Conrad's *Heart of Darkness*." Indeed, many scholars and
critics in the humanities currently subscribe to the view that
writing never takes shape in a vacuum; they explain that our
compositions are always influenced by other texts, whether
we are aware of such influence or not.

In the sciences, inquiry may begin with observation of natural phenomena. Famed science writer Lewis Thomas, for example, notices that two or three termites pick up pellets and move them with little discernable order or design. But as more termites join in, the group gains a "critical mass," able to build arches and other remarkably complex structures. Could it be, he asks, that termites communicate with one another? If so, how? In what sense do these termites possess intelligence?

The question that motivates your exploration needs to be formulated with care. Most teachers at the college level want you to do more than discover elements of plot or discern discrete phenomena. Therefore it isn't enough just to ask, "What happens to Mr. Kurtz at the end of *Heart of Darkness*?" A more meaningful question would be, "What drove Kurtz to do the things that he did?" and, "To what extent is Mr. Kurtz's demise predictable?" It isn't enough to ask, "What is a community's attitude toward establishing a waste disposal site in its neighborhoods?" You should also ask, "Why does a particular community object to such a site being built?" and, "What lessons can be learned by other communities that face a similar challenge?" A productive question requires adept use of the text or observable phenomenon under study as well as significant reflection. In other words, a fruitful question produces not only another visit to the subject at hand—the novel or the design plans for a waste disposal site—but the teasing out of *implications*, a key component, as we shall see, of the reflective process.

Asking fruitful questions also requires on your part an element of desire and a need to discover something. The most effective writing emerges from the writer's engagement with a subject, his or her wrestling to discover answers because the answers matter. If you happen to live in a community split by the prospect of a waste disposal site being built close by, you might invest a good deal of time and energy in discovering the reasons why family and friends are so anxious about the issue. And if you have put a lot into discovering the answer, it stands to reason that the writing will be that much more meaningful for you and your readers than if you had failed to connect with the question at hand.

Getting Started to Write: An Inquiry-based Process

In Chapter 1 we learned that inquiry is the foundation of study, reflection, and writing. What do you need to think about and do in order to get started to write? Even this first step can be thought of as a process:

1. Determine what you already know about a specific topic (your area of "expertise," you might say).

2. Evaluate the value and meaning of what you know, employing strategies that will help you narrow your subject.

3. Establish what you need to know.

4. When others frame a question for you (as in the case of teachers or supervisors), determine their expectations and the parameters of the assignment given.

Taking Stock: Determining What You Already Know about Your Subject

When asked by teachers or employers to undertake a subject, inexperienced writers often mistakenly assume that they know little that is useful in tackling that assignment. Perhaps this attitude is most evident in schools and colleges, where students are expected to take on the role of "expert learner," of someone who comes simply to acquire information and not to give it. But as a practical matter, we very likely bring to each writing task both experience and knowledge of a personal kind that can serve as valuable resources. What we already know can at least be a starting point for research and reflection. Although comical, this famous note from the bank robber Clyde Barrow to carmaker Henry Ford may serve as testimony to the power of personal and firsthand knowledge:

If you have difficulty starting a writing project, consider your own understanding and feeling about your subject: Do so either in some informal writing, or by simply "talking out" related personal knowledge. These questions are especially useful:

- What subject interests me most?
- What do I know firsthand about that subject already?
- What perspectives or feelings do I have about it?

Sometimes we draw on what we know of the knowledge of others. When Teresa, a student of marketing, began (in collaboration with another student) to write a modified plan for starting a pharmaceutical company in Poland after the fall of communism, she possessed a relevant resource: Her father, who worked in the area of international taxation, had told her many stories about the complex challenges of traveling and doing business abroad. Granted, not all students have access to knowledge about diverse cultures or technical expertise. Nevertheless no one comes to a writing task as a tabula rasa, a blank slate. Rather, each of us arrives at such a task with a range of experience and knowledge about the world.

Grounding the Theory

1. List three subjects that you know well (they could range from a statistical knowledge of a favorite sports team to a knowledge of all the lyrics on a preferred artist's CD). Choose one of the subjects in which you are an "expert." Write about the reasons why you chose that subject. In other words, write about your passionate connection to that subject. How do you feel about the subject?

2. Pick any subject that you are taking right now. On a sheet of paper draw two lines down the page to create three columns. In the far left column, list concepts from the subject that are entirely new to you; in the second column, jot down concepts also drawn from the subject but with which you have some familiarity. In the third column, write down everything you know about those concepts with which you are familiar. Finally, on a separate sheet, write down your judgment as to how much you already know about the subject. If you were reading the *Communist Manifesto,* you might put on the far left column the concepts "production" and "exchange." In the second column, you might indicate "bourgeoisie." Finally, in the third column, you could describe your understanding of "exploitation" in the workplace.

Working with What You Know

Mapping and Listing

Cognitive psychologists have taught us that people learn in a variety of ways. Many of us are visual learners, more comfortable with physical and visual cues than with verbal or symbolic ones. For writers who depend on the visual, mind or conceptual maps are very useful both as mirrors of thought processes and as shapers of such processes. *Mind maps* consist of idea clusters, each logically connected to the other. The illustration here shows how one student who is trying to begin a paper in psychology might start with a mind map about reasons for the "bystander effect"—the situation when people don't act as they witness a crime being committed:

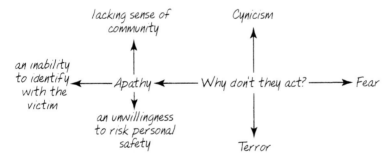

For writers who stare at a blank page in hopes of writing a polished first paragraph, creating a list might be the way to begin. Suppose you need to write a paper on the merits of sources of fuel other than oil and you don't know where or how to start. Why not begin by listing possible alternative sources?

Gasohol

Solar

Natural gas

Hydroelectric

Writing teachers sometimes call such strategies *prewriting,* but in fact this is as much writing as a full-blown paragraph would be. The difference, of course, is the first can get us to the second; it is a means to an end.

Nely, a student in a basic writing course, has the assignment of writing an essay that evaluates her course progress; this will become part of her *portfolio,* a collection of writings that she is to submit for a grade. A writer whose native language is not English, Nely takes the option of listing and mapping ideas—rather than attempting to start by drafting the essay. This is what she comes up with:

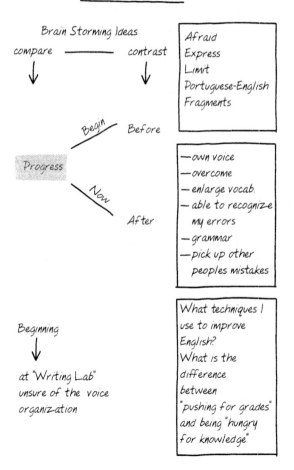

My Progress in English

Brain Storming Ideas

compare ———— contrast

Afraid
Express
Limit
Portuguese-English
Fragments

Begin Before

Progress

Now

After

—own voice
—overcome
— enlarge vocab.
— able to recognize
    my errors
—grammar
—pick up other
  peoples mistakes

Beginning

at "Writing Lab"
unsure of the voice
organization

What techniques I
use to improve
English?
What is the
difference
between
"pushing for grades"
and being "hungry
for knowledge"

Note how Nely clusters her ideas. First she highlights the word *progress* and then divides her topic into two, *Begin* and *Now*. She then begins to list additional subtopics that characterize or qualify her language abilities at the time (from *Afraid* to *Fragments* in the *Before* box). Nely is at a preliminary stage—we can see how sketchy the list is—as she writes down informal questions that she hopes will generate more thinking. But she is making real progress thinking out her paper.

Grounding the Theory

1. Construct a mind map for an assignment that you are working on from one of your classes. As with the model above, begin with a question and then provide tentative answers. Aim at providing at least two clusters.

2. Recent advances in medical technology have made it possible to implant a wireless mechanical heart in a patient whose own heart is failing. Try to construct a mind or conceptual map (using Nely's as a guide but designing your own distinctive map) that allows you to frame a question about such a mechanical heart. For example, your map might have as its center "wheel" the possible benefits (or harmful consequences) of such a device.

Discovering Detail: Asking Who? What? Where? When? Why? How?

Once you've begun to generate ideas through lists and clusters, your task then shifts to *developing* some of those ideas. Most teachers, regardless of their discipline, require that you take the time to spell out clearly the substance of your ideas. It does not matter that you are writing an explication of a poem or you are preparing a description of a lab experiment; your writing must be detailed. It must be *about* something.

You could of course simply begin to draft, and in the act of composing supply the substantive detail that your reader will need. Or you can content yourself early on (having given yourself the time to do so) with *asking generative questions* designed to elicit such detail. That's exactly what Nely does. After a mapping session that provides her with an approach to her topic (and a structure of *Before* and *After*), she asks and attempts to answer certain questions:

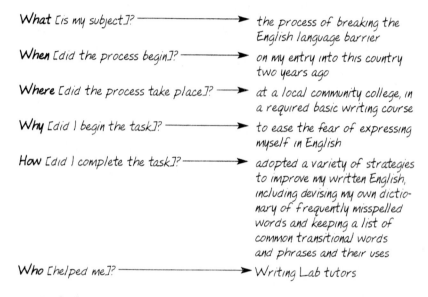

What [is my subject]? ⟶ the process of breaking the English language barrier

When [did the process begin]? ⟶ on my entry into this country two years ago

Where [did the process take place]? ⟶ at a local community college, in a required basic writing course

Why [did I begin the task]? ⟶ to ease the fear of expressing myself in English

How [did I complete the task]? ⟶ adopted a variety of strategies to improve my written English, including devising my own dictionary of frequently misspelled words and keeping a list of common transitional words and phrases and their uses

Who [helped me]? ⟶ Writing Lab tutors

Nely has not yet started to draft her essay, to be sure. But, she has arrived at a *structure* and, most important, has begun to fashion the *content* of her paper, all without writing a paragraph. That task—the composing of the actual essay—has become much less intimidating for Nely given the amount of writing and thinking she has already done. She knows her subject, knows the approach she wants toward her subject, and has begun to flesh out her argument by asking herself the right questions.

Grounding the Theory

1. Imagine that you're being asked to chart your development as a writer (as Nely needed to do). Use the Who? What? Where? When? Why? How? questions to develop detail on your subject.

2. Cut out an article from a newspaper. Put the piece to the test by asking the same questions. Does the writer provide the necessary detail? If not, what information is not provided?

Freewriting

Nely may want to do more low-pressure writing, and thereby explore her topic further, rather than attempt to compose a draft per se. Writing teachers have suggested for several decades now that so-called *freewriting* can liberate tentative writers who relentlessly edit or who censor themselves even before they have written a single word. Freewriting is usually done under the following conditions:

- The writing is informal and ungraded.
- It is timed and uninterrupted.
- The writer does not stop to cross out or edit the work but rather pushes on to generate as much language on the page as possible.

Within introductory composition courses, freewriting is often used in a very informal way to allow writers to discover topics of their own or to explore their feelings about a subject.

Deeper in the curriculum, students can turn to freewriting as a means of testing out certain ideas and areas of interest, or even just asking pertinent questions. When asked to reflect on what makes for a good teacher, one student, for example, produced this freewriting:

```
In   contrast   to   the   nasty   expression
"those who can't do, teach," I believe a
good teacher is one who has developed cre-
atively in his or her chosen area of ex-
pertise, who can "walk the talk," yet has
chosen to facilitate growth and learning
in others. A good teacher is passionate
about what he or she does, and is able to
```

```
communicate that enthusiasm to students.
I also believe a good teacher needs excel-
lent listening skills, and the ability to
stay flexible and to adapt teaching ap-
proaches as necessary to accommodate dif-
ferent learning styles. Most importantly,
a good teacher needs a sense of humor and
an effective stress-management program.
```

Through freewriting, a student is able to carve out a sub-ject for inquiry. In the example just given, the freewriting al-lows the student to break a large subject into smaller, man-ageable components (a good teacher has many qualities: passion, flexibility, good sense of humor. . . .) Indeed, the student begins the process of asking, and presenting possible answers to, critical questions.

Of course, no writing is ever "free." All writing, as we shall see in Chapter 5, is shaped by the pressures of purpose and au-dience (even if the purpose is to recollect the events of the day in a diary and even if the audience is just you). And freewrit-ing itself may be seen as the beginnings of a draft. Peter Elbow, a noted teacher of writing, suggests a variation of freewriting, which he calls *loop writing.* In loop writing, we begin to freewrite, testing out a variety of paths or subjects, and then try to steer ourselves back to what we feel is the most interesting and fruitful subject. Freewriting and its variations work for many because such writing carries low risk; writers give them-selves time to explore and perhaps even to develop ideas with-out needing to check in with an overly critical reader.

Grounding the Theory

1. Freewrite for five minutes to discover topics for writing in one of your other classes.

2. Review what you have written. Try to isolate a thread of an idea that interests you more than others. Resume freewriting, this time narrowing the focus to that particular thread.

Reading to Generate Ideas

We need to remember at the outset that the ideas we seek to generate or "invent" as writers are to some degree the products of a vast network of influences, from the people we have conversed with and observed, to the books, magazines, and newspapers we have read and the films, television shows, song lyrics, and Internet sites we have encountered. "Nothing can come of nothing," says Shakespeare's King Lear: Idea- and meaning-making don't occur in a vacuum, but rather as part of an ongoing conversation or exchange.

Our ability to be active and alert readers and listeners in these conversations can pay big dividends as we attempt to generate ideas of our own. To begin with, then, one way of generating ideas during a writing task is to become a *critical reader*, annotating as we go along. *Annotating* involves a full range of response, from replaying or summarizing what has been written to reacting with disagreement, agreement, or surprise. For example, imagine reading this excerpt from the work of the psychologist Jerome Bruner:

What does he mean that "science is not something that ex- ists out there"?

What we knew was that science is not something that exists out there in nature, but that it is a tool in the mind of the knower—teacher and student alike.

We understood that science was not "out there" in the natural world but rather that it exists in our minds as a means of understanding nature.

This is nonsense: facts are facts and science reveals those facts.

Let's annotate a more extended piece of writing. The following paragraphs are from the beginning of a book review written by Margaret Talbot.

Education
From "The New Counterculture"

by Margaret Talbot

In the 1980s, when newspapers and magazines first started reporting on parents who had rejected school in favor of teaching their

The 1980s seemed unlikely to produce the homeschooling phenomenon, especially given the increasing number of mothers employed outside the home.

The assumptions at work, and lack of specificity, in this paragraph are unsettling. Were most mothers, regardless of social class, employed out of the home? To whom is the writer referring when she mentions "recognized experts" and "paid caregivers"?

Contrary to expectations, the home schooling movement has grown.

children at home, it seemed that the movement would never last—or if it lasted, would never grow. More and more mothers were working outside the home. More and more parents, especially in the upper middle class, were fretting about their children's pusuit of academic excellence and healthy socialization, while simultaneously outsourcing the management of both to recognized experts and paid caregivers. It did not seem an auspicious time for a movement that demanded the intensive labor of mothers willing to forgo careers and income; that set little store by certification, licensing, degrees, and other signifiers of professional expertise; that took pride in a kind of rustic do-it-yourselfism; and that, even in its large, conservative Christian wing, held fast to the progressive-educational notion of not rushing kids into academics too early. Like so many other self-conscious reversions to the way of our forebears, the home-schooling movement seemed destined to sputter out.

Instead it has developed over the past decade or so into a surprisingly vigorous counterculture. In 1985 about 50,000 children nationwide were learning at home. Current estimates range from 1.5 to 1.9 million. (The former is probably the more reliable number, though precision is hard to come by because neither the census nor any other national survey distinguishes between homeschooled children and others.) By comparison, charter schools—the most celebrated alternative in public schooling—enroll only about 350,000 students. Patricia Lines, a former Department of Education researcher who has studied home schooling since the mid-1980s, points to evidence, such as Florida's annual survey of home schoolers, suggesting that the population of kids learning at home is growing by 15 to 20 percent a year. Moreover, home schoolers as a group are extraordinarily committed—not only to educating their children as they see fit but also to building and sustaining organizations. They have founded thousands of local support groups across the country, along with an influential lobbying and legal-defense organization, dozens of publishers and curriculum suppliers, and six nationally circulated magazines. By now it seems reasonable to agree with Lines that "the rise of homeschooling is one of the most significant social trends of the past half century."

As these examples demonstrate, an engaged reading of the passage will begin a process of meaningful and productive inquiry.

Grounding the Theory

1. Annotate a portion of a reading from one of your classes. Frame a significant question that could be the basis of an extended piece of writing.

2. Read and annotate the following essay by the scientist Lewis Thomas. From your annotations, frame questions that might lead to productive discussion of this passage.

Biology
"On Societies as Organisms"

by Lewis Thomas

Viewed from a suitable height, the aggregating clusters of medical scientists in the bright sunlight of the boardwalk at Atlantic City, swarmed there from everywhere for the annual meetings, have the look of assemblages of social insects. There is the same vibrating, ionic movement, interrupted by the darting back and forth of jerky individuals to touch antennae and exchange small bits of information; periodically, the mass casts out, like a trout-line, a long single file unerringly toward Child's. If the boards were not fastened down, it would not be a surprise to see them put together a nest of sorts.

It is permissible to say this sort of thing about humans. They do resemble, in their most compulsively social behavior, ants at a distance. It is, however, quite bad form in biological circles to put it the other way round, to imply that the operation of insect societies has any relation at all to human affairs. The writers of books on insect behavior generally take pains, in their prefaces, to caution that insects are like creatures from another planet, that their behavior is absolutely foreign, totally unhuman, unearthly, almost unbiological. They are more like perfectly tooled but crazy little machines, and we violate science when we try to read human meanings in their arrangements.

It is hard for a bystander not to do so. Ants are so much like human beings as to be an embarrassment. They farm fungi, raise aphids as livestock, launch armies into wars, use chemical sprays to alarm and confuse enemies, capture slaves. The families of weaver ants engage in child labor, holding their larvae like shuttles to spin out the thread that sews the leaves together for their fungus gardens. They exchange information ceaselessly. They do everything but watch television.

What makes us most uncomfortable is that they, and the bees and termites and social wasps, seem to live two kinds of lives: they are individuals, going about the day's business without much evidence of thought for tomorrow, and they are at the same time component parts, cellular elements, in the huge, writhing, ruminating organism of the Hill, the nest, the hive. It is because of this aspect, I think, that we most wish for them to be something foreign. We do not like the notion that there can be collective societies with the capacity to behave like organisms. If such things exist, they can have nothing to do with us.

Still, there it is. A solitary ant, afield, cannot be considered to have much of anything on his mind; indeed, with only a few neurons strung together by fibers, he can't be imagined to have a mind at all, much less a thought. He is more like a ganglion on legs. Four ants together, or ten, encircling a dead moth on a path, begin to look more like an idea. They fumble and shove, gradually moving the food toward the Hill, but as though by blind chance. It is only when you watch the dense mass of thousands of ants, crowded together around the Hill, blackening the ground, that you begin to see the whole beast, and now you observe it thinking, planning, calculating, It is an intelligence, a kind of live computer, with crawling bits for its wits.

At a stage in the construction, twigs of certain size are needed, and all the members forage obsessively for twigs of just this size. Later, when outer walls are to be finished, thatched, the size must change, and as though given new orders by telephone, all the workers shift the search to the new twigs. If you disturb the arrangement of a part of the Hill, hundreds ants will set it vibrating, shifting, until it is put right again. Distant sources of food are somehow sensed, and long lines, like tentacles, reach out over the ground, up over walls, behind boulders, to fetch it in.

Termites are even more extraordinary in the way they seem to accumulate intelligence as they gather together. Two or three termites in a chamber will begin to pick up pellets and move them from place to place, but nothing comes of it; nothing is built. As more join in, they seem to reach a critical mass, a quorum, and the thinking begins. They place pellets atop pellets, then throw up columns and beautiful, curving, symmetrical arches, and the crystalline architecture of vaulted chambers is created. It is not known how they communicate with each other, how the chains of termites building one column know when to turn toward the crew on the adjacent column, or how, when the time comes, they manage the flawless joining of the arches. The stimuli that set them off at the outset, building collectively instead of shifting things about, may be pheromones released when they reach committee size. They react as if alarmed. They become agitated, excited, and then they begin working, like artists.

Bees live lives of organisms, tissues, cells, organelles, all at the same time. The single bee, out of the hive retrieving sugar (instructed by the dancer: "south-southeast for seven hundred meters, clover—mind you make corrections for the sundrift") is still as much a part of the hive as if attached by a filament. Building the hive, the workers have the look of embryonic cells organizing a developing tissue; from a distance they are like the viruses inside of a cell, running off row after row of symmetrical polygons as though laying down crystals. When the time for swarming comes, and the old queen prepares to leave with her part of the population, it is as though the hive were involved in mitosis. There is an agitated moving of bees back and forth, like granules in cell sap. They distribute themselves in almost precisely equal parts, half to the departing queen, half to the new one. Thus, like an egg, the great, hairy, black and golden creature splits in two, each with an equal share of the family genome.

The phenomenon of separate animals joining up to form an organism is not unique in insects. Slime-mold cells do it all the time, of course, in each life cycle. At first they are single amebocytes swimming around, eating bacteria, aloof from each other, untouching, voting straight Republican. Then, a bell sounds, and acrasin is released by special cells toward which the others converge in stellate ranks, touch, fuse together, and construct the slug, solid as a trout. A splendid stalk is raised, with a fruiting body on top, and out of this comes the next generation of amebocytes, ready to swim across the same moist ground, solitary and ambitious.

Herring and other fish in schools are at times so closely integrated, their actions so coordinated, that they seem to be functionally a great multi-fish organism. Flocking birds, especially the seabirds nesting on the slopes of offshore islands in Newfoundland, are similarly attached, connected, synchronized.

Although we are by all odds the most social of all social animals—more interdependent, more attached to each other, more inseparable in our behavior than bees—we do not often feel our conjoined intelligence. Perhaps, however, we are linked in circuits for the storage, processing, and retrieval of information, since this

appears to be the most basic and universal of all human enter-
prises. It may be our biological function to build a certain kind of
Hill. We have access to all the information of the biosphere, arriv-
ing as elementary units in the stream of solar photons. When we
have learned how these are rearranged against randomness, to
make, say, springtails, quantum mechanics, and the late quartets,
we may have a clearer notion how to proceed. The circuitry seems
to be there, even if the current is not always on.

The system of communications used in science should provide
a neat, workable model for studying mechanisms of information-
building in human society. Ziman, in a recent *Nature* essay, points
out, "the invention of a mechanism for the systematic publication
of *fragments* of scientific work may well have been the key event
in the history of modern science." He continues:

> A regular journal carries from one research worker to an-
> other the various . . . observations which are of common
> interest. . . . A typical scientific paper has never pretended
> to be more than another little piece in a larger jigsaw—not
> significant in itself but as an element in a grander scheme.
> *This technique, of soliciting many modest contributions to
> the store of human knowledge, has been the secret of West-
> ern science since the seventeenth century, for it achieves a
> corporate, collective power that is far greater than any one
> individual can exert.* [italics mine]

With some alteration of terms, some toning down, the passage
could describe the building of a termite nest.

It is fascinating that the word "explore" does not apply to the
searching aspect of the activity, but has its origins in the sounds we
make while engaged in it. We like to think of exploring in science
as a lonely, meditative business, and so it is in the first stages, but
always, sooner or later, before the enterprise reaches completion,
as we explore, we call to each other, communicate, publish, send
letters to the editor, present papers, cry out on finding.

What Do You Need to Know?

After you have taken stock of what you already know, you begin to work with that knowledge. It now becomes necessary

to identify the gaps between what you know and what you need to know. Inquiry—and, more broadly, writing with consequence—require that you need and want to discover more about your writing subject. All the strategies that we've discussed so far should help lead the way toward discovering such a subject, but so much depends on your own curiosity and your own desire to find answers.

It can be helpful to set up a reading or observational log, in which you record your experience and your first steps toward framing questions for writing later on. Purchase a looseleaf binder as your notebook; this will allow you to pull out and replace entries, in case your teacher wants to review them along the way. Divide your log into five sections:

- Expectations and assumptions
- Surprises
- Confusion
- Contradictions
- Questions for further inquiry

Prior to starting to read or observe, jot down your expectations and a statement of what you know about your subject to this point. Then, when finished reading or observing, describe, in the appropriate part of your log, anything that surprised you along the way, any confusion you might be experiencing, inconsistencies, outright contradictions, and questions that have arisen during this process.

Grounding the Theory

1. Keep a reading or observational log for one of your classes. Try to come up with three to five questions for further inquiry.

2. Looking back at "The New Counterculture," write down some questions for which you need answers.

When Others Ask the Questions

It is safe to assume that most writing is driven not only by a
writer's own desire to say something but also by a desire to
satisfy a need suggested by someone else. In college, this
fact is self-evident, since the writing that is done there is in
direct response to teachers' prompting. But the same is
likely to be true in the workplace, since writing there is
prompted by a supervisor's or a colleague's or a client's
need to resolve a particular problem or meet some specific
demand. Inquiry still drives the writing, but when the inquiry is shared or originated by someone other than the
writer, it very much depends on the particular context of
classroom and workplace. Knowing, then, how to fashion a
question for writing hinges on the writer's understanding of
the *prompt,* the question or issue that the writing is to address. Let's look at an example of an assignment from an introductory management course. The task is to produce a
business plan, a form of writing done in both the classroom
and in the corporate world:

Sample Writing Assignment from an
Introduction to Management Course

Produce a business plan. A good business plan requires a good idea, appropriate research and analysis,
and a comprehensive and compelling argument for
why the business is likely to succeed.

The Idea

Your idea needs to be feasible and relatively low cost
(you probably can't afford to start an automobile fac-
tory). In coming up with an idea, use your personal
experience as a resource. For example, you may want
to focus on products or services that would appeal to
college students.

The Research

You will need to do two types of research for your project. First, you need to learn more generally about the type of business you plan to go into. To accomplish this you will need to do background research using the library and electronic resources. You may also find it helpful to interview people who are in similar businesses.

The second type of research relates specifically to your target market. Your business will only be profitable if there is a demand for your product/service and if you can satisfy that demand at a cost that is less than the selling price for your product/service. To determine if there is sufficient demand, you will need to develop a simple marketing survey.

The Plan

The business plan should provide a comprehensive and compelling story that would convince an investor that your business has potential.

The Final Version

The final version of the plan should include, among other elements:

A mission statement

An organizational and marketing plan

A financial analysis

An annotated bibliography

Clearly this assignment calls upon widely divergent ways of knowing. It asks the writer to demonstrate

- Procedural knowledge: how to develop a marketing survey

Responding to Writing Prompts: A Checklist

✓ **Read the prompt completely at least once, to get the lay of the land.** Often students do not understand instructions sufficiently and their writing suffers accordingly—because they spend too little time up front thinking about the form and intent of the assignment.

✓ **Consider your audience.** Remember that writing is, fundamentally, an act of communication with another. Understanding the needs and anticipating the questions of your reader is absolutely essential to making your writing work. An awareness of audience shapes everything from the language and tone that you use to the extent of evidence that you provide.

✓ **Underline terms that describe formal and organizational aspects of the writing.** Are you to write an academic essay? an annotated bibliography? a care plan? What are the expectations that go along with the genre that you are to use? The genres often vary from course to course, and with them so do the prompter's expectations.

- Reflective knowledge: a critical analysis of the findings
- Knowledge of the genre of the business plan itself: understanding the purposes and language usually associated with the different subsections of the plan, such as the mission statement, marketing plan, and financial analysis (as well as an annotated bibliography)

The writer's challenge is complex indeed: from inventing a company, to analyzing a target market, to promoting and marketing its product and, finally, projecting income and expenditures. Any effort to begin such a project must involve an understanding of the entire scheme and the processes involved.

Understanding the writing prompt when beginning to work on a project is crucial. You don't want to commit a great deal of energy to researching, reflecting, and writing on a project unless you understand the ground rules. As guidelines, I suggest following the practices in the checklist boxes on pages 58–59 when given detailed writing prompts.

Grounding the Theory

1. Analyze an assignment from one of your classes by using the checklists given on pages 58–59. Describe the teacher's expectations of the form and content of the project.

Responding to Discipline—Specific Writing Prompts: A Checklist

✓ **Underline procedural terms, that is, words that point to processes and activities, like *compare and contrast, survey, analyze,* or *argue.*** Too often, such terms take on a near-invisibility because we have seen them so often and have been called upon to engage in such processes again and again. But we need to make such terms visible: A failure to understand their intent may severely undermine our efforts to meet the demands of the writing task.

✓ **Underline (and annotate) technical terms, specific to the discipline or community in which the writing is being generated, and critical to the task itself.** An understanding, and accurate use, of the phrase *target audience,* for example, or *spreadsheet analysis* will be indispensable to an effective business plan.

✓ **Indicate questions, if you have them, in the margins.** Above all, inquire further of your prompter (teacher, colleague, supervisor) if you have any questions at all about what is being asked of you as you set out to do the writing task.

2. Read the following assignment taken from an introductory chem-
    istry course. Use the checklists to analyze the assignment.

What's Under the Kitchen Sink?

All of us have an amazing arsenal of chemicals in our
homes. To see this, simply venture into your kitchen, laundry,
bathroom, shop, garden shed, or garage, and begin reading
labels! Take a close look at these chemicals—specifically cleaning products. In groups of two, do short experiments in each
area, and then design and complete a study of your own
choosing. In the second week each group needs to carry out
controlled experiments in stain removal. Simulate washing
machines, automatic dishwashers, and test abrasives. Groups
should pool their data and arrive at conclusions useful to
them as consumers (e.g., the washing machine group decides
on the best cleaning conditions for the set of fabrics and
stains tested). The lab should end with oral reports by the
groups, which summarize the results of the controlled experiments in stain removal, and oral reports by each pair, which
give the results of the independent investigations done the
first week.

Disciplinary Perspective: History as Inquiry

What does it mean to frame a question in a particular subject
area or discipline? Do historians ask the same kinds of questions in their work as biologists in theirs? Our ability to ask
meaningful questions in various subject areas depends to a
great degree on how well we've adopted the ways of thinking
in those areas. The fact of the matter is, historians do differ a
bit from biologists in their mode of professional thinking, yet
both groups share a need to be able to pose significant questions for inquiry and research.

As part of an effort to understand how specialists frame questions in their fields, faculty in particular disciplines have been interviewed expressly for this book. You can hear them talk about the *ways of knowing* in those disciplines; the first interview follows. Then we meet the first of a number of students who, like you, are struggling to understand "what the teacher wants." They remind us that entry into a knowledge community sometimes poses stunning challenges.

Thinking Like a Historian:
An Interview with a Teacher of History

To the outsider, or nonspecialist, the work of a discipline often seems mysterious and inaccessible. To help remedy that situation, I asked Maureen Sowa, a colleague and teacher of U.S., Western, and Southeast Asian history, to talk with me about what it takes to get "inside" the field of history. With a Ph.D. in American history from Clark University, Maureen Sowa has taught at Bristol Community College in Fall River, Massachusetts, since 1989. A self-described storyteller, Professor Sowa uses oral histories in her classroom teaching and relies on them in her research as well. She is currently working on an oral history of the experience of American soldiers held captive in World War II concentration camps. We began by talking about what it means to think as a historian. The following excerpt from our conversation begins with her reply; the words in brackets represent my editing for clarity.

A. Thinking in the discipline required the evolution of higher critical thinking skills. I think the process began when I went to the University of San Francisco, a Jesuit university. [My instructors] consistently asked, "Why?" They consistently asked me to prove my analysis. And the first step of proving the facts is a first step to understanding history as inquiry. *History* is derivative of a Greek word meaning

Prove your analysis

"inquiry"—to ask "Why?" When I transferred to Hawaii, I took a course at the University of Hawaii, from Dr. Thomas Dowd Murphy, a crusty old Irishman who insisted that we think historically. I tried to figure out what he meant. It [finally] dawned on me that the important question in history was not who, what, when, [or] where, but [to understand] how and why things happened. The purpose of history is not to avoid repeating events but [to understand] how and why we do things here and now, to add context to the world in which we live. The gift of a historian, of critical thinking, is to look for the connections that are not obvious.

Q. Do you let students know how difficult it was for you to think historically?

A. Absolutely. I always tell them about Dr. Murphy. I had been the classic good student in high school—I could get by with short-term memory but never make the connection [between the "what" and the "why" events happened]. There's no right answer. In terms of history, I ask, "What's your thesis? Now support it with the evidence." Support is where the thinking historically comes in. History is a dialogue between the present and the past and the danger is to be too *presentist*, to apply the value of the present to the past.

Q. What way of thinking do you expect [from your students]?

A. [Students] have to think through their position, the nature of the society in which they lived; they have to understand context. It makes them connect in real ways to the past; the past has content. I asked a very interesting question in class the other day and got some interesting responses. I asked, "What is history and how do we know it?" "History is written down." "We know it through artifacts." And that was it. We had a good discussion. And I asked, Is that sufficient? Let me tell you a story about the Narragansetts, the loss of Narragansett lives during King Philip's War. Five hundred Narragansett men, women, and children were burned to death in the Great Swamp by New England colonial units. Is that a fight, a battle, or is it a massacre? You tell me what it is.

Ask yourself: how and why did these events occur?

Support your thesis

What is your bias?

The way we know history is through the lens of our own experience, our own perceptions, our own biases. My favorite final exam is: "You are being given the privilege of time travel. Select ten artifacts and explain to me how those artifacts represent the development of a civilization." I want [students] to think, not just to write mechanically sound essays. Another favorite is, "You have been given the privilege to invite three people to dinner from the group we have studied. Which would you invite? Why?" This is not the "great man" theory of history. If you want to bring back a woman from Deerfield, Massachusetts, from the 1700s, you can. What I am trying to teach them is that there are multiple prisms through which to look at facts.

Some of my colleagues will accuse me of being relativist, of believing that there is no concrete historical truth. To some degree that is so. History is a political construction. It's a construction of the period in which you live. Unfortunately, from K through 12, history is taught as an uncritical timeline, an acquisition of facts. It is a perfect vehicle to teach critical thinking at a very high level because you are asking yourself the fundamental questions: What do we know? How do we know it? And when we know it, what difference does it make that we know it? What are the cause and effect of this event? Those are the critical questions in the discipline of history.

What do you know, and why is it important?

Case Study

ANA PREPARES TO ENGAGE IN A CRITICAL INQUIRY OF COLUMBUS

The task of a professional historian seems light-years away from the chore that awaits students in a history class, who are just beginning to do historical analysis. After all, students rarely have the freedom to choose their own subjects for research. Moreover, they just as rarely have the opportunity to work with *primary sources* (material drawn from the period of history that is being studied). Instead they tend to work with historians' interpretations of events. Under these circumstances, how do students of history begin to frame their questions? Let's consider the case of Ana.

Ana's Background

Ana, on her way to majoring in psychology, is a full-time student on the brink of receiving her associate's degree. She has taken at least five different history courses and, for the most part, has enjoyed them. In our conversation, I asked Ana to recall the challenges posed by those courses. Was there an aspect of the courses that she couldn't crack or that seemed kind of daunting at first? In working on one assignment for a course in European history Ana admitted, "I made a mistake—I was thinking about the audience today rather than the audience at that time." In that work, she had to evaluate the purpose and effectiveness of a slave narrative. "The purpose didn't make sense to me," she admitted. "Had I placed it in the time that it was written for, then it [would have made] sense." When I asked Ana what advice she would give to students on beginning the work of writing in history, she said, "Go into the class as if you have no preconceptions; be open to a different interpretation." "Part of interpreting history," she added, "is putting things into context, purpose: why someone is telling a story."

Reading the Assignment

Ana's assignment in her European history course was complex. She was to compare the representation of Christopher Columbus in Hans Koning's *Columbus: His Enterprise* with a representation given in another book of her own choosing. She was given a series of questions to guide her consideration of each work:

- How factually accurate was the account?

- What was omitted that in your judgment would be important for a full understanding of Columbus?

- What motives does the book give to Columbus?

- What does the book get you to root for, and how do they accomplish that?

⬚ What function do pictures play in the book?

⬚ In your opinion, why does the book portray the Columbus/Indian encounter the way it does?

In requiring her to analyze each work, while at the same time comparing them, the task proved very challenging to Ana. Where should she begin? We will follow her through each phase of the assignment.

Organizing the Inquiry

1. What Did Ana Know? and How Did She Know It?

The Koning book introduces Ana to "a different side of Columbus," different from the purely heroic image of Columbus given in traditional narratives presented to her in earlier history courses. She had been told in those courses that Columbus had indeed discovered the New World and had done so out of motives that were public and not personal (in service of the King and Queen of Spain and of the Church). She had received this information mostly from textbooks, whose truthfulness and factual detail she had always taken for granted.

2. Outlining the Paper

Ana is beginning to rely on tried-and-true strategies for developing a line of inquiry. "I discover my thesis," Ana told me, "throughout the writing of the paper: I start jotting down ideas, how I feel about what I read." In her notes on the assignment focusing on the depiction of Columbus, she writes:

> Intro? name the books
> proof w/examples of details that show your opinion
> apply examples to each category

Although she prefers to "discover" her point during the writing of a paper, Ana is savvy enough to believe that her final paper needs an introductory paragraph to orient her reader, but she needs, by the same token, not to be narrowly confined by a simplistic thesis statement (one man is right, the other wrong). The question mark after "Intro" suggests her own uncertainty as to how formal an essay this work must be—if by "formal" we mean a piece of classroom writing that has a clear introductory paragraph, a body that supports the position taken, and a conclusion that sums it all up.

3. Ana Evaluates What She Knows and Inches Toward the Right Question

Hans Koning's unflattering treatment of Columbus's overweening ambition surprises Ana. She is led to reconsider the truthfulness of those early, textbook accounts. Clearly, Ana is being asked to read a text in a way that is entirely new to her. Instead of accepting what was written as authoritative she is being led to question why the story was being told and by whom. She later reflected

> What I realized as I struggled in my writing was each author's exposure and life experiences gave each of them their interpretation. Peter Sis [the author of *Follow the Dream,* the children's book that Ana selected] came from a country with walls [behind the Iron Curtain]; he was an immigrant. I could see how he could see Columbus as an explorer, how he broke down the walls. Koning was more of a social activist. He wrote his book for the Quincentennial celebration. Here are two authors who have very distinct impressions of one man.

Ana discovers that authors' political agendas—and cultural values—can shape the stories they tell. Peter Sis's own immigrant past becomes a lens through which to witness the Columbian adventure. Similarly, social activism and the time's critical reassessment of Columbus led Koning to write his damning account of the man and his voyage. The question that Ana is inching toward is this: To what extent do the values of a particular time and place and of the authors themselves affect the telling of history?

Framing a Question about the Past

1. According to Maureen Sowa, the study of history requires us to ask two critical questions: What do we know and how did we come to know it? Collect an artifact from your own neighborhood. What does the object say about the neighborhood or community? How do you know?

2. Following another assignment given by Professor Sowa, choose a person from history whom you have invited to dinner. What questions would you ask? Why?

3. Assume that you are collecting materials for a time capsule (a container to be buried, filled with representative objects from a particular time). What questions need to be asked to guide you in your selection?

For Extended Writing

1. Write a scenario of your own that invites the kind of inquiry that Professor Sowa talks about. Keep in mind the caveats that Professor Sowa and Ana offer: avoid the trap of "presentism," or assuming that the characters you've described share your own time's values and concerns. Keep historical context in mind.

2. Write a paper that contrasts two ways of looking at an important historical event that has occurred in your own lifetime. How do you account for the differences?

Framing Inquiry in the Extra-Curriculum: Memoirs

What a Memoir Is and What It Is Not

The writing of history is by no means limited to schools or colleges. Writing about the past may take a variety of forms—from statistical and demographic analysis to the journal writing that any of us might do at the end of a day. It may not surprise you to learn that such writing is exceedingly popular and prevalent in our culture. Indeed, writing about the past may be as thoroughly human an undertaking as reflection itself. After all, writers from all socioeconomic classes and cultures have for centuries committed to writing or to memory the record of the past.

We are using the term "extra-curriculum" to refer to the learning that takes place outside the classroom. Within this broad area, the *genre* or kind of historical writing known as *memoir* is especially popular. To write an effective memoir, you need to do the following:

- Try to focus on a narrow experience, a moment in time. Rather than describe a lifetime's worth of experience, try to single out a particular experience.

- Select an experience that has resonance for you—in other words, an experience that, in retrospect, had considerable impact on you and on others.

- Retell the experience in sharp, vivid detail.

- Draw out the significance of that experience, both for you and for your reader.

That last point is especially significant, since memoirs are by no means merely personal. They ought to have a public impact and function as well. Historians seek to account for the past not merely by studying the movements of the times but by inspecting the artifacts and records of local communities.

Limiting Your Subject: Knowing How to Ask the Right Questions

When composing a memoir, how do you know where to begin, or what to write about? This chapter has suggested a variety of approaches that you can take in conducting inquiry—as summarized on the next page.

Discovering Critical Questions about Which to Write: A Checklist

✓ Determine what you already know about specific topics (your expertise).

✓ Evaluate the value and meaning of what you know, employing strategies that will help you narrow your subject.

✓ Establish what you need to know

✓ When others frame a question for you (as in the case of teachers or supervisors), determine their expectations and the parameters of the assignment given.

I would add the following suggestions, specifically related to the challenge of writing about the past:

✓ Develop a historical context, paying attention to the details of the past.

✓ Acknowledge the effect of the present on the past, even as you construct such a context. In other words, be aware that the act of selecting events of the past is just that, a meaningful and subjective selection.

Taking a Closer Look

1. Relying on lists and on conceptual maps, begin to identify experiences of your own that could be the focus of a memoir. What questions need to be asked in order to determine the appropriateness of such experiences for a memoir?

2. Construct a timeline. One way of connecting the personal past with the public is to construct a time line encompassing your own life span so far. Begin by drawing a line across the width of the page. At one end, and under the line, indicate your birth year;

and on the other, also under the line, the current year. Above the line, begin to write down significant public events in your lifetime. Where do the public and private history converge?

3. Read the following passage, taken from historian L. S. Stavrianos's account of his own past and of a larger public history:

> I worked as a waiter in a skid-row restaurant to help stock the lean family larder. The restaurant was located in the beautiful city of Vancouver. There my impressionable young mind was confronted daily with the contrast between the destitution and misery of the customers I waited on and the visibly boundless riches of the province of British Columbia.
>
> —from *Lifelines from Our Past*

From this brief excerpt, it is possible to discern the process by which this historian framed a question about the past. What is the critical question implied here? How do you know it?

4. By listing them, take stock of key concerns that you might have of a public nature (concern about the gap between rich and poor, black and white, and so forth). Freewrite your recollection of how you came to hold such beliefs: What experiences helped form them?

5. Having answered all four of the previous steps, compose your own public memoir, adhering to the guidelines given on pages 68–69.

Chapter 3

Scholarship: What Has Been Done Before?

Relying on the Works and Voices of Others

Scholarship represents the significant knowledge accumulated over time on a particular subject. Although we are accustomed to think of scientific and literary breakthroughs as the product of individual geniuses who work completely in isolation, the fact is that knowledge emerges from the give-and-take of *scholarly conversation* (in print or at conferences, for example), guided by the accepted practice of the time. Current work done, for example, by Ian Wilmut and his colleagues in engineering mammals relies on their knowledge of attempts by other researchers to facilitate cell differentiation. Similarly, Charles Darwin stood on the shoulders of scientists such as Jean Baptiste Lemarck, whose theory that environment and use contribute to the development of species greatly shaped Darwin's theory of evolution. If we see knowledge-making as a product of conversations among knowledgeable communities, then it becomes possible to see the value and purposes of citing and listing one's sources in a research paper. The reasons for doing so are not merely to verify the sources used by student researchers but to make the crucial point that knowledge derives from the interaction and intermingling of many people.

Selecting Primary and Secondary Sources

We all know of the child's game in which one person whispers a message into the ear of another, who then passes that message along quietly to yet another, and so on. And we all know what invariably happens: The message changes in transmission. It changes because each new messenger is further removed from the original source and because each new "translator" receives the message through his or her own filter. What is transmitted is not without value, to be sure; we could even study each new message as an interpretation of the original, but we need to make distinctions among those various versions and certainly between them and the original source.

When using sources, it is essential that you recognize the difference between a *primary* (the initial message) and a *secondary* source (the message after it has been filtered through others). The easiest way to think about the difference is to think of a primary document as firsthand, produced in the time being studied (primary documents include maps, photographs, letters, drawings, memoirs, diaries, and court records), and a secondary source as secondhand, coming after the fact and offering interpretation (such as a film review or an interpretation of a poem).

Although each has its important uses, primary sources form the bedrock of our understanding. How different would our understanding of the Holocaust be, for example, if we did not have photographs taken by Allied soldiers as they liberated the Nazi concentration camps; official records left by the Third Reich as to the formulation of "The Final Solution," the organized scheme to eliminate the Jews; or the artwork, poetry, and memoirs of camp survivors? Interpretive or secondary sources are crucial if we are to understand an event of such magnitude, but without primary sources, all of us—experts and lay readers alike—would be at a loss. Also, since they convey the past in immediate ways, primary sources can potentially carry significant power and authority. All we need to do is think of Anne Frank's *Diary of a Young Girl* to realize the intensity of that power and the legitimacy of that authority.

But we are also dependent on secondary sources to learn more about the circumstances under which the *Diary* was written and how it found its way into print. Did Anne Frank revise her work? If so, in what way did the *Diary* change over time? How and by whom was the *Diary* found? How did it become published? These are questions of importance. We will find the answers by consulting scholars who have written about the making of the *Diary*.

But how do we know when to draw upon primary sources and when to call upon secondary accounts? There is no easy answer to that question. So much depends on our rhetorical purpose:

Why are we writing?

To whom are we writing?

What form will the writing take?

Ask yourself, how will my purpose in writing be fulfilled and enhanced by calling upon the voices of others—especially the voices of eyewitnesses to, and participants in, history?

Grounding the Theory

1. Which of the following would you consider a primary source? A secondary source? Why?

   a. A book review
   b. A taped interview
   c. An encyclopedia article
   d. A birth certificate
   e. An opinion poll

2. Imagine that you are studying the chronology and consequences of Jewish deportations during the Holocaust, and you come across the following account in the diary of a young Dutch girl (her name, you discover, is Anne Frank), dated October 9, 1942:

   > Our many Jewish friends and acquaintances are being taken away in droves. The Gestapo is treating them very roughly and transporting them in cattle cars to Westerbork, the big camp in Drenthe to which they're sending all the Jews. . . . If it's that bad in Holland, what must it be like in those faraway and uncivilized places where the Germans are sending them? We assume that most of

them are being murdered. The English radio says they're being gassed.

Describe everything that you learned from this passage about the subject of deportation. Discuss the advantages of such a source. Indicate, as well, any disadvantages.

Taking Reflective Notes: A Dialectical Notebook

Usually when students are asked to write with sources, much is said about the importance of taking good notes, and the implication is that notes are meant solely to reproduce what is said in source material. That is certainly one of the uses of note taking. Many of us have found it useful, for example, to rely on a system of note cards when working with written sources. One group of cards can be devoted to summarizing critical passages. Another can be used to contain exactly quoted passages of significance. And yet another can simply contain the full bibliographic references.

Summary, by its very nature, assumes that we have understood what we have summarized. As useful as the described note-taking techniques are, they actually do not by themselves make it easier for us to process and understand the material that has been read. More effective would be a system of note taking that helps us fashion a point of view and an interpretation about what we have read. One approach uses what is called the *dialectical notebook,* a tool first proposed by the composition theorist Ann E. Berthoff. It works this way: You set up, or purchase, a two-column notebook. In one column, you copy an excerpt from your reading that seems to confuse you or that you have a strong feeling about (of rejection or affirmation, or even ambivalence). You may choose to restate the main point in your own words, or you may choose to respond by offering your own assessment of what is said. Of course, you can use the margins of your reading as well (following what we have learned about annotating in Chapter 2). Here's an example of how a dialectical response might look:

The quoted passage:

Your response, partly summary, partly query:

The earth is currently in the midst of the sixth major extinction in the history of life.

The causes of earlier extinction events (e.g. the extinction of dinosaurs) are uncertain but probably reflected changes in the physical environment caused by such factors as meteor impacts or pulses of volcanism. By contrast, the current extinction event is biotically driven—specifically by human impact on land use, species invasions, and atmospheric and climatic changes.

(Chapin FS, Sala O, Burke I, Grime J, Hooper D, Lauenroth W, Lombard A, Mooney H, Mosier A, Naeem S, Pacala S, Roy J, Steffen W, Tilman D. Ecosystem consequences of changing biodiversity. Bioscience 48: 45–52)

If I understand this passage correctly, the writers assert that human activity has had as serious an impact on the biodiversity of this planet as did volcanic and meteoric explosions in the age of the dinosaur. Is there direct scientific evidence linking human land use with such extinctions? Or are the writers applying a political or "green" agenda to their research? In other words, are they predicting what is to happen or making it their mission to prevent a morally suspect exploitation by humans of the environment?

Note that the student has done more than summarize the passage: She has begun to critique it, speculating as to the writers' possible bias.

By reflecting on and reacting to a reading, you begin to process the information gathered and to fashion your own point of view. The dialectical notebook promotes genuine critical engagement with the research that you have done.

Grounding the Theory

1. How do you take notes? Describe the process that you've used in the past, taking care to spell out some of the challenges of taking notes while listening to what a teacher is saying.

2. Try using a dialectical notebook during one of your classes. Jot down a point or two that you find confusing and, after the fact, write your response to that point.

Summarizing to Understand Sources

What is a summary? And how do you go about writing one effectively? The first question is more easily answered than the second. When you write a *summary*, you reproduce, in your own words, the main points of a source. That may make summarizing seem very mechanical, just a replaying of what we have read or observed. But consider a different view of summary: The process has as much to do with the way you think and deal with the complexity of the text being summarized as with the rigid application of certain rules. It stands to reason that summarizing an article on a subject with which we are unfamiliar—a report in a professional journal written by and for biologists, for example—will pose more significant challenges than would conveying the essence of an article from a newspaper that we read every day or from a weekly news magazine.

A summary attempts to identify and provide the larger argument of a piece of writing. For example, a summary of the newspaper article on the disabled golfer Casey Martin reprinted in Chapter 1 (pages 24–27) might read this way:

> The U.S. Supreme Court ruled that disabled golfer Casey Martin may use a golf cart during tournaments.

The Court found that allowing Martin to use a golf
cart during tournaments amounted to a reasonable accommodation under the Americans with Disabilities
Act.

It becomes easier to write such a summary if you realize that
a newspaper article typically begins with the "lead-in," the
major news and reader-grabbing element of the story. But you
will also need to be aware of the fact that, while the article
seems to focus on the struggle of one golfer to achieve accommodation, the case must also be seen against the broader context of the Disabilities Act. Note that your summary need not
include the dissenting opinion in the case, since such information is not the focus of the piece itself.

Your ability to summarize hinges on the degree to which
you can do the following:

- Understand the format of the text that you are reading
- Understand specialized terms and concepts that appear
  in the reading
- Understand the contours of the argument

Understanding the Format

Your ability to summarize the news article about the disabled
golfer Casey Martin depends in part on how well you understand the structure of a news story. By contrast, the act of
summarizing the Americans with Disabilities Act (excerpted
in Chapter 1) might require that you distinguish between the
"FINDINGS AND PURPOSES" and "DEFINITIONS" sections.
Or consider the task of summarizing the article by Ian
Wilmut and his colleagues.

To do so appropriately, you would need some understanding of articles published in scientific journals. You
could be aided by your familiarity with the presence and purpose of the boldfaced abstract at the beginning of the article.

Your ability to grasp the meaning of Table 1 (comparing the number of pregnancies and lambs produced by cell type used) will help as well. You would need to know that detailed information about the methods used is included in the "Methods" section at the end of the article.

Genetics
Viable offspring derived from fetal and adult mammalian cells

by I. Wilmut, A. E. Schnieke*, J. McWhir, A. J. Kind*
& K. H. S. Campbell

Roslin Institute (Edinburgh), Roslin, Midlothian EH25 9PS, UK

* *PPL Therapeutics, Roslin, Midlothian EH25 9PP, UK*

Fertilization of mammalian eggs is followed by successive cell divisions and progressive differentiation, first into the early embryo and subsequently into all of the cell types that make up the adult animal. Transfer of a single nucleus at a specific stage of development, to an enucleated unfertilized egg, provided an opportunity to investigate whether cellular differentiation to that stage involved irreversible genetic modification. The first offspring to develop from a differentiated cell were born after nuclear transfer from an embryo-derived cell line that had been induced to become quiescent[1]. Using the same procedure, we now report the birth of live lambs from three new cell populations established from adult mammary gland, fetus and embryo. The fact that a lamb was derived from an adult cell confirms that differentiation of that cell did not involve the irreversible modification of genetic material required for development to term. The birth of lambs from differentiated fetal and adult cells also reinforces previous speculation[1,2] that by inducing donor cells to become quiescent it will be possible to obtain normal development from a wide variety of differentiated cells.

It has long been known that in amphibians, nuclei transferred from adult keratinocytes established in culture support development to the juvenile, tadpole stage[3]. Although this involves differentiation into complex tissues and organs, no development to the adult stage was reported, leaving open the question of whether a differentiated adult nucleus can be fully reprogrammed. Previously we reported the birth of live lambs after nuclear transfer from cultured embryonic cells that had been induced into quiescence. We suggested that inducing the donor cell to exit the growth phase causes changes in chromatin structure that facilitate reprogramming of gene expression and that development would be normal if nuclei are used from a variety of differentiated donor cells in similar regimes. Here we investigate whether normal development to term is possible when donor cells derived from fetal or adult tissue are induced to exit the growth cycle and enter the G0 phase of the cell cycle before nuclear transfer.

Three new populations of cells were derived from (1) a day-9 embryo, (2) a day-26 fetus and (3) mammary gland of a 6-year-old ewe in the last trimester of pregnancy. Morphology of the embryo-derived cells (Fig. 1) is unlike both mouse embryonic stem (ES) cells and the embryo-derived cells used in our previous study. Nuclear transfer was carried out according to one of our established protocols[1] and reconstructed embryos transferred into recipient ewes. Ultrasound scanning detected 21 single fetuses on day 50–60 after oestrus (Table 1). On subsequent scanning at ~14-day intervals, fewer fetuses were observed, suggesting either mis-diagnosis or fetal loss. In total, 62% of fetuses were lost, a significantly greater proportion than the estimate of 6% after natural mating[4]. Increased prenatal loss has been reported after embryo manipulation or culture of unreconstructed embryos[5]. At about day 110 of pregnancy, four fetuses were dead, all from embryo-derived cells, and post-mortem analysis was possible after killing the ewes. Two fetuses had abnormal liver development, but no other abnormalities were detected and there was no evidence of infection.

Eight ewes gave birth to live lambs (Table 1, Fig. 2). All three cell populations were represented. One weak lamb, derived from the fetal fibroblasts, weighed 3.1 kg and died within a few minutes of birth, although post-mortem analysis failed to find any abnormality or infection. At 12.5%, perinatal loss was not dissimilar to that occurring in a large study of commercial sheep, when 8% of lambs died within 24 h of birth[6]. In all cases the lambs displayed the morphological characteristics of the breed used to derive the nucleus donors and not that of the oocyte donor (Table 2). This alone indicates that the lambs could not have been born after inadvertent mating of either the oocyte donor or recipient ewes. In addition, DNA microsatellite analysis of the cell populations and the lambs at four polymorphic loci confirmed that each lamb was derived from the cell population used as nuclear donor (Fig. 1). Duration of gestation is determined by fetal genotype[7], and in all cases gestation was longer than he breed mean (Table 2). By contrast, birth weight is influenced by both maternal and fetal genotype[8]. The birth weight of all lambs was within the range for single lambs born to Blackface ewes on our farm (up to 6.6 kg) and in most cases was within the range for the breed of the nuclear donor. There are no strict control observations for birth weight after embryo transfer between breeds, but the range in weight of lambs born to their own breed on our farms is 1.2–5.0 kg, 2–4.9 kg and 3–9 kg for the Finn Dorset, Welsh Mountain and Poll Dorset genotypes, respectively. The attainment of sexual maturity in the lambs is being monitored.

Development of embryos produced by nuclear transfer depends upon the maintenance of normal ploidy and creating the conditions

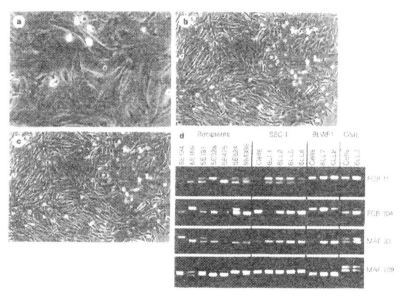

Figure 1 Phase-contrast photomicrograph of donor-cell populations: **a**, Embryo-derived cells (SEC1); **b**, fetal fibroblasts (BLWF1); **c**, mammary-derived cells (OME). **d**, Microsatellite analysis of recipient ewes, nuclear donor cells and lambs using four polymorphic ovine markers[22]. The ewes are arranged from left to right in the same order as the lambs. Cell populations are embryo-derived (SEC1), fetal-derived (BLW1), and mammary-derived (OME), respectively. Lambs have the same genotype as the donor cells and differ from their recipient mothers.

Table 1 Development of embryos reconstructed with three different cell types

Cell type	No. of fused couplets (%)*	No. recovered from oviduct (%)	No. cultured	No. of morula/ blastocyst (%)	No. of morula or blastocysts transferred†	No. of pregnancies/ no. of recipients (%)	No. of live lambs (%)‡
Mammary epithelium	277 (63.8)[a]	247 (89.2)	–	29 (11.7)[a]	29	1/13 (7.7)	1 (3.4%)
Fetal fibroblast	172 (84.7)[b]	124 (86.7)	-	34 (27.4)[b]	34	4/10 (40.0)	2 (5.9%)
			24	13 (54.2)[b]	6	1/6 (16.6)	1 (16.6%)§
Embryo-derived	385 (82.8)[b]	231 (85.3)	-	90 (39.0)[b]	72	14/27 (51.8)	4 (5.6%)
			92	36 (39.0)[b]	15	1/5 (20.0)	0

* As assessed 1 h after fusion by examination on a dissecting microscope. Superscripts a or b within a column indicate a significant difference between donor cell types in the efficiency of fusion ($P < 0.001$) or the proportion of embryos that developed to morula or blastocyst ($P < 0.001$).
† It was not practicable to transfer all morulae/blastocysts.
‡ As a proportion of morulae or blastocysts transferred. Not all recipients were perfectly synchronized.
§ This lamb died within a few minutes of birth.

Figure 2 Lamb number 6LL3 derived from the mammary gland of
a Finn Dorset ewe with the Scottish Blackface ewe which
was the recipient.

for developmental regulation of gene expression. These responses
are both influenced by the cell-cycle stage of donor and recipient
cells and the interaction between them (reviewed in ref. 9). A comparison of development of mouse and cattle embryos produced by
nuclear transfer to oocytes[10,11] or enucleated zygotes[12][13] suggests that
a greater proportion develop if the recipient is an oocyte. This may
be because factors that bring about reprogramming of gene expression in a transferred nucleus are required for early development and
are taken up by the pronuclei during development of the zygote.

If the recipient cytoplasm is prepared by enucleation of an
oocyte at metaphase II, it is only possible to avoid chromosomal
damage and maintain normal ploidy by transfer of diploid
nuclei[14,15], but further experiments are required to define the opti-
mum cell-cycle stage. Our studies with cultured cells suggest that
there is an advantage if cells are quiescent (ref. 1, and this work). In
earlier studies, donor cells were embryonic blastomeres that had
not been induced into quiescence. Comparisons of the phases of the
growth cycle showed that development was greater if donor cells
were in mitosis[16] or in the G1 (ref. 10) phase of the cycle, rather
than in S or G2 phases. Increased development using donor cells in
G0, G1 or mitosis may reflect greater access for reprogramming factors present in the oocyte cycoplasm, but a direct comparison of
these phases in the same cell population is required for a clearer
understanding of the underlying mechanisms.

Table 2 Delivery of lambs developing from embryos derived by nuclear transfer from three different donor cells types, showing gestation length and birth weight

Cell type	Breed of lamb	Lamb identity	Duration of pregnancy (days)*	Birth weight (kg)
Mammary epithelium	Finn Dorset	6LL3	148	6.6
Fetal fibroblast	Black Welsh	6LL7	152	5.6
	Black Welsh	6LL8	149	2.8
	Black Welsh	6LL9†	156	3.1
Embryo- derived	Poll Dorset	6LL1	149	6.5
	Poll Dorset	6LL2‡	152	6.2
	Poll Dorset	6LL5	148	4.2
	Poll Dorset	6LL6‡	152	5.3

* Breed averages are 143, 147 and 145 days, respectively for the three genotypes Finn Dorset, Black Welsh Mountain and Poll Dorset.
† This lamb died within a few minutes of birth.
‡ These lambs were delivered by caesarian section. Overall the nature of the assistance provided by the veterinary surgeon was similar to that expected in a commercial flock.

Together these results indicate that nuclei from a wide range of cell types should prove to be totipotent after enhancing opportunities for reprogramming by using appropriate combinations of these cell-cycle stages. In turn, the dissemination of the genetic improvement obtained within elite selection herds will be enhanced by limited replication of animals with proven performance by nuclear transfer from cells derived from adult animals. In addition, gene targeting in livestock should now be feasible by nuclear transfer from modified cell populations and will offer new opportunities in biotechnology. The techniques described also offer an opportunity to study the possible persistence and impact of epigenetic changes, such as imprinting and telomere shortening, which are known to occur in somatic cells during development and senescence, respectively.

The lamb born after nuclear transfer from a mammary gland cell is, to our knowledge, the first mammal to develop from a cell derived from an adult tissue. The phenotype of the donor cell is unknown. The primary culture contains mainly mammary epithelial (over 90%) as well as other differentiated cell types, including

myoepithelial cells and fibroblasts. We cannot exclude the possibility that there is a small proportion of relatively undifferentiated
stem cells able to support regeneration of the mammary gland during pregnancy. Birth of the lamb shows that during the development of that mammary cell there was no irreversible modification
of genetic information required for development to term. This is
consistent with the generally accepted view that mammalian differentiation is almost all achieved by systematic, sequential
changes in gene expression brought about by interactions between
the nucleus and the changing cytoplasmic environment[17].

Methods

Embryo-derived cells were obtained from embryonic disc of a day-
9 embryo from a Poll Dorset ewe cultured as described[1], with the
following modifications. Stem-cell medium was supplemented
with bovine DIA/LIF. After 8 days, the explanted disc was disag-
gregated by enzymatic digestion and cells replated onto fresh feed-
ers. After a further 7 days, a single colony of large flattened cells
was isolated and grown further in the absence of feeder cells. At
passage 8, the modal chromosome number was 54. These cells
were used as nuclear donors at passages 7–9. Fetal-derived cells
were obtained from an eviscerated Black Welsh Mountain fetus recovered at autopsy on day 26 of pregnancy. The head was removed
before tissues were cut into small pieces and the cells dispersed by
exposure to trypsin. Culture was in BHK 21 (Glasgow MEM; Gibco
Life Sciences) supplemented with L-glutamine (2 mM), sodium
pyruvate (1 mM) and 10% fetal calf serum. At 90% confluency, the
cells were passaged with a 1:2 division. At passage 4, these fibro-
blast-like cells (Fig. 1) had modal chromosome number of 54. Fetal
cells were used as nuclear donors at passages 4–6. Cells from mammary gland were obtained from a 6-year-old Finn Dorset ewe in the
last trimester of pregnancy[18]. At passages 3 and 6, the modal chromosome number was 54 and these cells were used as nuclear
donors at passage numbers 3–6.

   Nuclear transfer was done according to a previous protocol[1].
Oocytes were recovered from Scottish Blackface ewes between 28
and 33 h after injection of gonadotropin-releasing hormone
(GnRH), and enucleated as soon as possible. They were recovered
in calcium- and magnesium-free PBS containing 1% FCS and
transferred to calcium-free M2 medium[19] containing 10% FCS at
37 °C. Quiescent, diploid donor cells were produced by reducing
the concentration of serum in the medium from 10 to 0.5% for 5
days, causing the cells to exit the growth cycle and arrest in G0.

Confirmation that cells had left the cycle was obtained by staining with antiPCNA/cyclin antibody (Immuno Concepts), revealed by a second antibody conjugated with rhodamine (Dakopatts).

Fusion of the donor cell to the enucleated oocyte and activation of the oocyte were induced by the same electrical pulses, between 34 and 36 h after GnRH injection to donor ewes. The majority of reconstructed embryos were cultured in ligated oviducts of sheep as before, but some embryos produced by transfer from embryo-derived cells or fetal fibroblasts were cultured in a chemically defined medium[20]. Most embryos that developed to morula or blastocyst after 6 days of culture were transferred to recipients and allowed to develop to term (Table 1). One, two or three embryos were transferred to each ewe depending upon the availability of embryos. The effect of cell type upon fusion and development to morula or blastocyst was analysed using the marginal model of Breslow and Clayton[21]. No comparison was possible of development to term as it was not practicable to transfer all embryos developing to a suitable stage for transfer. When too many embryos were available, those having better morphology were selected.

Ultrasound scan was used for pregnancy diagnosis at around day 60 after oestrus and to monitor fetal development thereafter at 2-week intervals. Pregnant recipient ewes were monitored for nutritional status, body condition and signs of EAE, Q fever, border disease, louping ill and toxoplasmosis. As lambing approached, they were under constant observation and a veterinary surgeon called at the onset of parturition. Microsatellite analysis was carried out on DNA from the lambs and recipient ewes using four polymorphic ovine markers[22].

Received 25 November 1996; accepted 10 January 1997.

Endnotes

1. Campbell, K. H. S., McWhir, J., Ritchie, W. A. & Wilmut, I. Sheep cloned by nuclear transfer from a cultured cell line. *Nature* 380, 64–66 (1996).

2. Solter, D. Lambing by nuclear transfer. *Nature* 380, 24–25 (1996).

3. Gurdon, J. B., Laskey, R. A. & Reeves, O. R. The developmental capacity of nuclei transplanted from keratinized skin cells of adult frogs. *J. Embryol. Exp. Morph.* 34, 93–112 (1975)

4. Quinlivan, T. D., Martin, C. A., Taylor, W. B. & Cairney, I. M. Pre- and perinatal mortality in those ewes that conceived to one service. *J. Reprod. Fert.* 11, 379–390 (1966).

5. Walker, S. K., Heard, T. M. & Seamark, R. F. *In vitro* culture of sheep embryos without co-culture: successes and perspectives. *Therio* 37, 111–126 (1992).

6. Nash, M. L., Hungerford, L. L., Nash, T. G. & Zinn, G. M. Risk factors for perinatal and postnatal mortality in lambs. *Vet. Rec.* 139, 64–67 (1996).

7. Bradford, G. E., Hart, R., Quirke, J. F. & Land, R. B. Genetic control of the duration of gestation in sheep. *J. Reprod. Fert.* 30, 459–463 (1972).

8. Walton, A. & Hammond, J. The maternal effects on growth and conformation in Shire horse–Shetland pony crosses. *Proc. R. Soc. B* 125, 311–335 (1938).

9. Campbell, K. H. S., Loi, P., Otaegui, P. J. & Wilmut, I. Cell cycle coordination in embryo cloning by nuclear transfer. *Rev. Reprod.* 1, 40–46 (1996).

10. Cheong, H.-T., Takahashi, Y. & Kanagawa, H. Birth of mice after transplantation of early-cell-cycle-stage embryonic nuclei into enucleated oocytes. *Biol. Reprod.* 48, 958–963 (1993).

11. Prather, R. S. *et al.* Nuclear transplantation in the bovine embryo. Assessment of donor nuclei and recipient oocyte. *Biol. Reprod.* 37, 859–866 (1987).

12. McGrath, J. & Solter, D. Inability of mouse blastomere nuclei transferred to enucleated zygotes to support development *in vitro*. *Science* 226, 1317–1318 (1984).

13. Robl, J. M. *et al.* Nuclear transplantation in bovine embryos. *J. Anim. Sci.* 64, 642–647 (1987).

14. Campbell, K. H. S., Ritchie, W. A. & Wilmut, I. Nuclear-cytoplasmic interactions during the first cell cycle of nuclear transfer reconstructed bovine embryos: Implications for deoxyribonucleic acid replication and development. *Biol. Reprod.* 49, 933–942 (1993).

15. Barnes, F. L. *et al.* Influence of recipient oocyte cell cycle stage on DNA synthesis, nuclear envelope breakdown, chromosome constitution, and development in nuclear transplant bovine embryos. *Mol. Reprod. Dev.* 36, 33–41 (1993).

16. Kwon, O. Y. & Kono, T. Production of identical sextuplet mice by transferring metaphase nuclei from 4-cell embryos. *J. Reprod. Fert. Abst. Ser.* 17, 30 (1996).

17. Gurdon, J. B. The control of gene expression in animal development (Oxford University Press, Oxford, 1974).

18. Finch, L. M. B. *et al.* Primary culture of ovine mammary epithelial cells. *Biochem. Soc. Trans.* 24, 369S (1996).

19. Whitten, W. K. & Biggers, J. D. Complete development *in vitro* of the preimplantation stages of the mouse in a simple chemically defined medium. *J. Reprod. Fertil.* 17, 399–401 (1968).

20. Gardner, D. K., Lane, M., Spitzer, A. & Batt, P. A. Enhanced rates of cleavage and development for sheep zygotes cultured to the blastocyst stage in vitro in the absence of serum and somatic cells. Amino acids, vitamins, and culturing embryos in groups stimulate development. *Biol. Reprod.* 50, 390–400 (1994).

21. Breslow, N. E. & Clayton, D. G. Approximate inference in generalized linear mixed models. *J. Am. Stat. Assoc.* 88, 9–25 (1993).

22. Buchanan, F. C., Littlejohn, R. P., Galloway, S. M. & Crawford, A. L. Microsatellites and associated repetitive elements in the sheep genome. *Mammal. Gen.* 4, 258–264 (1993).

Acknowledgements. We thank A. Colman for his involvement throughout this experiment and for guidance during the preparation of this manuscript; C. Wilde for mammary-derived cells; M. Ritchie, J. Bracken, M. Malcolm-Smith, W.A. Ritchie, P. Ferrier and K. Mycock for technical assistance; D. Waddington for statistical analysis and H. Bowran and his colleagues for care of the animals. This research was supported in part by the Ministry of Agriculture, Fisheries and Food. The experiments were conducted under the Animals (Scientific Procedures) Act 1986 and with the approval of the Roslin Institute Animal Welfare and Experiments Committee.

Correspondence should be addressed to I.W. (e-mail Ian.Wilmut@ bbsrc.ac.uk).

Understanding Specialized Language in a Reading

Writers in particular disciplines rely on shorthand and specialized vocabulary, terms, and concepts known to those who work in that knowledge community. Summary requires comprehension of such terms. Looking again at the Wilmut article, you would do well to understand terms such as *progressive differentiation* and *nuclear transfer.* A failure to grasp all such technical terms need not prevent you from gaining the gist of the piece, but a complete understanding of such terms is a signal that you have thoroughly entered the scholarly conversation.

Understanding the Contours of the Argument

Perhaps most crucial of all is your ability to distinguish between the peaks and the valleys of a text. In others words, you need to be able to sift out a writer's main points from the detail supporting those points. In some sense, the process of summarizing comes down to the *strategic way* in which you read. Do you, for example, read a paragraph with the knowledge that the topic sentence (the controlling idea of that paragraph) usually comes early or late in that paragraph? Consider this essay by the semanticist, S. I. Hayakawa. Do you see how Hayakawa follows the contours of a conventional essay by stating in the first paragraph the view against which he is arguing? Do you also see how Hayakawa uses dialogue to support his view? Finally, are you aware that Hayakawa returns to his theme, language as play, in the closing?

Semantics
Words and Children

by S. I. Hayakawa

Those who still believe, after all the writing that semanticists have done, that semantics is a science of words, may be surprised to learn that semantics has the effect—at least, it has had on me and on many others—of reducing rather than increasing one's preoccupation with words. First of all, there is that vast area of nonverbal communication with children that we accomplish through holding, touching, rocking, caressing our children, putting food in their mouths, and all of the little attentions that we give them. These are all communication, and we communicate in this way for a long time before the children even start to talk.

Then, after they start to talk, there is always the problem of interpretation. There is a sense in which small children are recent immigrants in our midst. They have trouble both in understanding and in using the language, and they often make errors. Many people (you can notice this in the supermarkets, especially with parents of two- and three-year-old children) get angry at their children when they don't seem to mind. Anyone standing within earshot of one of these episodes can tell that the child just hasn't understood what the mother said. But the mother feels, "Well, I said it, didn't I? What's wrong with the child that he doesn't understand? It's English, isn't it?" But, as I say, the child is a recent immigrant in our midst and there are things that the child doesn't understand.

There are curious instances. Once, when our daughter was three years old, she found the bath too hot and she said, "Make it warmer." It took me a moment to figure out that she meant, "Bring the water more nearly to the condition we call warm." It makes perfectly good sense looked at that way. Confronted with unusual formulations such as these which children constantly make, many of us react with incredible lack of imagination. Sometimes children are laughed at for making "silly statements," when it only requires understanding their way of abstracting and their way of formulating their abstractions to see that they are not silly at all.

Again, when our daughter was three years old, I was pounding away at my typewriter in my study and she was drawing pictures on the floor when she suddenly said, "I want to go see the popentole."

I kept typing.

Then I stopped and said, "What?!"

She said, "I want to see the popentole."

"Did you say *popentole?*"

I just stopped. It was a puzzle to figure out, but I did. In a few seconds I said, "You mean like last Saturday, you want to go to Lincoln Park and see the totem pole?"

She said, "Yes."

And what was so warm about this, so wonderful about it, was that having got her point across she played for another twenty minutes singing to herself, happy that she had communicated. I didn't say to her, "Okay, I'll take you next Sunday to see the popentole." The mere fact that she'd made her point and got it registered was a source of satisfaction to her. And I felt very proud of myself at the time for having understood.

One of the things we tend to overlook in our culture is the tremendous value of the acknowledgment of message. Not, "I agree with you" or "I disagree with you" or "That's a wonderful idea" or "That's a silly idea," but just the acknowledgment, "I know exactly what you've said. It goes on the record. You said that." She said, "I want to go see the totem pole." I said, "Okay, you want to go see the totem pole." The acknowledgment of message says in effect, "I know you're around. I know what you're thinking. I acknowledge your presence."

There is also a sense in which a child understands far more than we suspect. Because a child doesn't understand words too well (and also because his nervous system is not yet deadened by years spent as a lawyer, accountant, advertising executive, or professor of philosophy), a child attends not only to what we say but to everything about us as we say it—tone of voice, gesture, facial expression, bodily tensions, and so on. A child attends to a conversation between grown-ups with the same amazing absorption. Indeed, a child listening is, I hope, like a good psychiatrist listening—or like a good semanticist listening—because she watches not only the words but also the nonverbal events to which words bear, in all too many cases, so uncertain a relationship. Therefore a child is in some matters quite difficult to fool, especially on the subject of one's true attitude toward her. For this reason many parents, without knowing it, are to a greater or lesser degree in the situation of the worried mother who said to the psychiatrist to whom she brought her child, "I tell her a dozen times a day that I love her, but the brat still hates me. Why, doctor?"

"Life in a big city is dangerous," a mother once said to me. "You hear so often of children running thoughtlessly out in the street and being struck by passing cars. They will never learn unless you keep telling them and telling them." This is the communication theory that makes otherwise pleasant men and women into nagging parents: You've got to keep telling them; then you've got to remind them; then tell 'em again. Are there no better ways to teach children not to run out into the street? Of course there are. I think it was done in our family without words.

Whenever my wife crossed the street with our boy Alan—he was then about three—she would come to a stop at the curb whether there was any traffic in sight or not, and look up and down the boulevard before crossing. It soon became a habit. One day I absentmindedly started crossing the street without looking up and down—the street was empty. Alan grabbed my coat and pulled me back on the curb to look up and down before we started out again. Children love to know the right way to do things. They learn by imitation far more than by precept.

The uncritical confidence that many people place in words is a matter of constant amazement to me. When we were living in Chicago there was a concrete courtyard behind our apartment house. I heard a great deal of noise and shouting out there one day, and I looked out and saw a father teaching his boy to ride a bicycle. The father was shouting instructions: "Keep your head up. Now push down with your left foot. Now look out, you're running into the wall. Steer away from it. *Steer away from it!* Now push down with your right foot. Don't fall down!" and so on and so on. The poor boy was trying to keep his balance, manage the bicycle, obey his father's instructions all at the same time, and he looked about as totally confused as it is possible for a little boy to get. One thing we learn from general semantics, if we haven't learned it some other way already, is that there are limits to what can be accomplished in words. Learning to ride a bicycle is beyond those limits. Having sensed those limits, we become content to let many things take care of themselves without words. All this makes for a quieter household.

The anthropologist Ray Birdwhistell has undertaken a study that he calls "kinesics,*" which is the systematic examination of gesture and body motion in communication; this is a rich area of concern about which many students of human behavior have been much excited. But there is a danger in going too far in this direction—in going overboard to the extent of saying that words are of *no* importance. There are thousands of things children must know and enjoy that it is not possible for them to get *without* words.

The sense of what one misses through the lack of words has been brought home to us by the fact that our second boy, Mark, now twenty-nine, is seriously mentally retarded. At the age of six he was hardly able to talk at all. Now he talks quite a bit, but his speech is very difficult to understand; members of the family can understand it about half the time. He was always able to understand words with direct physical referents—watch, glass of water, orange juice, record player, television, and so on. But there are certain things that exist only in words, like the concept of the future. I remember the following incident when he was six years old. He came across a candy bar at ten minutes to twelve when lunch was just about to be served. I tried to take it away from him and said, "Look, Mark, you can have it right after lunch. Don't eat it now. You can have it right after lunch." Well, when he was six all he could understand was that it was being taken away from him *now*, and the idea that there was a future in which he'd have it back was something he just couldn't get at the time. Of course, the concept of futurity developed later, but it took him much longer to develop it than it took the other children.

For human beings, the future, which exists *only in language*, is a wonderful dimension in which to live. That is, human beings can readily endure and even enjoy postponement; the anticipation of future pleasures is itself a pleasure. But futurity is something that has no physical referent like "a glass of water." It exists only in language. Mark's frequent frustrations and rage when he was younger were a constant reminder to us that all the warmth and richness of nonverbal communication, all that we could communicate by holding him and feeding him and patting his head and playing on the floor with him, were not enough for the purpose of human interaction. Organized games of any kind all have linguistically formulated rules. Take an organized game like baseball. Can there be a baseball without language? No, there can't. What's the difference between a ball and a strike? There are linguistically formulated rules by which we define the difference. All systematic games, even much simpler games that children play, have to have a language to formulate the rules. An enormous amount of human life is possible only with language, and without it one is very much impoverished.

---

*Ray Birdwhistell. *Kinesics and Context*. Philadelphia: University of Pennsylvania Press, 1970.

Keep in mind that you want to capture the author's key point and the substantive arguments used in support of that point.

Grounding the Theory

1. Using the checklist as a guide, prepare a summary of "Imagine That!" by Steven Pinker.

Biology
Imagine That!

by Steven Pinker

What shape are a beagle's ears? How many windows are in your living room? What's darker, a Christmas tree or a frozen pea? What's larger, a guinea pig or a gerbil? Does a lobster have a mouth? When a person stands up straight, is her navel above her wrist? If the letter *D* is turned on its back and put on top of a *J*, what does that combination remind you of?

How to Summarize: A Checklist

I would suggest the following as a way to produce a sound summary:

✓ **Read the original text thoroughly first, without marking it up.** This is the first go-around, as you get the lay of the land. Read for the big picture first before you work on understanding the component parts.

✓ **Put the text aside and write down your sense of the major point being made.** To create a sense of independence from the text (and your own empowerment as a reader), try to remember the gist of what you have read. Doing so will jump-start the processing of information that is required in writing an effective summary. It will also make it less likely that you will insert exact words and phrases from your source—which are normally not included in a pure summary.

✓ **Return to the passage and read it again, this time underlining critical points in the reading and any terms that are unfamiliar to you.** Keep in mind that writers are not out to bury their meaning. They usually choose to insert key ideas where they can best be viewed and remembered—in the early and later portion of the piece and in the beginning and ends of paragraphs.

✓ **Restate in your own words what you have underlined.** Use your underlining to produce an outline or blueprint of the author's argument.

✓ **Revisit the original passage, taking care to compare your reading to your outline.** This move will ensure that you have captured the essence of the article you are summarizing.

✓ **Draft, in paragraph form, a full summary, developing points from your outline.**

Most people say that they answer these questions using a "mental image." They visualize the shape, which feels like conjuring up a picture available for inspection in the mind's eye. The feeling is quite unlike the experience of answering abstract questions, such as "What is your mother's maiden name?" or "What is more important, civil liberties or a lower rate of crime?"

Mental imagery is the engine that drives our thinking about objects in space. To load a car with suitcases or rearrange the furniture, we imagine the different spatial arrangements before we try them. The anthropologist Napoleon Chagnon described an ingenious use of mental imagery by the Yanomamö Indians of the Amazon rainforest. They had blown smoke down the opening of an armadillo hole to asphyxiate the animal, and then had to figure out where to dig to extract it from its tunnel, which could run underground for hundreds of feet. One of the Yanomamö men hit on the idea of threading a long vine with a knot at the end down the hole as far as it would go. The other men kept their ears to the ground listening for the knot bumping the sides of the burrow so they could get a sense of the direction in which the burrow ran. The first man broke off the vine, pulled it out, laid it along the ground, and began to dig where the end of the vine lay. A few feet down they struck armadillo. Without an ability to visualize the tunnel and the vine and armadillo inside it, the men would not have connected a sequence of threading, listening, yanking, breaking, measuring, and digging actions to an expectation of finding an animal corpse. In a joke we used to tell as children, two carpenters are hammering nails into the side of a house, and one asks the other why he is examining each nail as he takes it out of the box and throwing half of them away. "They're defective," replies the second carpenter, holding one up. "The pointy end is facing the wrong way." "You fool!" shouts the first carpenter. "Those are for the other side of the house!"

But people do not use imagery just to rearrange the furniture or dig up armadillos. The eminent psychologist D. O. Hebb once wrote, "You can hardly turn around in psychology without bumping into the image." Give people a list of nouns to memorize, and they will imagine them interacting in bizarre images. Give them factual questions like "Does a flea have a mouth?" and they will visualize the flea and "look for" the mouth. And, of course, give them a complex shape at an unfamiliar orientation, and they will rotate its image to a familiar one.

Many creative people claim to "see" the solution to a problem in an image. Faraday and Maxwell visualized electromagnetic fields as tiny tubes filled with fluid. Kekulé saw the benzene ring in a reverie of snakes biting their tails. Watson and Crick mentally rotated models of what was to become the double helix. Einstein imagined what it would be like to ride on a beam of light or drop a penny in a plummeting elevator. He once wrote, "My particular ability does not lie in mathematical calculation, but rather in visualizing effects, possibilities, and consequences." Painters and sculptors try out ideas in their minds, and even novelists visualize scenes and plots in their mind's eye before putting pen to paper.

Images drive the emotions as well as the intellect. Hemingway wrote, "Cowardice, as distinguished from panic, is almost always simply a lack of ability to suspend the functioning of the imagination." Ambition, anxiety, sexual arousal, and jealous rage can all be triggered by images of what isn't there. In one experiment, volunteers were hooked up to electrodes and asked to imagine their mates being unfaithful. The authors report, "Their skin conductance increased 1.5 microSiemens, the corrugator muscle in their brow showed 7.75 microvolts units of contraction, and their heart rates accelerated by five beats per minute, equivalent to drinking three cups of coffee at one sitting." Of course, the imagination revives many experiences at a time, not just seeing, but the visual image makes a mental simulation especially vivid.

Imagery is an industry. Courses on How to Improve Your Memory teach age-old tricks like imagining items in the rooms of your house and then mentally walking through it, or finding a visual allusion in a person's name and linking it to his face (if you were introduced to me, you would imagine me in a cerise leisure suit). Phobias are often treated by a kind of mental Pavlovian conditioning where an image substitutes for the bell. The patient relaxes deeply and then imagines the snake or spider, until the image— and, by extension, the real thing—is associated with the relaxation. Highly paid "sports psychologists" have athletes relax in a comfy chair and visualize the perfect swing. Many of these techniques work, though some are downright flaky. I am skeptical of cancer therapies in which patients visualize their antibodies munching the tumor, even more so when it is the patient's support group that does the visualizing. (A woman once called to ask if I thought it would work over the Internet.)

But what *is* a mental image? Many philosophers with behaviorist leanings think the whole idea is a terrible blunder. An image is supposed to be a picture in the head, but then you would need a little man et cetera, et cetera, et cetera. In fact, the computational theory of mind makes the notion perfectly straightforward. We already know that the visual system uses a 2½-D sketch which is picturelike in several respects. It is a mosaic of elements that stand for points in the visual field. The elements are arranged in two dimensions so that neighboring elements in the array stand for neighboring points in the visual field. Shapes are represented by filling in some of the elements in a pattern that matches the shape's projected contours. Shape-analysis mechanisms—not little men—process information in the sketch by imposing reference frames, finding geons, and so on. A mental image is simply a pattern in the 2½-D sketch that is loaded from long-term memory rather than from the eyes. A number of artificial intelligence programs for reasoning about space are designed in exactly this way.

A depiction like the 2½-D sketch contrasts starkly with a description in a language-like representation like a geon model, a semantic network, a sentence in English, or a proposition in mentalese. In the proposition *A symmetrical triangle is above a circle*, the words do not stand for points in the visual field, and they are not arranged so that nearby words represent nearby points. Words like *symmetrical* and *above* can't be pinned to any piece of the visual field; they denote complicated relationships among the filled-in pieces.

One can even make an educated guess about the anatomy of mental imagery. The incarnation of a 2½-D sketch in neurons is called a topographically organized cortical map: a patch of cortex in which each neuron responds to contours in one part of the visual field, and in which neighboring neurons respond to neighboring parts. The primate brain has at least fifteen of these maps, and in a very real sense they are pictures in the head. Neuroscientists can inject a monkey with a radioactive isotope of glucose while it stares at a bull's-eye. The glucose is taken up by the active neurons, and one can literally *develop the monkey's brain* as if it were a piece of film. It comes out of the darkroom with a distorted bull's-eye laid out over the visual cortex. Of course, nothing "looks at" the cortex from above; connectivity is all that matters, and the activity pattern is interpreted by networks of neurons plugged into each cortical map. Presumably space in the world is represented by space on the cortex because neurons are connected to their neighbors, and it is handy for nearby bits of the world to be analyzed together. For example, edges are not scattered across the visual field like rice but snake along a line, and most surfaces are not archipelagos but cohesive masses. In a cortical map, lines and surfaces can be handled by neurons that are highly interconnected.

The brain is also ready for the second computational demand of an imagery system, information flowing down from memory instead of up from the eyes. The fiber pathways to the visual areas of the brain are two-way. They carry as much information down from the higher, conceptual levels as up from the lower, sensory levels. No one knows what these top-down connections are for, but they could be there to download memory images into visual maps.

So mental images *could be* pictures in the head. Are they? There are two ways to find out. One is to see if thinking in images engages the visual parts of the brain. The other is to see if thinking in images works more like computing with graphics or more like computing with a database of propositions.

Evaluating Source Material

Once you have read and understood the content of your source material, you are faced with the important task of determining the relevance, validity, and credibility of that material. Keep in mind that your research question will serve as the standard by which to evaluate a source's usefulness. How would the material contribute to your thesis? Not all sources are equally credible, just as not all authors are equally authoritative. How do you know whom to trust? How do you know which argument is the most convincing? These are not easy questions to answer, but it is possible to set up guidelines for evaluation. Some suggestions can be found in the checklist on the following page.

Given the tremendous amount of material that now comes our way via the World Wide Web, the challenge of sorting and sifting sources has become even more formida-

Evaluating the Credibility of a Source: A Checklist

✓ **Consider the author's background as a claim for expertise.** What credentials does the author have that lend credibility to the writing?

✓ **Determine the author's purpose in writing the piece.** Does the author claim to be neutral or unbiased? Or is the author advocating a particular point of view? What is that point of view?

✓ **Visualize the audience for which the piece is intended.** Is the writing meant for readers of a specific knowledge community? Or is it aimed at a more general readership? How successfully does the writer meet the needs and expectations of the audience?

✓ **Evaluate the extensiveness, relevance, currency, and credibility of the evidence provided.** How convincing is the evidence brought to support the writer's purpose? Has any relevant detail been excluded? If so, what difference might the inclusion of such materials produce?

ble and more urgent. On the following page you will find a set of questions you can ask about information from Web sites.

Grounding the Theory

1. Go to the reference room of your local library and discover as much as you can about Steven Pinker, the author of the essay on mental images. How does knowing more about him affect your judgment as to his authority and expertise? Should we believe what he writes? Why?

2. Locate two sites on the World Wide Web, one a government location and the other a commercial site. Using the checklist on

---

Evaluating the Credibility of a Source on the Web: A Checklist

✓ **Authority:**

Who publishes this Web page?

What makes her or him an authority on the subject?

Does he or she cite experience or credentials?

Is she or he accredited or endorsed by a reputable organization?

If an educational background is given, are the educational institutions accredited?

Does the article contain footnotes?

Does material copied from other sources appear to be fully credited?

✓ **Scope:**

Who is the intended audience?

What time period is covered?

What geographical area is covered?

Is there a cultural bias?

---

evaluating Web sources, evaluate each site on the basis of its authority, scope or purpose, currency, and accuracy.

Writing with Sources

Writing with consequence requires that scholarship be put to the service of a particular purpose or line of inquiry (as we have defined that process in Chapter 1; see page 11). In other words, while scholarship may be available for anyone sufficiently inquisitive, willing, and able to acquire it, the premise of this chapter is that scholarship ought to be utilized as sources for writing. How you use your sources will be determined by your own purpose.

Is this information a part of a more comprehensive source? If so, who abridged it and why?

✓ **Currency:**
What is the date on the Web page?
How frequently is it updated?
Is some of the information obviously out of date?

✓ **Accuracy:**
Are the facts known to be reliable?
Have you checked any of the data with other sources known to be accurate?
Is the coverage objective? If not, is the bias clearly stated?

✓ **Commercialism:**
Is the presenter selling something (a product or an idea)?
Does the URL have a .com label?
Does the page have a corporate sponsor?
Are there any hidden costs?
Do you have to enter personal information in order to proceed?

Do you need to	*If so, use*
Give your readers the gist of the entire source?	Summary
Give details about one specific matter from the source?	Paraphrase
Refer in passing to a well-established work in the field as reference or background to the topic you are writing about?	Reference
Convey the author's meaning and voice?	Quotation

Whether summarizing, paraphrasing, referencing, or quoting from a source, you are obliged both to acknowledge the source itself and to be faithful to that source. A purposeful use of quotation will make it less likely that you will plagiarize your source. *Plagiarism* involves the appropriation of someone's words or ideas—intentionally or not—so as to make them appear your own. It is important to be accurate when using sources because scholarship and research are built on the foundations established by others. If your own use of a previous study is not accurate, then others after you may build on a shaky foundation. Moreover, correctly acknowledging the work of others affirms that scholarship is an expression of a larger conversation going on in a discipline or area of research. Your work is part of that conversation.

Referring to Key Works

Researchers know that their credibility in advancing a research problem and solution rests on their knowledge of and use of existing data and source material. Partly for this reason, researchers often refer to key work that has already been done on their subject. When you need to acknowledge significant work, you can use a reference, including a citation that will allow readers to locate the source themselves. A reference may be given explicitly within your sentence:

Jones had traced this effect in an earlier study (1998).

Or a reference may be restricted to the citation only (the listing in parentheses of the author and date of a work that you used to make a statement):

In vitro fertilization (IVF) is a valuable tool for assessing functionality and for studying the success or failure of gamete interaction in the domestic cat and its wild relatives (Wildt et al. 1992).

In either case, the message is clear: Significant work has been done previously and now needs to be acknowledged. The point here is two-fold: You *refer to* sources in their entirety (rather than paraphrase a portion or quote an excerpt) and you *select* sources for their significance to your topic and purpose.

To write with consequence requires legitimacy and authority, and using references properly helps provide these essential qualities. In other words, your ability to reference relevant and important work already done on your subject signals to your reader that you are a member of a knowledge community. Even more important, referencing works judiciously allows you to sharpen your own perspective (for the reader's benefit and your own) in relation to work already done. The question that reviewers ask of manuscripts submitted to journals is typically this: How does this current study add to our knowledge of the subject? The referencing of prior work allows a writer to make that kind of distinction.

Summarizing for Readers

As a practical matter, writers summarize their sources not only to gain a better grasp of these sources themselves but also to provide necessary information for their readers. Writers rely on summary when source material requires distillation—in other words, when the reader needs to get to the gist of an article or book rather than be distracted by details. It is important that writers not overuse summary, however. Such overuse may in effect drown out the writer's own point of view.

You should also take care that your summary restates the source's main points *in your own words*. Here are examples of (1) an effective summary, which captures the gist of a source in the researcher's own words, and (2) a plagiarized summary, in which the researcher uses the language of the source without acknowledgment. First, read the excerpt.

Original passage from "The American Geographies" by Barry Lopez

To do this well, to really come to an understanding of the specific American geography, requires not only time but a kind of local expertise, an intimacy with place few of us ever develop. There is no way around the former requirement: If you want to know, you must take the time. It is not in books. A specific geographical understanding, however, can be sought out and borrowed. It resides with men and women more or less sworn to a place, who abide there, who have a feel for the soil and history, for the turn of leaves and night sounds. Often they are glad to take the outlander in tow.

Effective summary

The best way of gaining familiarity with a place, writes Barry Lopez, is to live in that place, or to seek out those who live there (68).

The summary brings out Lopez's main point: that knowledge of a location comes from inhabiting that space.

Plagiarized summary

If you want to know about a place, you need to take the time to know it. It cannot be found in books.

The plagiarized version is flawed for several reasons. First, it is not an accurate summary; it omits Lopez's point that "a specific geographical understanding . . . can be sought out and borrowed" (68). It also draws upon the exact wording and phrasing of the original without using quotation marks. Because of the lack of quotation marks, it gives the impression that the words are the writer's own, rather than someone else's.

Paraphrasing Specific Passages

A *paraphrase* is a restatement in your own words of a particular passage in roughly the same length as the original passage. In contrast, summaries are typically much briefer than
the original work. The purpose of a paraphrase is to offer the
gist of a specific passage or excerpt. As with summary, you
must take special care not to plagiarize the original.

Original passage from "The American Geographies" by Barry Lopez

People in America, then, face a convoluted and ultimately destructive situation. The land itself, vast and
differentiated, defies the notion of a national geography. Yet Americans are daily presented with, and
have become accustomed to talking about, a homoge-
nized national geography, one that seems to operate
independently of the land, a collection of objects appearing in advertisements, as a background in movies,
and in patriotic calendars.

Effective paraphrase

Americans confront a difficult challenge, writes Barry
Lopez. While geographical features of America are diverse and not easily categorized, the media and popular culture routinely give Americans simplified and
false representations of American geography (71).

Note how the paraphrase retains Lopez's contrast between
America's diverse geography and the simplification produced by the media.

Plagiarized paraphrase

Americans face a destructive situation. The land defies any easy idea of a national geography. However,

> Americans are daily given images of a national geography, including objects that appear in advertisements, movies, and calendars.

Plagiarism mars this paraphrase because words and phrases are taken directly from the original, without acknowledgement of the source. No citation has been included, nor any reference to Lopez.

Quoting Word for Word from Sources

A quotation is a rendering of someone else's ideas verbatim, or word for word. A quotation may consist of a single word or several paragraphs. As a practical matter, we quote from a source when we feel that the author's own words have a significant impact on our argument. For example, if we were to write a paper on the magical qualities of American spaces, we would be hard-pressed to write more eloquently than Barry Lopez on the subject: "They are mysteries upon which we impose names" (68).

Similarly, although it is possible to paraphrase the following sentences from Steven Pinker's article on mental imagery, for example, we ought to recognize the special power of Pinker's own voice, style, and authority contained within the words given to us:

> Imagery is an industry. Courses on How to Improve Your Memory teach age-old tricks like imagining items in the rooms of your house and then mentally walking through it, or finding a visual allusion in a person's name and linking it to his face (if you were introduced to me, you would imagine me in a cerise leisure suit).

Note that it is not only *what* Pinker says that affects us but *how* he says it. The brief assertion at the beginning contrasts with the lumbering sentence that follows it. Moreover, the matter-of-fact tone is nicely subverted by the parenthetical statement about Pinker himself, who, we can be sure, does not wear leisure suits, cerise or otherwise. It is worth nothing that the excerpt, taken out of context, implies a different message from the point of the essay as a whole. The passage seems to suggest that memory is a mental phenomenon, the product, at times, of our own will to remember. In fact, Pinker argues, images are produced by the play of neurons on our cerebral cortex. All this brings me to make this claim about quoting from source material: We quote to make a special impact on our readers, but we do so with the full knowledge and understanding of the writer's intentions and stylistic choices.

As a general rule, it is best to introduce a quotation and to follow it with a statement of its significance. Doing so prevents "floating" quotations—that is, quoted material whose purpose is not clear and whose connection to the main argument is left for the reader to surmise.

Effective uses of quotation

"If only folks would turn off the TV and start attending PTA meetings," writes Teda Skocpol, we would become once again a community of citizens rather than a collection of isolated individuals (171).

Are insects capable of behavior that resembles that of humans? According to the biologist Lewis Thomas, it is altogether incorrect "to imply that the operation of insect societies has any relation at all to human affairs" (592). Thomas's caveat reminds us to beware the trap of seeing the world as merely reproducing human behavior.

In each example, note how the quotation is embedded within the writer's own sentence.

When and How to Quote Sources: A Checklist

Generally speaking, keep the following rules in mind when you quote:

✓ **Know why you want to quote in the first place.** From the very start, you need to have a handle on your own purposes for quoting and on the meaning of the words you wish to quote.

✓ **Always quote a passage exactly as it appears in the original, down to the last punctuation mark; if an error of any kind appears, use brackets with the word "sic" inside—[sic]—meaning "just so."** Accuracy and authenticity matter. When you quote from a source, your reader must feel assured that what he or she is seeing is exactly what the original author produced.

✓ **When inserting your own words into a quotation, always use brackets—[ ]—to let your reader know that the brack-**

Ineffective use of quotation

People just don't care enough to vote or to become informed about significant legislation: "Television was certainly a major factor" (Skocpol 176).

A gap exists between the writer's own statement and the quotation pulled in for support of that statement. To explain the use of the quotation, the writer could have composed something like this:

People just don't care enough to vote or to become informed about significant legislation. Among the causes, writes Theda Skocpol, is the media practice of focusing on matters other than the civic: Televi-

eted words are not the original author's. Sometimes, as you try to integrate the source material into your own writing, or as you take the passage from its context, you may need to insert words for easier reading. Again, use brackets to let your reader know what is yours and what comes from another writer.

✓ Use a series of three dots, called points of ellipsis, when you are skipping words in your quotation. Be especially careful when omitting words from your source since doing so may change the meaning of the passage. Indicate with an ellipsis— . . . —those omissions.

✓ Integrate your quotation seamlessly within the argument that you are making. Embed your source material judiciously within your own writing. Inserting a quoted phrase in your own sentence can be very effective, as can the careful insertion of a longer passage within your paper. Pick your spots with care.

sion, with its ratings-driven scheduling, was "a major factor" (176).

Integrating Your Ideas and Source Material

Bringing together your source material and your own written argument in a meaningful way represents a huge challenge. Think about it: Not only do you need to be sure about your own thesis or research question and to be able to muster a series of arguments on behalf of that thesis; you then must find just the right places to call upon authoritative evidence for support. To prepare for the successful synthesis of source material, ask yourself the following questions:

- What is my purpose in the paper?
- How do the various pieces of my argument fit?
- What are my sources telling me in the aggregate?
- What are they telling me individually?
- Where might I judiciously place or refer to those sources?

As I stated in the previous section, introducing quotations and following them with a statement of significance goes a long way toward integrating source materials. Teachers often refer to this approach as *sandwiching*, putting your quotations between two of your own sentences. In doing so, you are integrating the source material thoughtfully within your own writing, demonstrating to your reader that you have mastered that material. Take, for example, this excerpt from a student-produced pamphlet on the dangers of teenage drinking:

> One of the biggest problems is teenage drinking and driving. Not only are teenagers inexperienced at driving, but combining this inexperience with drinking is deadly. According to a study done by the U.S. Surgeon General, "[T]he death rate for 15- to 24-year-olds is higher today than it was 20 years ago: [t]he leading cause of death is drunk and drugged driving" (Mothers Against Drunk Driving). This tragedy has occurred even as life expectancy for all other age groups has dramatically increased.

Notice how the student skillfully weaves the quoted material within the body of his own writing.

In the writing done for academic communities, the integration of source material is most obviously seen as part of a *literature review*, a survey of previously done studies that have relevance to the project being discussed. Consider this passage from an essay on the subject of writing and civic commitment:

> It has been suggested that our contemporary society is faced with a moral crisis, partly owing to an inability to find common points of agreement with which to discuss morality or moral resources to inform such discussions. For example, Kurt Spellmeyer calls the fragmentation of discourse and the dismantling of public space so that it is no longer public—producing the demise of the social imagination—the "overriding predicament of our times" (268). Cornel West agrees, lamenting our contemporary inability to imagine interconnected lives amid racial and cultural differences (8–12).

The writer uses a quotation and a reference in the service of establishing the central point: that contemporary society is fragmented.

Citing Your Sources

When you rely directly on source material—whether as reference, quotation, summary, or paraphrase—you are expected to cite your source (indicating, within parentheses, the source that you are using) and to disclose the full bibliographic information in a list of references or works cited. The name of the list depends on the subject you write in and the rules of that discipline for citing sources, as we will see below. Citations accompany all references to sources, so that your reader has the opportunity to go back to the source materials that you have used. Failure to cite your sources amounts to plagiarism.

   Each discipline has its own conventions for citing sources. Clear reasons exist for such differences. In some of the scientific fields, preference is given, for example, to the year in which a work is published (the year is included in parenthetical citations and is included early in a listing of works as part of a bibliography). In those fields, advances are often published in journals that appear frequently, rather than as book-length studies, which can take a year or more to publish. The year is crucial in determining the currency of the information provided. The prominent placement of publication date in the formats used in psychology and biology suggest the fast-moving advances within those fields.

Below are brief examples of citation formats from three professional organizations: the Modern Language Association (MLA), the American Psychological Association (APA), and The Council of Science Editors (CSE). You should consult the appropriate style manual for the discipline in which you are writing for complete information:

MLA Handbook for Writers of Research Papers. 5th ed. By Joseph Gibaldi, 2000 [http://www.mla.org]

Publication Manual of the American Psychological Association. 5th ed, 2000. [http://www.apastyle.org]

The Council of Science Editors (CSE), 1994. [http://www.councilscienceeditors.org/]

Typical entries from each citation style are provided—for a book, a journal, and an online source. After each example of an in-text citation, the full bibliographic listing is given as it would appear at the end of your paper (alphabetically by author's last name). For comprehensive information, please consult the appropriate style manual.

Modern Language Association (MLA)

Book
In Gans's working-class population, the roles of husband and wife were clearly differentiated (50-52).

Work Cited
Gans, Herbert J. <u>The Urban Villagers</u>. 2nd ed. New York: Free, 1982.

Periodical

Campisi found that the influence of Italian culture was growing weaker, with more and more cultural values shaped by the larger society rather than by the family (443-49).

Work Cited

Campisi, Paul J. "Ethnic Family Patterns: The Italian Family in the United States." American Journal of Sociology 53 (1948): 443-49.

Online Source

These days, Shakespeare's works are readily available on the Internet (Gray).

Work Cited

Gray, Terry A., ed. Shakespeare's Works. 10 April 2001. Retrieved 23 Nov. 2001 from the World Wide Web <http://shakespeare.palomar.edu/works.htm>

Various situations call for slightly different ways of citing sources. For example, if the author is unknown, a shortened title of the work is given in the body of the paper, and the Works Cited entry for that source begins with those same words so readers can find the full publication information. See the *MLA Handbook for Writers of Research Papers,* 5th edition, for further information.

American Psychological Association (APA)

Book

According to a longitudinal study of the high school class of 1972, thirty-four percent dropped out within their first two years (Ecklund & Henderson, 1981).

Reference

Ecklund, B.K., & Henderson, L. B. (1981). *Longitudinal study of the high school class of 1972.* Washington,

DC: National Institute of Education. (ERIC Document Reproduction Service No. ED311222).

Periodical

Bishop and Snyder (1976) noted grades and money as the major pressures that account for the differences between resident and commuter students.

Reference

Bishop, J. B., & Snyder, G. S. (1976). Commuters and residents: Pressures, helps and psychological services. *Journal of College Student Personnel, 17,* 232–235.

Online Source

According to Chou et al. (1993), both technology and traditions have use in the classroom.

Reference

Chou, L., McClintock, R., Moretti, F. & Nix, D. H. (1993). *Technology and education: New wine in new bottles: Choosing pasts and imagining educational futures.* Retrieved August 24, 2000, from Columbia University, Institute for Learning Technologies Web site: http://www.ilt.columbia.edu/publications/papers/newwine1.html

The Council of Science Editors (CSE)

The Council of Science Editors offers two alternative citation styles. The citation sequence style relies on numbered citations. The author-year system is exemplified here.

Book

Most of the work with fossil followers goes directly into comparative morphology of living angiosperms (Cronquist 1968).

Reference

Cronquist, A. The evolution and classification of flowering plants. Riverside Studies in Biology. Boston: Houghton Mifflin; 1968.

Periodical

The third fossil flower is most widespread (Dilcher and Crane 1984).

Reference

Dilcher, DL; Crane, P.R. In pursuit of the first flower. NatHist. March: 57-60.

Online Source

According to one study (Wolf and Green 1999), the actions of certain proteases are highly regulated.

Reference

Wolf BB, Green DR. Suicidal tendencies: apoptopic cell death by caspase family proteinases. J Biol Chem [serial online] 1999; 274 (29): 20049-52. Available from: Journal of Biological Chemistry Website via the Internet (http://www.jbc.org/).

Grounding the Theory

1. Practice the "sandwich" approach to quoting sources by using a sentence from Pinker's article. Remember to introduce the quotation by referring to the author and to provide additional commentary after quoting. Finally, consult a style manual and cite your source. Provide a corresponding Works Cited or References entry.

2. Citing sources that appear in the World Wide Web has made documentation complex. Go to the Web site of the American Psychological Association (http://www.apa.org) and research the proper

way to cite electronic sources. Then go to your five favorite Web sites. Create a reference list with those sites, following the APA format.

Bibliographical Indexes in the Disciplines

Part of what it means to be professionalized in a field is to become familiar with the significant work to date on a particular problem or subspecialty. Professionals and students alike may consult a variety of indexes in their search for relevant research studies. Please consult a reference librarian for even more precise information as to how to locate these indexes. Libraries vary in terms of the database services to which they subscribe. Here is a sampling, drawn from indexes in the study of language and literature, social sciences, and the biological sciences and business:

Humanities

Art
New Dictionary of Modern Sculpture

Oxford Companion to Art

Drama
New York Times Theatre Reviews

Modern World Drama: An Encyclopedia

Film
Guide to Critical Reviews

New York Times Film Reviews

History
Cambridge Ancient History

CRIS (Combined Retrospective Index to Journals in History)

Harvard Guide to American History
New Cambridge Modern History

Language and Literature
Biography Index
Book Review Digest
Contemporary Authors
Current Biography
Essay and General Literature Index
MLA International Bibliography
Oxford Companion to American Literature
Oxford Companion to Classical Literature
Oxford Companion to English Literature
Twentieth Century Authors

Music
Grove's Dictionary of Music and Musicians
Music Index

Philosophy
The Concise Encyclopedia of Western Philosophy and Philosophers
Encyclopedia of Philosophy

Online Databases in the Humanities
Comprehensive Dissertation Abstracts
EBSCO's Academic Search Elite
Historical Abstracts
Humanities Index
MLA Bibliography

Social Sciences

Anthropology
Abstracts in Anthropology
Anthropological Index

Criminal Justice
Criminal Justice Abstracts
Criminal Justice Periodicals Index

Psychology
Author Index to Psychological Index and Psychological Abstracts
Cumulative Subject Index to Psychological Abstracts
Psychological Abstracts

Sociology
Poverty and Human Resources Abstracts
Rural Sociology Abstracts
Social Sciences Index
Sociological Abstracts

Online Databases in the Social Sciences
Psychological Abstracts
PsychINFO
ERIC
Sociological Abstracts
PAIS International

Natural Sciences

General Science
General Science Index
Science Citation Index

Chemistry

Analytical Abstracts

Chemical Abstracts

Encyclopedia of Chemistry

Engineering

Engineering Encyclopedia

Engineering Index

Environment Index

Biology

Biological Abstracts

Encyclopedia of the Biological Sciences

Index Medicus

Mathematics

Index to Mathematical Papers

Mathematical Reviews

Physics

Astronomy and Astrophysics Abstracts

Encyclopedia of Physics

Online Databases in the Natural Sciences

BIOSIS Previews

MEDLINE

SCISEARCH

Life Sciences Collection

Business

Business Periodicals Index

Moody's Industry Review

Standard and Poor's Register of Corporations

Wall Street Journal Index

Online Databases in Business
Business Software Database

ABI/Inform

Grounding the Theory

---

1. Ask your reference librarian how to access *EBSCO's Academic Search Elite*. Drawing upon a topic from one of your classes, do a keyword search to find one full-text article on the subject. Describe in detail the process that you followed, especially as you narrow your search.

2. Consult the Social Sciences Index to find three journal articles on one of these subjects:

    a. Alzheimer's disease
    b. Anorexia nervosa
    c. Attention-deficit disorder

Disciplinary Perspective: Scholarship and Authority in Biology

Like their colleagues in other disciplines, scholars of biology rely on past authority or precedent, build on such precedent (if only to qualify the claims of others, or even refute such claims), and offer their work for scholarly scrutiny. To lay a foundation, I've asked a teacher of biology to comment broadly on the ways that his discipline uses the authority of the past.

Working as a Biologist: An Interview with a Teacher of Biology

Trained to study the molecular biology of tumor viruses, John Bennett has taught full-time at Clark College since 1996. He received his doctorate from Loyola University of Chicago, where he isolated a gene that might play a role in the development of Hodgkin's disease. His teaching responsibilities include General Biology, a First-Year Seminar (required of all entering students), and Research and Methods. Professor Bennett believes strongly in the need to stay current in the literature of his field and to read work in other areas "not directly related" to his own research interests.

Q. What kinds of writing do your students do?

A. In the Research and Methods course, [students] produce outlines, identify hypotheses, summarize abstracts and articles. A couple of related exercises are used to help the students distill abstracts down to a single hypothesis statement. They must identify five articles related to a topic of interest and identify the hypothesis for each, then write an underlying hypothesis for all five articles.

In the biology seminar, students observe how professionals construct scientific literature, develop an argument, and support [it] with data. Prior to an in-class assignment, the students are given an article from *BioScience* and told to read it and address several questions. The questions focus the students on various aspects of paper construction from structure of the introduction, development of a hypothesis, and support of a position. During class the students were given the

[margin note: Identifying hypotheses in sources]

[margin note: Understanding the structure of a source]

article in twenty pieces. Their assignment is to work in groups to reconstruct the article.

Q. Can you comment more specifically on the scholarly work of biologists? For example, nonscientists often naively speak of science as "proving" a fact to be true, in an absolute sense. What would biologists say about that process?

Identifying gaps in information

A. Scientific questioning is a critical aspect of the education of biology students. They must learn to identify gaps in information and how to obtain the information that will help to fill those gaps. A significant skill that biology students must learn is how to control an experiment. Controls are aspects of an experiment that demonstrate a true positive and a true negative result. Proper controls allow an investigator to determine if the results of an experiment are meaningful. Improper controls may lead an investigator to develop false conclusions. This may represent the key difference between scientists and nonscientists, [the need] to identify controls.

Testing information to see if it is accurate

[Take, as an example,] a pregnancy test. Usually a urine sample is applied to an indicator. If the indicator changes color, that would indicate pregnancy. But to be conclusive, this test should be controlled. To control for the quality of the indicator, some urine from a pregnant woman should be applied to some indicator to demonstrate the right positive response. Likewise, urine from a woman who is not pregnant should be applied to some indicator to demonstrate a negative response. If both the positive and negative responses work appropriately, then we would have confidence that the test sample results would be reliable.

Can the results be reproduced?

Q. How important is the idea of replicability to a project in your field?

A. Reproducibility is an important aspect of science. If results cannot be reproduced, then the results are likely to be considered invalid.

To be accepted in the scientific literature, one must clearly demonstrate data supporting a hypothesis. This is closely related to the concept of controls that we discussed earlier. Again, that is a difficult point for students to grasp initially. It is easy for the untrained biologist to suggest that "that is obvious; therefore I do not have to demonstrate it." Wrong. Rigor is the essence of good science. Okay, clarity is very important too. But students need to adapt to the concept that findings must be demonstrated before they are accepted. Without such rigor, it becomes nearly impossible to determine if a hypothesis has been adequately addressed.

Q. Are students aware that biological knowledge is built on previous work and is continually revised?

A. Beginning students in the sciences often assume that the textbooks are highly authoritative. It seems to me that they hold the concept that "We know almost everything except there are a few more questions about cancer and HIV." This is not the case. Although our information about many biological systems has been well studied, there are often many questions about how systems are regulated. With every new biological fact that is discerned, more questions are raised. We will always have questions to ask.

New questions will always arise

Case Study

REFERENCING SOURCES IN BIOLOGY

Not unlike the practice in other disciplines, biologists who publish their findings first must acknowledge the relevant work already done on the problem. A biologist's report thus uses as a foundation the work of others and adds its contribution to the development of the field. Consider, for example, the now-famous paper by a group of Scottish researchers led by Ian Wilmut reporting on the cloning of the sheep named Dolly (the complete text is given on pages 79–88).

The paper lays its groundwork by acknowledging work already done. At the same time, the authors note the room for further advancement of knowledge through this particular study.

In acknowledging the importance of a previous study that reported the transfer of differentiated cells in amphibians, Wilmut's group announces its debt to such work. But just as quickly, the group notes the limitations of the previous work: Researchers were unable to develop their specimens beyond the tadpole stage. The question of whether an adult can be cloned through such transfer thus remains open. The current study, then, takes on the challenge of answering that question and thus advancing knowledge. This same group had earlier reported success in producing live lambs after disabling the growth of differentiated cells.

Because of the cumulative nature of work in biology and in the other sciences, referencing of previous work is essential. Moreover, when Wilmut and his team write that their work "reinforces previous speculation"—namely that putting donor cells to sleep, as it were, would permit "normal development"—they are obliged to indicate where such speculation occurred (including their own landmark work on the subject). A research trail is thus created—to be scrutinized by researchers to come.

A Student Writes about Her Research

Although students who write about their research do not necessarily break new ground, their ability to survey the work already done on their subject serves to familiarize them with the ongoing debates within the field—and perhaps exposes them to the notion that knowledge in the biological sciences is often tentative. As Professor Bennett remarked, "With every new biological fact that is discerned, more questions are raised."

One student had to confront this fact about the field when asked to do a research paper on the effects of global warming on the planet's biological diversity. Rather than merely assert the latest findings on the species, she took stock of the questions that remain to be answered:

> Public perceptions to the contrary, debate about the causes, extent, and consequences of global warming continues to work its way through the scientific community. Theories abound as to the catalyst for such warming, ranging from corporate policy (Nemecek 1999) and indiscriminate logging (Nepstad et al. 1999) to erratic behavior of the sun itself (Pierce 1999), and "species invasion" (Chapin et al. 1998). The extent of the warming has itself been difficult to establish, with surface temperatures needing to be reconciled with readings from satellite imagery (Gaffen et al. 2000). Nevertheless, such assumed climactic changes have been seen as contributing to a new range of extinctions (Bernarde 1992; Aitken 1998).

Notice that the student makes explicit reference (using the CSE author-year system) to particular researchers for the purpose of presenting scientific debate. Most notable of all is the student's realization that the debate over climactic warming, like so much of science, is ongoing. This is, ultimately, her point, and the scholarship is used efficiently to bring that point out.

Grounding the Theory

1. Option A: Using the paper by Ian Wilmut's group as a key paper, search the *Science Citation Index* for related studies. Then from the list of citations select one and locate its abstract in *Biological Abstracts*. Describe the details of your search, including information as to how to locate information in the indexes as well as your chosen citation and the paper's abstract.

Option B: Choose a subject of interest to you from the social sciences. Locate a relevant article using the Social Sciences Index.
Describe the details of your search.

2.   Read the following article from *Scientific American*. Analyze the essay in terms of audience and purpose. What is the writer's purpose? Who is the intended reader? How do you know?

Protecting the Nation's Water Supply

Long before the recent terrorist attacks, some researchers began developing ways to assess and address threats to the U.S. water infrastructure.

In the six weeks that have passed since September 11, Americans
have stopped taking many things for granted. Among other worries, we no longer assume that our airports are safe from hijackers
or our mail from bioterrorists. Federal agencies are moving quickly
to put new, stricter security measures in place. But when it comes
to protecting water reservoirs, researchers at the Department of Energy's Sandia National Laboratory are already one step ahead. For
the past few years they have worked on sophisticated means to
identify vulnerabilities in the nation's water infrastructure, as well
as technologies to detect in real time contamination of the water
supply.

"We started exploring the possibility of working together [with
the Environmental Protection Agency (EPA) and the American Water Works Association Research Foundation (AWWARF)] to enhance the security of America's water infrastructure—supply, treatment and distribution—well before the September 11 attacks on
the World Trade Center and the Pentagon," Sandia scientist Jeffrey
Danneels says. His efforts, which have taken on a new urgency
since the recent terrorist attacks, have focused on establishing
a program to target problem areas on-site at utilities and train
the personnel to minimize any risks. He held a workshop for
AWWARF and the American Water Works Association (AWWA)
this past November and has more scheduled to begin this month.

Danneels modeled his program after one Sandia initially created to support the U.S. nuclear security mission and that has
since been adapted to assess the threat of terrorist attacks on gov-

ernment buildings, air force bases, nuclear power plants, nuclear processing facilities, prisons and federal dams. The EPA is most interested in analyzing the water distribution systems that serve the country's 340 largest cities. Because many of these systems are more than 60 years old, they have different structures and therefore different security concerns. Danneels says utilities must follow three basic steps to evaluate their own individual vulnerabilities: They must assess how well their system detects a problem, how well it can delay the spread of the problem and how well it can ultimately respond to the problem.

Where at least the first step is concerned—detection—some of Danneel's colleagues at Sandia may soon provide real help. Cliff Ho and Bob Hughes have created a novel real-time gas- and water-quality monitoring system, made up of a tiny sensor array and weatherproof casing. Whereas traditional monitoring involves collecting samples of water, gas or soil and sending them for laboratory analysis, which can cost from $100 to $1,000, the new device performs its testing in situ and sends its results—via a computer at a collection station—to an interactive Web site.

"The electronic sniffer is a unique monitor that can be put directly underground—in groundwater or soils where the humidity reaches nearly 100 percent—and detect toxic chemicals at the site without taking samples to the lab," Ho explains. "It has the capability of detecting in real time undesirable chemicals being pumped into the water supply accidentally or intentionally. It will be able to monitor sites containing toxic chemical spills, leaking underground storage tanks and chemical waste dumps, potentially saving millions of dollars a year in the process."

The sensor array contains a collection of different chemiresistors to detect a range of volatile organic compounds (VOCs). To make the chemiresistors, Hughes first mixed commercial polymers that had been dissolved in a solvent with conductive carbon particles. He then painted this inklike mixture onto electrodes in specially designed microfabricated circuits. If VOCs are present, the polymers absorb the compounds and swell, which in turn changes the electrical resistance in the circuit. The swelling and change in resistance correspond to the concentration of the VOC. Once the chemical is removed, the polymers shrink back to normal. "By using four different kinds of polymers—one for each sensor—we think we can detect all solvents of interest," Hughes says.

Ho and other team members devised the weatherproof packaging for the chemiresistor chip—without which the device could not be placed in water or underground. "The package is modular, like a watertight flashlight, and is fitted with O-rings," Ho explains. "It can be unscrewed, allowing for easy exchange of components." All told, the casing, constructed of stainless steel, measures a mere three centimeters in diameter. Chemical vapors pass through the casing to the chemiresistor array through a small window covered with a waterproof Gore-Tex membrane. When the device is placed in water, VOCs will partition across the membrane into the gas phase.

The scientists recently placed the sensor at Sandia's Chemical Waste Landfill to see how well the device works outside the lab. There it is suspended about 60 feet down a screened well and logs data every hour. This field test will last for several weeks or months, and others are planned at Edwards Air Force Base and the Nevada Test Site. From the experiments, Ho, Hughes and their colleagues hope to determine the sensor's life span, as well as its performance when temperature, pressure and humidity vary.

"Over the next few years I expect we will see this invention being applied to DOE sites that require monitoring, remediation and/or long-term stewardship of contaminated sites, which currently spend millions of dollars for off-site analysis of manual samples," Ho adds. "This device can also be applied to numerous commercial sites and applications, such as gas stations, which include more than two million underground storage tanks that require monitoring to satisfy the EPA requirements."

And the electronic sniffer may offer at least part of the solution toward safeguarding the national water infrastructure. "A low security level might mean hiring a security guard and installing some detection features around critical assets, and that won't cost a lot," Danneels says. "But to stop a fairly organized group from committing a terrorist act could be extremely expensive."

—Kristin Leutwyler

For Extended Writing

1. Write a summary of a chapter in one of your course textbooks or readings. As you do so, reference your source and incorporate relevant quotations within your summary. Remember to cite and list your source as well.

2. Identify a subject from any of your courses about which you'd like to learn more. Using any of the indexes described in this chapter, locate three sources about your subject. Compose a bibliography, listing the sources in proper bibliographic format (MLA or APA, for example). After each source, summarize the argument of each source and evaluate its usefulness for anyone who might want to know more about your chosen subject.

Scholarship in the Extra-Curriculum: The Advocacy Pamphlet

In this chapter, we have seen that scholarship matters—in part to establish the writer's credibility in a subject, but also to acknowledge the cumulative nature of knowledge-making. But scholarship is important not only in the academic community; it also has a role in what I have been calling the "extra-curriculum"—the places beyond schools and colleges where people work and live. And, although we often think of scholarship as somehow removed from the concerns of everyday life, consider the view that the issues that most concern us—our health and the health of our communities and of our planet, for example—are best engaged from a scholarly and informed perspective.

One kind of public writing that demonstrates my point is the *advocacy pamphlet*, a genre aimed at both informing the public and encouraging it to act on behalf of a pressing public issue. The latter (action) cannot occur responsibly without the former (information). The best pamphlets rest on solid scholarship, granting the public access to valuable sources on the focused issue. Here are two examples of student-produced pamphlets, one urging better wages for child care workers and the other on addressing the dangers of drinking while driving.

Under Paid
Childcare Workers

What You
Should Know

Problem

Many children are dropped off everyday to childcare providers because their parents must work for economic and other reasons. Parents want the best care for their children but fail to recognize a troubling trend with many childcare workers. The turn-over rate in this profession is tremendous. Childcare workers are grossly underpaid and because of this they are forced to leave their employment as childcare workers for other jobs with higher wages.

What many parents do not know is that an essential element for quality childcare is the quality and consistency of the caregiver. With the high turn-over in this profession, the children who are cared for are the ones that are hurt by this. Childcare workers have such an important job in teaching tomorrow's future, our children. Shouldn't they be compensated for such an important responsibility.

Child Care Work
Force Profile

Who are the child
care teaching staff?

97% are female
41% have children
10% are single parents

- Child care teaching staff earn an average of $6.89 per hour or $12,058 per year (based on 35 hours per week and 50 weeks per year) (data from Cost, Quality and Child Outcomes in Child Care Centers, Technical Report 1995, salary data are in 1993 dollars).

- Only 18 percent of child care centers offer fully paid health coverage to teaching staff.

- Although they earn lower wages, child care teachers are better educated than the general population.

- One-third of all child care teachers leave their centers each year.

- Family child care providers who care for and educate young children in their homes also have very low earnings. Providers earn $9,528 annually after expenses (data from The Economics of Family Child Care Study, a forthcoming publi-cation from Wheelock College, earnings in 1996 dollars). Unregulated providers, who care for fewer children and are offered fewer supports, earned just $5,132 after expenses. (qtd. in Profile)

Solution

Many childcare workers are forced from a job that they love and are well qualified for because of such poor wages. They must leave their employment because they must provide for their own

families. Not only are the childcare workers cheated from their job, but so too are the children they are caring for. As stated earlier an essential component of quality childcare is the consistency of the caregiver. With such a high turnover in the profession there is anything but consistency. The solution to end this trend is to raise the wages given to childcare workers and to give them incentives to stay in their current jobs.

A solution to this trend is to support the United Child Care Union. Studies have shown that unionized childcare workers "made $1.44 per hour more than non-unionized workers" and that turnover rates for unionized workers were much less than those of non-unionized workers. (Burbank)

Childcare workers should be entitled to and deserve fair wages. Please support them in their efforts to attain what they rightly deserve, higher wages. Not only will they benefit but also the children that they care for.

Works Cited

"A Profile of the Child Care Work Force." Home Page. December 3, 2000. Child Care Bulletin. <http://nccic.org/ccb/ ccbja97/workforc.html>.

Burbank, John. "Moving Beyond the Market: A Proposal for Education Linked State Subsidies for Childcare Workers' Wages." Economic Opportunity Institute. December 3, 2000. <http://www.econop. org/ECE-1994Proposal- PolicyComparisons. htm>.

"Channel 2000-Report Finds Childcare Scarce." Home Page. December 3, 2000. <http://kcbs2.com/ news/stories/news- 19991207-234704. html>.

"Child-Care Workers Begin to Nurture Fledgling Union." December 3, 2000. <http://www. csmonitor.com/ durable/1998/07/14/ p3s1.htm>.

Teenage Drinking and Driving

What Every Parent Needs to Know

The Problem:

Every single injury and death caused by drunk driving is totally preventable. Unfortunately, traffic crashes are the largest cause of death for ages 6 to 28 with almost half being alcohol-related.

One of the biggest problems is teenage drinking and driving. Not only are teenagers inexperienced at driving, but combining this inexperience with drinking is deadly. "The U.S. Surgeon General reports that life ex-pectancy has improved in the U.S. over the past 75 years for every age group except one: the date rate for 15- to 24-year-olds is higher today than it was 20 years ago. The leading cause of death is drunk and drugged driving (Underage Drinking Information Parents Need to Know).

General Statistics:

* 35% of children in the fourth grade report having been pressured by their classmates to drink; by the time they reach the sixth grade, 49% have been pressured (Underage Drinking Information Parents Need to Know).

- 33% of nearly 200,000 students surveyed said that they are not disciplined routinely when they break the rules pressured (Underage Drinking Information Parents Need to Know).

- Alcohol use is the number one drug problem among young people (qtd. in MADD Statistics: Safety Belts).

- 26 million teenagers don't know that a person can die from an alcohol overdose (qtd. in MADD Statistics: Safety Belts).

- 8 young people a day die in alcohol-related crashes (qtd. in MADD Statistics: Safety Belts).

- During a typical weekend, an average of 1 teenager dies each hour in a car crash. Nearly 50% of those crashes involve alcohol (qtd. MADD Statistics: Safety Belts).

The Solution:

Without the proper education, guidance and discipline, teenagers will continue the destructive act of drinking and driving. Where should we start? Parents should start by educating their children about the consequences of drugs and alcohol. As noted under the general statistics, a large percentage of teenagers are not disciplined after breaking the rules. Parents should maintain a disciplinary structure in their home to help prevent their children from the turning to drugs and alcohol.

Education and Prevention Programs should be offered through the school systems. By receiving the proper education at home followed by additional programs on drinking and driving at school, teenagers will be well aware that their actions have consequences and that these consequences can be deadly to themselves and others.

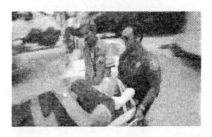

Besides educating our youths about the consequences of drinking and driving, the state laws need to be revised and enforced.

Due to the increase in drinking and driving fatalities, the state laws should be revised to include some of the following:

- Automatic license revocation appears to be the single most effective measure to reduce drunk driving. Not only is license revocation effective, but we should remember that driving is a privilege, not a right (qtd. in Drinking and Driving).

- Automatic license revocation along with a mandatory jail sentence appears to be even more effective than just automatic license revocation (qtd. in Drinking and Driving).

- Passing mandatory alcohol and drug testing in fatal crashes would promote successful prosecution of drunk and drugged drivers (qtd. in Drinking and Driving).

If teenagers realize that they will have to pay heavily if they break the rules, they might even think twice before drinking and driving.

Works Cited:

Mothers Against Drunk Driving. Home page. April 25, 2000. <www.madd.org>.

MADD Statistics: Safety Belts. Home Page. April 25, 2000. Mothers Against Drunk Driving. <www.madd.org/stats/stat_youth.shtml>.

MADD Statistics: General Statistics. Home Page. April 25, 2000. Mothers Against Drunk Driving <www.madd.org/stats/stat_gen.shtml>.

Underage Drinking Information Parents Need to Know. Home Page. April 25, 2000. Mothers Against Drunk Driving <www.madd.org/under21/youth_issues.shtml>.

Drinking and Driving. Home Page. April 28, 2000. <www2.potsdam.edu/soc/hansondj/DrinkDrive/DrinkingDriving.html>.

Producing an Action-Based Advocacy Pamphlet: A Checklist

The action-based advocacy pamphlet usually contains the following components:

✓ Description of the issue

✓ Background of the problem

✓ Currently proposed solutions

✓ Solicitation of help

✓ Clear and practical steps to enlist that assistance

✓ Contact information and a list of significant sources

While not an academically produced research paper, the advocacy pamphlet attempts to use the techniques and motives of research to address real-word, urgent concerns.

Taking a Closer Look

1. Although our discussion of developments in biology has focused on what occurs in lab and school settings, the preservation of our biological and natural resources is a very public matter that affects us all. Our literacies in such matters—our ability to identify, process, and critique the available information on threatened sites throughout the world, and our ability to mount an effective written response to such threats—may define our role as activist citizens in the new century. Our written advocacy of such causes, given the capability of the World Wide Web to create community, mount campaigns, and to effect change, may in fact have real and tangible results.

   To familiarize yourself with some of the more pressing environmental issues nationally, access the World Wide Web site of the Environmental Working Group (http://www.ewg.org/). Founded in 1993 and based in Washington D.C., the EWG works in collaboration with a wide variety of public interest groups to help keep us informed about pressing environmental concerns. Identify an issue that affects your own community, and design an action-based advocacy pamphlet to address that concern. If you prefer not to produce a pamphlet, simply follow the structure as laid out above.

2. Access the Rainforest Action Network on the World Wide Web (http://www.ran.org/) and click on the "action alert" icon. Read about a currently pressing environmental issue and write and design an action-based advocacy pamphlet (or simply follow the structure above) on preserving the rain forests of the world.

Chapter 4

Research: Gathering New Data

What Is Research?

As we learned in the previous chapter, scholarship is comprised of the knowledge that has already been gained and shared. Research, on the other hand, aims to discover or make new knowledge. In their pursuit of new knowledge, researchers have acquired considerable expertise in the methods of collecting data—through training and through observation. Social scientists may, for example, know how to design an effective survey or a questionnaire that will yield up significant data (which, in turn, they will know how to interpret and from it to extract meaning). Or biologists may know how to set up a laboratory experiment, from knowledge of appropriate instruments to knowing how to design control groups. This kind of knowledge is called *procedural;* there is an understanding not only of the "what" but also of the "how." Literary scholars may juxtapose a text (fiction or nonfiction, prose or poetry) next to a writer's journal or perhaps examine two works by the same author as a means of discovering knowledge about a writer or the conditions under which a text has been produced.

At first glance, you might think you have little in common with researchers who do original work. After all, you are a student and not an expert in the subject you are taking. You may feel that you are not expected to discover knowledge, to contribute to the conversation taking place amongst the scholars in your discipline. But is it necessarily true that as a student you can't have the experience of legitimately generating new data? In other words, is it possible for you, while a student, to feel the rush of discovery and the sense of competence in using methods that lead to that discovery? The message of this book is: It is more than just possible.

Writing with consequence assumes that writing done in the classroom and outside the classroom can have genuine significance beyond the getting of a grade. In fact, there is quite a variety of colleges, universities, corporations, and funding agencies that promote undergraduate research. Here is a brief list of such institutions and agencies, all located on the World Wide Web:

Abbott Laboratories Summer Internship Program (http://abbott.com/career/internships.html)

Undergraduate Research Opportunities at the University of Pittsburgh (http://www.pitt.edu/~urop/)

The Council on Undergraduate Research (http://www.cur.org/)

National Undergraduate Research Observatory at Northern Arizona University and Lowell Observatory (http://www.nuro.nau.edu/)

Summer Undergraduate Research Opportunities at The University of North Carolina at Chapel Hill (http://www.med.unc.edu/pmbb/sure.htm)

Howard Hughes Undergraduate Research Program at the University of Illinois (http://www.life.uiuc.edu/hughes/)

A visit to the University of Pittsburgh site will offer you access to an archive of previous undergraduate research projects, including the following:

- Alternative gene splicing designed to avoid the development of certain cancers

- A study of the menstrual cycles in macaques to determine the role of the menstrual cycles in women's susceptibility to the HIV infection

Undergraduates are presenting their research at conferences, publishing papers in professional journals, and working as interns at scientific laboratories. Undergraduate research has become something other than visiting the library and doing a subject search through the library's collections. Undergraduates are becoming involved in the collecting of data for the purpose of making knowledge. The process is a "searching out," a means of discovery.

Even within a single discipline there may be more than one way of doing research. In the field of history and psychology, for example, some researchers rely on *quantitative data,* others on *qualitative methods,* and still others employ both kinds. The study of an historical period may depend, in other words, on an analysis of infant mortality rates but may also involve the interpretation of journals and memoirs written at the time. Similarly, study of the effect of birth order calls upon statistical investigations as to the occurrence of certain behavioral traits, but it may also benefit from description of individual cases.

The first kind of research—quantitative—employs statistical evidence to support researchers' claims and draws upon a random sample in order to make more extensive generalizations. Researchers may rely on questionnaires to gather data—on, for example, the percentage of households that have access to the Internet. They may also discover information through direct observation in a lab environment—the transfer rate of differentiated (ready to be cloned) cells to a living organism. Quantitative data is usually represented in the forms of tables and charts, as in these examples of a bar graph and a line graph (both representing hypothetical data taken from a lab exercise on yeast fermentation).

Qualitative research, on the other hand, attempts to study human phenomena in naturalistic settings. Such research draws heavily upon focus groups, interviews, and case studies. For example, one qualitative study of gangs in Los Angeles and Ventura counties used interviews of gang members, their parents, police, and community members; photographs of the neighborhood; and authoritative secondary sources. Unlike a quantitative study, which from a sampling or discrete experiment tries to predict the behav-

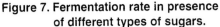

Figure 7. Fermentation rate in presence of different types of sugars.

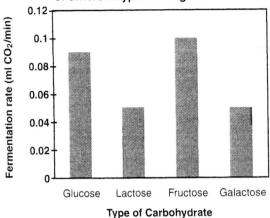

Figure 8. Rate of respiration in presence of different amounts of sugar.

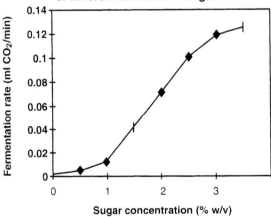

Spilatro, Steve. "Yeast on the Rise: Investigative Study Fermentation in the Introductory Biology Curriculum." Retrieved on 6 June 2002 from http://www.cur.org/rl2000/pdf/ystferm.pdf.

iors or outcomes of a large group, qualitative research makes no such prediction—although, as we shall see, such research may create inferences about the larger group. Qualitative research aims to provide a richly textured description and analysis of the subject. Consider this excerpt from the study referred to above of L.A. gang members:

> The female gang-affiliated members came from the same dysfunctional environment and noxious types of homes as the male members interviewed in this research.
>
> They expressed a preference for gang-affiliated males, and a good many voiced distaste for men who wore suits and ties. Others said they weren't sure why they were attracted to the gang guys. Many had not been treated right, yet they went back to the gang male, or became involved with another one. On the positive, though satirical side, one female said, "They don't let no one mess with them," and this toughness was, at least for her, a desirable trait.
>
> Many females had poor relationships with their parents.
>
> Angela: "I hate my mother, and I hate my step-father even more. Hijola!"
>
> Comments of this sort were commonplace.
>
> Hallcom, Dr. Francine. "Gang Girls" in *An Urban Ethnography of Latino Street Gangs in Los Angeles and Ventura Counties.* Retrieved on 2 June 2002 from http://www.csun.edu/~hcchs006/ table.html.

Proponents of each kind of research are often at odds philosophically. Advocates of quantitative research argue that only through careful control of the field studied and through rigorous statistical analysis can objective judgments be made about a research problem. Those who support the qualitative approach state that such objectivity is neither possible nor reliable, but rather what ought to be studied is the human experience itself, in all its complex richness. Later in this chapter you will be able to try your hand at both kinds of research—to determine for yourself the relative advantages and disadvantages of each approach.

Research Instruments

The Interview

Among the humanities, social sciences, and business fields, a common method for collecting data is the interview. The interview method belongs under the category of "qualitative research" because it focuses on the subjective experience of an individual. Used in both specialized and popular research, the interview might be found in the pages of an academic journal such as the *Journal of Advanced Composition* or televised every week on a popular TV program like *60 Minutes*. An interview is usually recorded so as to make a written record or transcript possible.

An effective interview requires a great deal of preparation. You must, first of all, have a clear and manageable purpose. Since your selection of an *informant* and your line of questioning both depend on that purpose, an interview has very little point without prior research and reflection. As explained in Chapter 2, your desire to answer a question or to test a hypothesis will drive the research engine. Nevertheless, the selection of a worthwhile topic is but the beginning. The checklist on pages 147 and 148 provides some other considerations to think about.

Grounding the Theory

---

1. In this excerpt from an interview of MIT's Steven Pinker (whose work on mental imagery we have seen in Chapter 3), Harvey Blume of *Wired* magazine focuses on Pinker's fascinating view of the brain's evolution. How would you evaluate Blume's interview skills?

    Wired: How has computer science contributed to the field of evolutionary psychology?

    Pinker: Traditional evolutionary explanations of the mind have been very crude, relying on things like "territorial imperative" and "sex drive." Given the complexity and richness of human thought, that's not a satisfactory answer. But if what evolved is a complex set of information processing mechanisms—neural circuitry designed for intricate computation—then you can have both the richness of human thought and a scientific framework to make sense of it.

W. So the brain is a naturally evolved neural computer. Who shares that view?

P. Virtually everyone in cognitive science, from Marvin Minsky to Noam Chomsky. It's actually easier to point to the people who think the brain is not a neural computer—they are flamboyant, though few in number and unrepresentative.

It's hard to ignore that our brains are made of information processors. Down to a neuron's axon and molecules, the nerve cell is designed to be an information carrier. Too often we think of neurons as bean counters, but they're much more like sophisticated chips or microcomputers. And if neurons are like chips, when you wire up a hundred billion of them you get a very powerful computational device. That's the only explanation for how a hunk of matter can do intelligent things—unless you think there's a special kind of substance necessary for intelligence, which would mean robots and artificial intelligence cannot be created.

W. Does this mean that to build smart machines we should study the evolution of the human brain?

P. The answer is an emphatic yes. Nature has been doing R&D much longer than humans, and engineers often learn from the natural world. For example, composite materials like fiberglass or carbon fiber, which embed filaments in a matrix, are based on the design of wood. Genetic algorithms are obviously based on natural selection. And stereophotography, used in aerial reconnaissance, is based on stereovision in animals.

2. Imagine that you are going to interview a person whose accomplishments you admire. Compose a short list of questions from which you might draw to conduct the interview, ordering the questions in the sequence that you might ask them.

Conducting an Interview: A Checklist

✓ **Give yourself time.** The logistical work of locating interview subjects, scheduling interviews (to meet not only your needs but the timetables of your informants), preparing (if appropriate) to record the session, holding the interview session, and producing a written transcript requires a great deal of time.

✓ **Do the necessary research before the interview.** Information begets more information. When you, the interviewer, are informed and prepared, your questions will elicit even more relevant and useful information. Find out as much as you can about your project and your interview subject before you step into that interview room.

✓ **In your selection of informants, aim not only for appropriateness but for a diversity of perspectives.** You want to interview someone who will offer you relevant insights into your project. The last thing you want to do is to waste your time or that of your informants. Contact the appropriate agencies and consult experts in the field about likely subjects to interview. Try to field a range of perspectives, if possible. Social scientists use the term *triangulation* to denote the use of multiple vantage points. The "truth" is most efficiently arrived at through a variety of perspectives.

✓ **Inform your interview subjects beforehand about the nature and scope of your project and the extent of their involvement.** Obtaining informed consent is crucial. In the light of what history has taught us about the unethical use of human subjects for experimentation, researchers in a variety of disciplines have outlined ethical guidelines in conducting researching involving human subjects (see, for example, *Guidelines and Principles of the Oral History Association*, Pamphlet No. 3, Oral History Association, 1992). Interview subjects must be made aware of the full scope of your project and be given the right to refuse to discuss certain subjects and even to remain anonymous.

✓ **With the informants' consent, be prepared to record the session or, in the absence of consent, to find an efficient and accurate method of note taking.** Because of the difficulties of conducting an interview while at the same time accurately recording what transpires, interviewers need to be able to rely on a mechanical means of recording the session (with the subject's approval) or find a reliable method of taking notes (perhaps relying on another to do so). As a precaution, please make certain to test your recording equipment before the interview.

✓ **Come to the interview with a short list of questions, but be prepared to ask follow-up questions and to initiate questions that occur to you during the interview.** The importance of listening carefully to your interview subject cannot be overstated. You can avoid the purely scripted interview by listening and being ready to ask critical follow-up questions.

✓ **Prepare an accurate written record of the interview.** This process can be terribly time-consuming, but it is crucial. Without an authoritative written record of the interview session, you may miss some of the nuances and perhaps some of the gaps that become obvious only when the written record is reviewed.

✓ **Give your interview subject an opportunity to review the transcript and the way you will use the session in your project.** On ethical grounds—but also on the principle of accuracy—allow your informant to review the session's transcript and any rendering of the session in your work. If you are composing an oral history, for example, share with your informant a draft of the work as a whole, showing the context within which you've embedded your informant's words. Perhaps the best justification for doing so is to view you and your informant as collaborators on the project. Both are necessary to a successful outcome.

Types of Surveys

Surveys greet us everywhere these days—on the phone, on the Internet, and, less frequently, in a mailing. The surveying of *focus groups*—small samplings of individuals whose attitudes are studied for a company's or agency's marketing purposes—is commonplace. A survey might ask us questions about our views on voting initiatives or the television programs that we watch. Although we normally don't give much thought to how surveys are designed and reviewed, in fact they are systematically constructed. They differ in kind and function, as you can see from this listing of different designs.

Cross-section Surveys

Rather than exhaustively studying all the members of a particular group, surveys facilitate the collection of information by selecting a random sampling of that group. A cross section includes all the subgroups within the larger community that is studied. When studying the incidence of a certain kind of cancer among a community that resides near the scene of chemical spillage, researchers might survey a cross section that includes various age-*cohorts*, single heads of households as well as two-parent households, and a range of social and economic classes. (A cohort is a group of people with some statistical characteristic—such as age—in common.)

Stratified Surveys

If you were interested in focusing on a particular subgroup within the field studied—say, the amount of exercise per week done by 10- to 15-year-olds in a community—you could survey that subgroup along with others in the community, drawing upon a random sampling in each. You would then be comparing specific strata within the larger grouping.

Preparing a Survey: A Checklist

✓ **Begin by collecting demographic information** (gender, marital status, income, education, and so on). Such information will serve as *predictor variable*. In other words, they will allow you to factor in such considerations in determining why your subjects responded the way that they did.

✓ **Avoid biased or leading questions** ("Is Vice President Gore a sore loser?"). You want to collect data, not create responses to suit your own research needs.

✓ **Decide what type of response you seek.** Do you wish to use an *open-ended response* ("What is your view about the medicinal use of marijuana?"), a *closed response* ("How often do you exercise per week?: Not at all/one to three times/five or more"), or a *partially limited response* ("What kinds of music do you listen to? Check all that apply: New Age/R&B/Hip Hop/Other").

✓ **If using a rating scale** (from one to five, from very weak to very strong), **make it manageable** (not overly long or complex) and clearly label the end points. Such scales have appeal because they are easily computed.

✓ **Group related questions together.** It may frustrate and confuse your informant if s/he must move back and forth in subject matter.

✓ **Ask precise questions.** If your intent is to gauge the impact of video games on teen violence, it would make little sense to ask a question about television use, unless you planned to suggest a correlation between video and television.

Longitudinal Surveys

Longitudinal surveys study the same or similar groups of people over a lengthy period of time. Some surveys gather information about a cohort but use different samples or representatives—in order to track patterns or trends among the group as a group. Other surveys study the same group and the same sampling within that group over time, to track changes and patterns among individuals as well as the cohort.

Designing a Survey

When researchers need to collect data in writing, they typically design a survey, with carefully crafted questions aimed at eliciting key pieces of information. See the checklist on the facing page for some tips to consider.

Grounding the Theory

1. The classroom has become a popular site for surveying. Take, for example, the following survey that tries to assess the role of technology in the classroom. Evaluate the effectiveness of the survey, using the criteria given in the checklist.

Pedagogical Focus: Online Assessment Questionnaire

In order to best evaluate how students feel about the application of technology in the classroom, students will be invited to respond to questions similar to the following. Responses to these statements will be used to manipulate future course offerings so that pedagogical advantages are leveraged:

- I was able to access Internet-based class resources.
  (agree strongly) a b c d e (disagree strongly)

- The professor had an appropriate knowledge of the technologies used in this class.
  (agree strongly) a b c d e (disagree strongly)

- The technologies used were well integrated into course material.
  (agree strongly) a b c d e (disagree strongly)

- The professor responded in an appropriate amount of

time to my e-mail.
(agree strongly) a b c d e *(disagree strongly)*

▓ Course *news groups* were helpful.
(agree strongly) a b c d e *(disagree strongly)*

▓ I started this course knowing very little about the World
Wide Web.
(agree strongly) a b c d e *(disagree strongly)*

▓ I enjoyed the virtual group projects in this course.
(agree strongly) a b c d e *(disagree strongly)*

▓ I am more comfortable using the Internet than before this
class.
(agree strongly) a b c d e *(disagree strongly)*

▓ I prefer traditional classroom teaching techniques, i.e.,
blackboard only, no Internet, etc.
(agree strongly) a b c d e *(disagree strongly)*

▓ On-line video recordings of class lectures where helpful.
(agree strongly) a b c d e *(disagree strongly)*

▓ The quality of on-line presentations was acceptable.
(agree strongly) a b c d e *(disagree strongly)*

"Pedagogical Focus: Online Assessment Questionnaire." Computer Enhanced Education. Retrieved 2 June 2002 from http://
www.ece.gatech.edu/academic/computer_education/intro.html.

2. Design a survey for a course that you are currently taking.

The Observational Notebook

Surveys are, of course, not the only ways to collect data. *Observation*, whether with the naked eye or with the assistance of
a telescope or microscope, can yield significant discoveries.
One instructor in a chemistry department effectively uses a
certain classroom assignment to test the power of observation. He asks his students to observe a candle that has been lit
and to write down 50 characteristics they have perceived.
The human eye constructs even as it perceives the world; it

makes something as well as records what is "out there." How
many items can you notice when asked to observe an object
for a lengthy period of time?

Observational notebooks—the written record of a researcher's observations—are used, with variations, in a wide
variety of disciplines, including fields as diverse as astronomy, biology (in the rendering of laboratory results), art (in
the form of sketches drawn from observing natural settings or
museum pieces), and anthropology (in field notes). In an astronomy course, for example, you might be asked to record
your observations of the night sky, providing the following
information:

- Specific location
- Date and time
- Description of viewing conditions
- Rendering of the object observed
- Indication of the instrument used

As an example, take a look at the following entry in a student's observational notebook:

Date: October 19, 2000
Time: 1700 UT (1:00 PM EST)
Location: Bristol Community College (Building "E"-Rooftop)
Sky Conditions:
     Transparency: Moving clouds
     Seeing Conditions: Relatively good when the clouds
     passed; sky was clear
     Any Influence by Moon: No; it was daylight
     Light Pollution: No; it was daylight
Instrument Used:
     Mead 10" Schymidt Cassegrain Reflector-FL>:
     2800mm/Mg: 70x/Eyepiece: 40mm (sun filter was used)
Objects Observed:
     List of Objects Observed: Sun/Sunspots/Moon

Details on Objects Observed: Although some of us had to wait for the clouds to pass in order to observe the sun, it was well worth the wait. The sun, closest star to Earth, is 93,000,000 miles away from Earth. It looked much like one would expect, that is, a bright orange ball in the sky. The thrill lay in the ability to observe sunspots on the sun so clearly. V:-26.75/ Spectral Type: G2 (Yellow). [The V (apparent magnitude = the apparent (not actual) brightness of the sun and the G (Spectral Type or classification = the temperature classification) Spectral Classification is as follows : O B A F G K M R N S 'O' is the hottest star and 'S' is the coolest.] Sunspots are regions of the sun where the magnetic field is especially strong and are cooler regions of the sun. Each sunspot has a dark center called the umbra, and less dark region called penumbra. I also noticed that the moon was visible, looking like a white transparency in the sky.

Grounding the Theory

1. Review the sample observational notebook above. Describe what each section does and why it is important.

2. Visit a local planetarium to discover as much as you can about the features of the night sky at this time of year. Then, over a series of several nights, compile an observational notebook by carefully jotting down what you have observed.

3. Adapt the observational notebook approach to other research purposes. For example, you might use it to study the demographics of mall shoppers, or to sketch the layout of your own classroom.

The Case Study

The tools that we have discussed so far—surveys, interviews, and observational notebooks—may all be called upon to produce a single form of research and analysis: the _case study_. Often associated with psychology, the case study has achieved prominence in such disparate fields as business management,

Designing a Case Study: A Checklist

In designing a case study, you need to follow various steps:

✓ **Construct a theoretical perspective.** Although a case study focuses, by its very nature, on a narrowly defined subject, researchers who employ such studies usually attempt to frame a case study by positing a theoretical view. For example, in a case study of the L.A. gang scene, the researcher suggests a theoretical view in the very first sentence: "The female gang-affiliated members came from the same dysfunctional environment and noxious types of homes as the male members interviewed in this research." She posits some connection between gang affiliation and a dysfunctional home environment.

✓ **Determine your goals.** Keep in mind that in designing a case study, you are trying to depict a particular, localized subject in a natural setting. You cannot hope to achieve an immediately generalizable study that fits all sizes. Be practical and work within clearly defined limits.

✓ **Select a subject.** Choose as your subject a concern that wholly engages you. Keeping in mind that you will be both observer and participant in the study, you need to feel comfortable speaking with and being among the subject(s) of your study.

✓ **Select appropriate methods of collecting data.** How will you record what you observe? What technical resources will you use (video/audio recorders, for example)? In an effort to achieve "triangulation" (that is, obtaining a range of perspectives in order to maximize the accuracy of your data) and context, will you consult a variety of sources, including written documents? Have you informed your subject of the purpose and scope of your study and obtained consent to use your subject as the focus of your research (see pages 199–200, informed consent)?

✓ **Compose your case, taking care to provide critical context as well as richly layered description of your subject.** Like a camera that begins with panorama but gradually narrows its angle of vision, your case study ought to provide needed context before zeroing in on your subject.

computer science, and public health. In business, for example, a case study might focus on one company's efforts to diversify its product line; in computer science, a software program might be tested in a particular office environment; and in public health, incidents of disease prevention might be studied by examining preventive methods in a single community.

The case study, a form of qualitative research, attempts to provide an in-depth study of an individual, community, or institution, drawing from a wide array of both primary and secondary sources. Whether done by the anthropologist reporting on the rituals of a cultural community, or the marketing specialist studying the management style of a particular company, the case study gives what ethnographers (those who make written records of the activities of particular cultures) call *thick descriptions* of the subject studied. Such studies do not aim for replicability but rather seek to test theories by constructing in considerable detail the real-life activities of a community. A case study, for example, of a group of firemen in lower Manhattan, coping with the aftermath of the 9/11 terrorist attacks, aims to capture the activities of that particular community but does not necessarily claim to present data on other firemen.

Evaluating Research Methods

When should you use a particular research method? That depends on what you want to know.

If you wish to ...	*Use ...*
Highlight the perspective of individual informants	Interviews
Gather statistical evidence	A survey
Test your hypothesis against observed phenomena	An observational notebook
Study a large problem within a naturalistic setting	A case study

Grounding the Theory

1. Design, research, and write a case study that focuses on a subject drawn from your own community. You might choose to write about the clients who frequent a tattoo shop or regular visitors to an online chat room. Remember, though, to provide a hypothesis or theoretical perspective ("The act of obtaining a tattoo amounts to a statement of independence," for example) from the very start as a way of framing your case study.

2. Read the case study entitled, "Student Participation in a Discussion-Oriented Online Course." Describe the methods of research used (such as field observation or surveys). Employing similar methods, conduct and report on a case study of a discussion in one of your own courses, whether face-to-face or online or a combination of both.

Student Participation in a Discussion-Oriented Online Course: A Case Study

Abstract

Online course offerings are expanding. Although many are independent *study* courses with some contact with instructors and other students, discussion-oriented courses are also delivered on the Web. This *study* examined the nature of student participation in one such course. Access to course materials varied widely from student to student but reflected an overall commitment to learning. Student posts to the threaded discussion were very focused on the course content. Participation in the course changed while students served as course moderators, suggesting the positive effect such a role may have on learning and community building. A strong sense of community was established as students engaged in dialogue with each other and with the instructor. (Keywords: community, computer conferences, computer-mediated communication, moderator, online course, online learning.)

Distance learning has been around for centuries. It has evolved from primarily text-based correspondence courses to videotape-based instruction and now to compressed video transmission that allows for two-way audio and video connections between the teacher and the learner (Schlosser & Anderson, 1994). Because of advances in hardware and software, the *Internet* also can be an effective distance learning medium.

Computer-mediated communication has the potential to transform education by creating learner-centered instructional environments (Van Gorp, 1998). Van Gorp suggests, "The Web is now more than an area to access and post information: It is a place to interactively communicate and construct knowledge" (p. 12). Computer conferencing can be used to foster intellectual development, learner autonomy, and equal opportunities for students to participate in discussion (Cifuentes, Murphy, Segur, & Kodali, 1997). Furthermore, "Computer conferencing provides students with opportunities to elaborate on and defend their positions to other students and to negotiate meaning with teachers and fellow students" (Cifuentes et al., p. 186).

The body of knowledge about how students engage in learning in online courses is rather modest at this time. Because the use of telecommunication tools in higher education course work has the potential to address teaching and learning in ways that are different from traditional instruction, it is critical to develop a solid understanding of what transpires during courses offered through this delivery medium.

This *study* examined the nature of student participation in an online course. Several research questions were examined:

- In what ways did students choose to access and engage course materials?
- How did students participate during the week in which they moderated the discussion?
- What was the content of the students' bulletin board posts?
- How did student participation contribute to the class as a community of learners?

Method

The Course
EDIT 5110, Social Perspectives of Technology in Education, was a 2-unit graduate course offered in fall 1998 at California State University Stanislaus. It was a required course for students pursuing a

master of arts in education with emphasis in educational technology. There were no face-to-face class meetings; however, it was not an independent *study* course. Collaboration and discussion were incorporated into the online course design.

Each week, students read articles dealing with social, ethical, or legal perspectives of technology, and they completed an online quiz designed to assess their understanding of the articles' content. Students were required to post at least two messages per week to the online bulletin board. Each class member moderated or comoderated one of the weekly discussions, which took place after the quiz on the topic had been completed. In addition, students wrote a position paper and took a midterm examination with a partner, and they completed an individual project dealing with a social issue regarding technology in education. For class purposes, the week began at 12:01 a.m. Sunday and ended at midnight Saturday. EDIT 5110 was the only course in the master's program offered entirely online.

The first requirement of the semester was for students to post a biography to the course bulletin board, an exercise to acquaint them with class members and also to familiarize them with the Web site's features. Social, ethical, and legal topics were selected for their timeliness and discussion potential. Several controversial topics were purposely included so that multiple perspectives could be shared and understood. Some examples included the neutrality of technology, gender and technology, and filtering in relation to freedom of speech.

All online interaction was controlled through a course Web site that students accessed using a browser and a password. The software, WebCT (1996–1999), allowed for threaded discussions (asynchronous), live chats (synchronous), and quizzes. All communications and contributions were stored and tracked for analysis after the semester concluded.

Participants

Fourteen graduate students were enrolled in the course, 10 females and 4 males. All were K-12 teachers, with experience varying from less than 1 year to more than 20 years. All students were interested in obtaining a master of arts in education with emphasis in educational technology. EDIT 5110 was the first online course taken by each of the students, though some had engaged in other Web-based activities prior to their enrollment.

Data Collection and Analysis

The *study* was primarily a qualitative analysis of student participation in the course. Statistical analyses were performed on some of the data to gain a more comprehensive understanding of what transpired. The purpose of the *study* was to understand how students chose to engage themselves with the course materials and with each other.

All of the bulletin board contributions during the semester were collected and coded. E-mail messages sent to the course instructor were saved and tabulated. Surveys were sent to all class members at the end of the semester to gather information regarding student perception of the online course experience, and three students chose to write follow-up analyses of their participation.

Observations and Interpretations

Accessing Course Materials

One of the reasons online courses have become popular is that students can participate when it is convenient for them to do so. In this course, bulletin board posts and quizzes needed to be completed by midnight each Saturday, providing flexibility based on individuals' schedules and preferences. Most of the students in the course accessed the class Web site several times each week and contributed far more messages to the bulletin board than were required. During a 15-week time period, students posted a total of 1,025 messages to the bulletin board. Most posts were made on Saturdays than any other day; however, other than a midweek lull on Tuesdays, students participated in the discussions throughout the week (Figure 1). Computer conferencing systems extend class time,

S	159
M	113
T	91
W	112
R	159
F	128
Sa	263

Figure 1 Number of student posts to the bulletin board by day of the week.

which may lengthen the time students spend engaged in course content (Cifuentes et al., 1997).

As varied as the day of the week in which students posted messages was the time of day in which they participated. Most of the students were teaching during daytime hours on weekdays; this resulted in fewer posted messages during daytime hours than evening hours on weekdays. This pattern continued during the weekends as well (Figure 2).

Students primarily accessed course materials from their home computers. Access from their school computers or campus computers was relatively minimal (Figure 3). Campus computers were the primary access option for two students who did not have access to the Web at home. These two students checked the course Web site fewer times throughout the week than did students with Web access at home.

Students actively participated in the class. They were required to post a total of 27 messages during the semester. Table 1 indicates that the average number of posts per student was 73 messages. The table also indicates how many of the 1,458 total posts (which included student posts, instructor posts, and visitor posts) each student read. The number displayed in WebCT (1996–1999) could exceed 1,458 if students read posts multiple

0–4 am	29
4–8 am	18
8 am–noon	127
noon–4 pm	208
4–8 pm	346
8 pm–midnight	297

Figure 2 Time of day in which student posts were made to the bulletin board.

Home	74.38
School	14.68
Campus	10.75

Figure 3 Location of computers used to access course materials, by percent of total access.

Table 1 Summary of Involvement in the Class Bulletin Board, by Student

Legend for Chart:

A – Gender

B – Number of Posts

C – Average Number of Lines per Post

D – Number of Posts Read

E – Number of Total Hits

A	B	C	D	E
F	35	14	1,156	1,347
F	27	12	499	576
M	78	19	1,356	1,746
M	37	8	682	827
F	59	13	1,406	1,584
F	121	15	1,394	1,649
F	221	10	1,695	1,999
M	63	12	1,009	1,160
F	109	14	1,441	1,792
F	42	13	522	624
F	38	20	471	648
F	20	16	409	486
M	41	18	1,022	1,151
F	125	10	1,508	1,817
Average	73	14	1,040	1,243

times. The Number of Total Hits column in the table indicates the combined total of number of articles read, the number of posts made, and the number of course Web site accesses (which linked them to the bulletin board, synchronous chat, quiz section, and course calendar).

Student participation varied from person to person, which happens in all classroom settings, but the online medium gave each of them a voice (Piburn & Middleton, 1998; Schlagal, Trathen,

& Blanton, 1996; Thomas, Clift, & Sugimoto, 1996). Some of the students chose not to read all of the posts. In a traditional class format, students are less likely to ignore verbal responses from students than they were in the online class. In EDIT 5110, students were unaware that the number of posts they read could be tracked. It is possible that some of them may have read a higher percentage of the posts had they known this. On the other hand, the number of posts became quite large, one of the possible dangers of online learning (Kimball, 1995). There was no direct relationship between course grade and reading each message, so students may have completed other tasks for the course in lieu of reading all messages.

The correlation between the number of posts a student contributed and the average number of lines per his or her posts was $r = -0.318$, a moderately negative relationship between the two factors. The students who were the most frequent contributors to the class bulletin board had somewhat shorter messages than did the students who made fewer posts. The students who were very active in the discussion often wrote one- or two-line reactions to other messages. Those who were less active did not tend to exhibit this behavior as frequently.

WebCT (1996–1999) includes a synchronous chat feature, which can be tracked by the instructor. Although students were encouraged to use this option as they worked with their partners on the position paper and midterm essay, only two chat room conversations were initiated for this purpose. Most of the students visited the chat rooms early in the semester to see how they were designed but did not view the feature as an appealing option for course communication. Instead, most pairs collaborated by e-mail only, while a handful of face-to-face meetings and phone conversations facilitated the development of these projects.

Involvement as a Moderator
A review of the literature regarding online learning indicated that students became more involved and responsible for their participation when the entire course was not instructor driven (Cifuentes et al., 1997; Rohfeld & Hiemstra, 1995). For this reason, each class member was responsible for moderating or comoderating the discussion for one week. Moderator duties were assigned based on student topic preferences.

Early in the semester, students read two articles outlining the responsibility of the moderator to prepare them for their role. It was up to individual students, however, to decide how to perform while assigned the position. Table 2 indicates that students' participation in the class changed during the week of their moderator obligation. The number of posts made by moderators during their assigned week averaged 14.5, whereas students each posted an average of

Table 2 Comparison of Student Participation During Moderator and Nonmoderator Weeks

Legend for Chart:

A – Student
B – Number of Posts During Moderator Week
C – Average Posts per Week During Nonmoderator Weeks
D – Average Lines per Post During Moderator Week
E – Average Lines per Post During Nonmoderator Weeks

A	B	C	D	E
1	7	2.33	20	12
2	6	1.75	13	12
3	17	5.08	25	18
4	9	2.33	7	8
5	12	3.92	14	13
6	35	7.17	18	13
7	15	17.17	16	9
8	21	3.50	13	11
9	28	6.75	19	12
10	4	3.17	19	12
11	11	2.25	22	19
12	N/A [*]	N/A [*]	N/A [*]	16
13	9	1.67	20	17
14	19	8.83	12	9
Average	14.5	4.76	17	13

* This student's participation was affected by personal matters not related to the class, and she eventually withdrew.

only 4.76 messages per week during periods when they were not moderating the discussion. This was a highly significant difference, t = 4.261, p less than .0011, df = 13. In addition, students' posts were significantly longer during weeks when they were moderating the discussion, t = 5.019, p less than .0003, df = 13.

The student moderators provided "the intellectual impetus, the ideological framework from which the discussion would progress" (Tagg, 1994, p. 43). Students took their role very seriously, as indicated by these differences in participation. On completion of the course, one student reflected, "The duties of the moderator really allowed us to follow one discussion so carefully that we literally behaved as the instructor. I enjoyed the fact that the instructor had enough confidence in students to engage [us] in this process." The moderator role not only facilitated a learner-centered environment but also served as an empowering opportunity for students.

Content of Posts

There were several ways in which the contents of the bulletin board messages were examined. One analysis was based on the work of Thomas et al. (1996), who coded computer-mediated conversations into one of five focus areas: articles, content, technical, procedural, or nonacademic. EDIT 5110 messages were coded into one or more of those categories.

Posts that were coded as article were those containing material that specifically mentioned one of the article authors or included content directly from one of the readings. A sample message coded this way was posted by one of the nonmoderators. She said, "The Leslie article from last week stated that in many ways, telecommunications can blur certain social distinctions such as race, disabilities, gender, social status, physical appearance." The student went on to explain how this can also have negative connotations. Another student post that was coded in this category said, "I found Stoll's article witty, and I agree he seems to have a love/hate relationship with technology." Both of these posts directly referred to information that came from assigned readings.

Information that was related to the course readings but was not directly elicited by one of them was coded as content. One student wrote, "Seriously, has anyone else heard of any potential damage-causing cookies? Our readings this week said nothing about this issue. Keeping track of my Web use without my permission is one thing, but sending me 'bad cookies' is another." Another content post begins, "So then what happens to the idea of the school acting in loco parentis? Is *Internet* access different from curriculum access? Should we have unfiltered *Internet* access if the filters do not work?" The questions posed by the student were generated after reading and thinking about one of the articles.

The last three categories were less related to curriculum than the previous two categories. Technical posts were those messages containing information or questions about the use of the course Web site. An example included, "Did anyone else have problems accessing the course site last night?" Another student wrote, "Can I ask a favor of the group? Maybe it's my latent ADD, but I sometimes get a little foggy during some of these longer responses that seem to be getting more prevalent. Would it be possible to throw in a paragraph or a skipped line on occasion?"

Procedural posts were those containing announcements, logistical information, and information about course requirements. These were primarily posts by the instructor to let students know what articles they needed to read and tasks necessary to complete during the week.

The fifth category, nonacademic, included messages that did not directly relate to the class. Some of these were personal messages between students, such as "Nice to see you are back for another class, SS." Another student wrote, "Fun use of technology—speaking of microwaves—I just heard this today. You can have a grape race in a microwave. Line up the grapes at one end. Close the door and start it up! The moisture in the grapes is supposed to cause them to run to the other side . . .)" Although there was a thread in which microwaves were included in the discussion, this post obviously deviated from the academic content.

Based on the Thomas et al. (1996) categories, the bulletin board messages were, overall, very focused on course content (Table 3). Student posts that were related to the content of the readings or to the articles themselves comprised 85% of the total student messages. The content of the bulletin board messages in the online course was more focused on academics than the messages that were sent to a listserv used in a science and mathematics teaching methods course (Piburn & Middleton, 1998). However, the online medium was used only as a supplement to instruction in that *study* rather than as the sole delivery mechanism. The degree to which student contributions relate to actual content may depend highly on the purpose of the computer-mediated communication.

Table 3 Percentage of Instructor and Student Posts Based on Thomas, Clift, and Sugimoto's (1996) Categories

Legend for Chart:

A – Article

B – Content

C – Technical

D – Procedural

E – Nonacademic

	A	B	C	D	E
Instructor	12.7	62.5	7.0	9.7	8.1
Students	14.9	69.7	4.4	1.9	9.1

There were relatively few posts related to technical issues, partly because of student experience with technology and also because WebCT (1996–1999) was relatively easy to use. The bulk of the technical posts related to America Online disconnections during quizzes, bulletin board features, and occasional server problems. The other main technical thread was a student-initiated request to eliminate old bulletin board messages in an effort to decrease the number of viewable messages.

The bulk of posts in the nonacademic category related to the scheduling of two social gatherings: one at a conference and one after the semester ended. Other posts in this category dealt with information about the Miller Analogies Test, an exam required for acceptance into the master's program, and ride sharing to another class that many of the students were taking.

An additional coding system was used to analyze the verbal interactions included in the messages. Bellack, Kliebard, Hyman, and Smith (1966) conducted a three-year *study* of the teaching process through an analysis of the verbal interaction between teachers and students. They examined what the speakers said and how that dialogue contributed to the class. Although the *study* was done more than three decades ago, their observations serve as a basis for language patterns in classrooms. It is possible that the shift to more student-centered learning has changed the interactions between teachers and students since the 1966 observations. Many college courses, however, are still delivered by lecture and would likely yield similar findings.

Bellack and colleagues (1966) categorized the verbal interactions into four categories, called pedagogical moves:

▓ Structuring: Setting the context for behavior by initiating or stopping interaction. An example is to begin class by focusing on a topic or problem.

▓ Soliciting: Verbal prompts designed to elicit a verbal response. Questions, commands, imperatives, and requests fall under this category.

▓ Responding: Addressing soliciting moves.

▓ Reacting: Responses caused indirectly by structuring, soliciting, or responding.

Clarification, synthesis, and expanding on ideas serve as reacting moves, while a responding move is always elicited by a solicitation.

Each bulletin board message was coded with one or more of these pedagogical moves. In the Bellack et al. (1966) *study*, teachers performed 61.7% of the moves. In EDIT 5110, the teacher performed only 29.6% of the moves, while students performed the remaining 70.4%. This mirrored Piburn and Middleton's (1998) findings regarding the ratio of faculty to student contributions to their listserv, indicating the potential of Web-based instructional media to change the role of the teacher.

Table 4 displays the comparison of the verbal interactions of students and the instructor based on move type. Distinct differ-

Table 4 Percentage of Move Types by Instructor and Students in the Online Class

Legend for Chart:

A – Structure
B – Solicit
C – Respond
D – React
E – Percent of All Moves

	A	B	C	D	E
Instructor	4.6	5.4	5.7	13.9	29.6
Students	4.9	14.7	7.9	42.9	70.4
Percent of All Moves	9.5	20.1	13.6	56.8	100.0

ences were found between the interactions in the online course. Piburn and Middleton's (1998) *study*, in which the listserv was used as a supplement to instruction, and Bellack and colleagues' (1966) observations in a traditional classroom. In traditional classrooms, teachers solicited and reacted (22.8% and 22.6% of all interactions), whereas the teachers' role in the two online media environments included only a small percent of soliciting moves (5.4%). In the online course, teacher moves were balanced between structuring (4.6%), soliciting (5.4%), and responding (5.7%). In the traditional class, teachers performed 4.75 times more soliciting moves than structuring moves, and 6.5 times more soliciting moves than reacting moves. Likewise, in the listserv, the teachers performed no structuring moves, while the number of responding moves was 4.2 times higher than the number of soliciting moves. The online learning medium may promote diverse instructor roles.

Among students, the online group generated a much higher percentage of reacting moves (42.9% of all communication) than in the other two groups (23.9% in the listserv, and 5.7% in the traditional classroom). In the online course, each structuring and soliciting move often elicited responses or reactions from multiple students.

An online setting often provides less restrained communication between students than does a more traditional setting, and it allows students to function without the influence of a dominant point of view such as that of the teacher or other class member (Buckley, 1997). The difference in moves made by teachers and students in the various class settings supports this position. Students seem to take control more in electronic conversations, consistent with constructivist approaches where teachers and students take on different classroom roles (Piburn & Middleton, 1998).

Class as Community
Because online students do not share a physical connection to their classmates, community building needs to occur differently than it does in traditional classes. However, studies indicate that communities do develop among students involved in computer-mediated conferencing systems (Herrmann, 1998; McDonald & Gibson, 1998; McGinnis, 1996; Schlagal et al., 1996). An examination of what contributes to a sense of community can help strengthen online course design.

One measure of the sense of community among the students is the use of class members' names in bulletin board messages. Of the

1,025 student posts, 448 messages (44.1%) included the mention of 500 class member names (some messaged contained more than one name). Referring to other class members is a strong indicator that students felt connected with their classmates (Paulsen, 1995). It is likely that students repeatedly included others' names because of the unified atmosphere it created among and between class members.

Because visual and verbal cues are absent from online learning environments, it is common for groups to develop some way of expressing their emotions and feelings (Cifuentes et al., 1997). In some cases, students may use emoticons, computer keystrokes that resemble things like smiley faces, to help convey meaning. In EDIT 5110, emoticons were used in only 5.3% of the posts. It is possible that this was because of the large percentage of posts related to the course content. When students did use emoticons, it was mostly to lighten the tone. Some people believe that the use of emoticons has a "flattening" effect on the emotional content of a message (Buckley, 1997). One student wrote, "I enjoy having the opportunity to think things through before writing to an audience of 'peers.' However, I am finding it challenging to not have the opportunity to interact with you face-to-face. I find that I miss the 'humanity' of it all . . . the real laughs and chuckles vs:)."

The "humanity" component came up repeatedly in discussions, as in the above quote. One student wrote, "I agree that the in-depth level of interaction between us cannot occur in spontaneous classroom debate or dialogue. (But I still miss not hearing the emotion in the voices, and especially not being able to put faces with the opinions!)." Students appreciated the passionate messages that were made possible because of the reflection time facilitated through the medium. Conversely, the physical presence of others could not fully be replicated online. Related to how physical presence contributes to class community, one student observed:

> As I was sitting waiting for the famous Tuesday night class to begin, I was struck by the fact that many of us who had engaged in some rather serious discourse online were just sitting and chatting about rather innocuous topics when we came face to face. Now granted, the class had not begun, and we were not in a formal seminar, but it seemed rather ironic, or interesting, that when we did get in a setting where we could read each others faces, and hear sarcasm, etc. (all the things that we said were missing from

posted messages) that not much was happening on an intellectual level.

It appeared that, though the students felt they were missing out on the human component of traditional classes, their perception of the interactions that take place in the face-to-face setting did not necessarily parallel the reality.

The author of one of the required readings suggested posting messages using a pen name to provoke discussion in online courses (Paulsen, 1995). After reading the article, a female student requested the creation of an account for "Darren Smith," which she would manage. A biography was posted for this fictitious class member, a conservative, somewhat chauvinistic male who was thinking about becoming a teacher. Messages under his name were posted throughout the semester, often containing content that generated lots of discussion among class members. Though Darren's name was never listed on the course Web site where completed partner products were posted, the possibility that he was fictitious did not occur to class members. Darren's real identity was revealed at a social gathering after the semester had ended. Several students were amused, especially in light of some of Darren's opinions. This feeling was not shared by all, however. One male student was offended to find out that Darren was not a real person. In a reflective analysis after the completion of the class, he wrote:

> When I learned that a fictitious character had been added to our class, I understood the motivation of expanded perspective for group discussion, but felt duped. I expended considerable personal energy trying to help restore this make-believe person's place or credibility in the group. (I truly sweat over the comments I posted in an attempt to reconcile this wayward sheep, though I wondered how he could have been so "stupid" or unaware.) I was not amused to learn that I had befriended or come to the aid of a figment of someone's imagination.

Because online communities are based largely on trust between and among students and instructors (Cifuentes et al., 1997), the process of introducing false identities to provoke discussion is questionable. In this *case*, the discussion was very rich without the introduction of a "provoker." Other techniques suggested by

Paulsen, such as the use of student moderators and visiting experts, might be more conducive to community building. If fictitious students are created to spur discussion, it is suggested that class members be informed up front.

Two topics during the course generated a fair amount of disagreement and friction between students: gender issues related to technology and filtering. These disagreements actually contributed to the development of the class community. The gender discussion unfolded over approximately a 3-week period. The first week was a discussion of the neutrality of computers/technology and included several gender-related issues. The next set of articles dealt with gender from a critical theory perspective. The third week focused on equity in general, and certainly gender was one aspect included with this topic.

The critical theory articles, in particular, addressed societal issues that went beyond the use and creation of technology. Many students contributed passionate messages to the bulletin board during this discussion, some of which were uncomfortable for others to read. A post from the "imposter" student suggesting that the natural role of the female is to be in the home initiated one controversial discussion thread. A male student responded, "I was afraid that you'd 'started something' here! Now, I'm wanting to come to your aid—I think it's that 'male-bonding' thing!?!" He went on to gingerly but effectively infuse his opinion with that of the imposter and three female students who had previously reacted to the message. This student did not defend the initial post but rather offered another interpretation of the discussion that had transpired. He concluded the message by suggesting that the males in the class wear "heavy armor" for the next few days.

Ironically, in a long-term *study* of community building on a listserv, conflict occurred during a gender-related discussion of invited speakers to a conference (Herrmann, 1998). The tone on the listserv was different during this part of the discussion than it was at other times. It took a suggestion to disband the listserv to resolve the conflict. Although EDIT 5110 would not have ended because of disagreements, students' willingness to participate in future discussions may have been compromised by the dissenting ideas. Instead, it created a stronger bond between class members, as they negotiated meaning and understanding with each other. Comments such as, "Sorry, DC, I respectfully disagree," were common.

The class became enough of a community for class members to inform others when they would be away from the discussion. One student wrote, "Oh, by the way, I'm signing off for a few days. I'm moving (ugh!) and my telephone service won't be connected." Another wrote, "I'm off on a deer-hunting trip, so I will miss all of the chatter for the next four or five days." Students apologized for technical or other difficulties that limited their participation. It is unlikely that they would have felt compelled to share this information if they had not felt a sense of community or if they believed their posts were merely perfunctory.

McDonald and Gibson (1998) explored group dynamics and development in a computer conferencing course. Their results showed that specific criteria could be identified regarding group dynamics and that these patterns are manifested in both face-to-face and computer conferencing environments. Though the *study* here did not focus on these patterns specifically, it was clear that a community of learners developed among and between class members.

Discussion

The proliferation of online courses requires an understanding of the unique learning environment that computer-mediated communication facilitates. Awareness of student participation patterns can help online course designers capitalize on the strengths of the medium.

Access to course materials varied widely from student to student but reflected an overall commitment to learning. The number of student posts to the bulletin board far exceeded expectations. Students checked in throughout each week to more effectively follow the discussion threads. Readily available Web access is an obvious consideration in such courses; in fact, home computers are almost a necessity for students to participate to the extent that they did in EDIT 5110. In traditional class settings, students sometimes are reluctant to contribute, either because they do not want to lengthen the class or because they feel their response will not reflect what they want to say. The flexible participation schedule afforded by computer-mediated communication tools can lengthen the time in which students are engaged in class material, while the reflection time may encourage more widespread participation by all students.

Despite the availability of a synchronous chat feature, students did not choose to arrange live conversations with their classmates. They preferred the more time-independent communication facilitated through the bulletin board and e-mail. Synchronous chats should be scheduled only when they are necessary to build student understanding.

Requiring student participation as a moderator, after providing students with a foundation regarding what the role entails, can have a positive effect on discussions. Moderators posted more and longer messages than when these students were not moderators. The use of student moderators eliminated the need for the instructor to assume the leadership role alone. It is likely that moderator responsibilities also contributed to students' sense of community, because acting as moderator was a common experience for all class members.

Online courses can certainly foster discussion related to course content. A very high percentage of posted messages dealt directly with the required readings. The online medium facilitated a shift in the traditional student and teacher functions in the class. The students took an active role in the course. The medium may not only facilitate student participation but also encourage instructors to change their role as the teacher.

The Web-based delivery medium did not inhibit the development of the class as a community. In many ways, it actually contributed to the formation of a cohesive group. Students referred to each other in their bulletin board posts, indicating an effort to maintain the dialogue as conversation rather than as distinct and unconnected messages. Though they could not read facial expressions or gestures, students' written responses were such that class members could interpret meaning, emotion, and sarcasm. Because the development of online communities is based largely on trust, care must be taken to maintain this atmosphere throughout the course. In EDIT 5110, this trust may have been breached through the introduction of a fictitious student.

One of the best examples of community development surfaced during an extended discussion of gender issues related to technology. Though student opinions were often in opposition, class members were very respectful of each other and made an effort to at least understand the alternative view. Traditional class structures sometimes encourage emotional outbursts, whereas the online medium enabled students to respond with passionate, but well-supported positions. All voices were heard, not just those of the most vocal students.

There is still much to learn about the effect of online courses on student learning. Course designs that allow for flexible student-centered participation may effectively take advantage of the learning environments that can be facilitated through online course tools.

References

1. Bellack, A. A., Kliebard, H. M., Hyman, R. T., & Smith, F. L. (1966). *The language of the classroom.* New York: Teachers College Press.
2. Buckley, J. (1997). The invisible audience and the disembodied voice: Online teaching and the loss of body image. *Computers and Composition,* 14(2), 179–188.
3. Cifuentes, L., Murphy, K. L., Segur, R., & Kodali, S. (1997). Design considerations for computer conferences. *Journal of Research on Computing in Education,* 30(2), 177–201.
4. Herrmann, E. (1998). Building online communities of practice: An example and implications. *Educational Technology,* 38(1), 16–23.
5. Kimball, L. (1995). Ten ways to make online learning groups work. *Educational Leadership,* 53(2), 54–56.
6. McDonald, J., & Gibson, C. C. (1998). Interpersonal dynamics and group development in computer conferencing. *The American Journal of Distance Education,* 12(1), 7–25.
7. McGinnis, J. R. (1996). Promoting an electronic community with the use of communication technology in a graduate elementary science methods class. *Journal of Elementary Science Education,* 8(1), 39–63.
8. Paulsen, M. F. (1995). Moderating educational computing conferences. In Z. L. Berge & M. P. Collins (Eds.), *Computer mediated communication and the online classroom: V. III: Distance learning* (pp. 81–89). Cresskill, NJ: Hampton Press.
9. Piburn, M. D., & Middleton, J. A. (1998). Patterns of faculty and student conversation in listserv and traditional journals in a program for preservice mathematics and science teachers. *Journal of Research on Computing in Education,* 31(1), 62–77.
10. Rohfeld, R. W., & Hiemstra, R. (1995). Moderating discussions in the electronic classroom. In Z. L. Berge & M. P. Collins (Eds.), *Computer mediated communication and the online classroom, V. III: Distance learning* (pp. 91–104). Cresskill, NJ: Hampton Press.
11. Schlagal, B., Trathen, W., & Blanton, W. (1996). Structuring telecommunications to create instructional conversations

about student teaching. *Journal of Teacher Education, 47*(3), 175–183.

12. Schlosser, C., & Anderson, M. (1994). *Distance education: Review of the literature.* Washington, DC: Association for Educational Communications and Technology.
13. Tagg, A. C. (1994). Leadership from within: Student moderation of computer conferences. *The American Journal of Distance Education, 8*(3), 40–50.
14. Thomas, L., Clift, R., & Sugimoto, T. (1996). Telecommunication, student teaching, and methods instruction. An exploratory investigation. *Journal of Teacher Education, 47*(3), 165–174.
15. Van Gorp, M. J. (1998). Computer-mediated communication in preservice teacher education: Surveying research, identifying problems, and considering needs. *Journal of Computing in Teacher Education, 14*(2), 8–14.
16. WebCT [Computer software]. (1996–1999). Vancouver, BC: WebCT Educational Technologies.

By Dawn M. Poole, California State University Stanislaus

Dr. Dawn Poole is an associate professor of educational technology at California State University Stanislaus. Her research interests include online learning and technology integration into the K-12 curriculum. (Address: Dawn M. Poole, Advanced Studies in Education, 801 W. Monte Vista Avenue, Turlock, CA 95382; dpoole@toto.csustan.edu.)

Disciplinary Perspective: Doing Research in Psychology

Making Knowledge: An Interview with a Teacher of Psychology

A published poet with experience in clinical psychology and a teacher of sociology and psychology, Chris Gilbert has unique perspectives from which to view the relationship between doing research and writing about it. As he explained to me in our interview, language used in his courses provides a "lens" through which to view the world. A study of that lens or perspective yields up a genuine understanding of the methods used by researchers in the field. He is a firm believer in the importance of giving students the chance to assume the role of researchers, rather than remain merely consumers of research. Chris is currently engaged in an ethnographic study of African-American families that focuses on the development of attitudes toward schooling. "How does parenting set the stage," he asks, "for perspectives on being a student?" We began our conversation by looking at the research methods in psychology.

Q. What are the conventional research methodologies in your field?

A. Psychology is such a big area that there is not one way of doing it. The research method depends on the question that you are asking. Once you have a question and especially a hypothesis that you are testing, then you develop a set of procedures or steps that allow you to put the question to the test, involving a control and varying other factors to see the effects of such factors. Some questions have to do with the "typical" person: Large numbers of people are tested and evaluated and examined. Their responses are averaged. That's one method in psychology, the conventional approach. Other methods assume that you have a representative population to begin with. And if you study a single individual in depth as a case study, that person will give you a rich source of information, telling you what other people are like and how they see the world.

Research methods

Q. A case study gives you rich detail, a thick description, of an individual, but does it give you a basis from which to generalize beyond the case?

A. In doing a case study, you are assuming certain things about the world—that this person in front of you has a form of mentality that is replicated in the mentality of other peo-

Case studies

ple. [It assumes] that there is form to the world. If you have
that piece of sand, it is emblematic of the world.

Q. Can you talk about the research projects that you have
students do? What steps are involved in the research?

A. One of the things that I have done in introductory psychology courses is [have students do] the work of an experiment, the kind of work that psychologists actually do. One of
the experiments that I have had students do is one on "bystander apathy" and "diffusion of responsibility." They are
the kinds of phenomena that students can do research on
without a lot of research technology and a lot of apparatus.
Can they extrapolate on a particular study [previous studies
on the subject] to their hypotheses of variables that affect human behavior? In one class, I had a couple of students who
decided to test to see whether people would be more likely to
help, to offer a donation, if they were touched. That was their
hypothesis, that by touching the bystanders, they'd get bigger
donations [to the Salvation Army]. They volunteered with
the Salvation Army and got the Salvation Army uniform and
bucket. The money that they received they donated to the
Salvation Army. They [set up] a control situation, in which
they did not touch the subjects in their experiment. They
identified randomly sampled people, had a number of controls as far as weather, time of day and so on. They found that
touching resulted in greater giving. Touching matters.

    Part of their work was not just to carry out the experiment
but to write it up in journal article form, explaining with a rationale a reason for their hypothesis, read material having to
do with bystander apathy and material having to do with altruism and human touch.

Q. Are you showing students a way of knowing as well as a
way of writing?

A. There's a kind of lens that the language provides, a kind
of psychological lens for seeing the world, a social psychology perspective from which they were working that privi-

Student
experiments

Disciplinary
perspective

leges the situation. [From that perspective, a person might say] that situational factors are more important than personality. They are learning a whole new way of thinking about themselves and the world because of the kind of language being used. The unit of analysis is not the individual—the id, ego—but the situation, the bigger chunk. That's the beauty of psychology. We go from the biological level to the group level [from] hormonal influences, and influences of neural transmitters [to group processes].

Case Study

ROBYN'S RESEARCH ON BIRTH ORDER AND PERSONALITY

Can research performed by students for a classroom assignment be expected to employ the various methods that I have described in this chapter? Let's look at the experience of one student who undertook such a project.

Robyn's Background

Robyn, a peer tutor in our college's writing lab, knows both from observing the experience of students who come to the lab with such work and from her own classroom experience that writing a research paper poses terrific challenges:

- Selecting an engaging and workable topic
- Locating and processing relevant and credible sources
- Composing a fluent and focused draft that integrates such sources.

Each in itself is daunting enough, but to have to put it all together requires a great deal of guidance and a great deal of discipline.

Robyn had experience in doing library research as part of her work in our college's required first-year composition course. "My instructor held one of our classes in the library where we were shown how to access the various resources there," she writes. It was for this course that Robyn wrote her first research paper.

Preparing the Research Paper

For her work in a course in child development, Robyn discovers that while some of the skills she acquired in her composition courses carry over to her assignment in psychology, the bar has in some sense been raised. Not only does she need to write about a "specific topic of interest in child psychology," she will be expected to design her own research study. Robyn describes the task this way:

> First I needed to formulate and submit to my instructor a research question. Like a thesis statement in an essay, this question would be the focus of my study. In addition, I was required to use at least three scholarly sources for my references, which meant that articles from popular magazines and obscure Internet sources were out. I decided to use [our college's] databases to search for professional literature on my topic. . . .

Format

The paper itself is to conform to the following format:

1. **Title page:** Illustrate the question being studied.
2. **Abstract:** Briefly summarize the study.
3. **Introduction:** Briefly introduce the main idea of the study.
4. **Statement of the Reason(s)—for selecting the topic of your study:** Present a summary of the reasons for choosing the topic.
5. **Literature Review:** Review at least three scholarly articles or books relevant to the study.
6. **Present Study:** Provide a detailed description of the study, stating the theory you used, the hypothesis you are

testing, and the operational definitions for all independent variables and dependent measures. Describe as well the sample used and all measuring instruments. Follow American Psychological Association (APA) ethical guidelines for obtaining informed consent from your research subjects.

7. **Summary of Results and Conclusions:** Summarize your results and draw your conclusions, referring to tables and graphs where appropriate.

8. **References:** Include a list of all references, following the APA Style Guide (see pages 113–114).

9. **Appendix:** Include consent forms, drawings, tables, questionnaires and the like.

Her teacher, clearly, "expects her students to write their papers as do professionals in the field." The project seems far removed, in one sense, from the more generic library research that Robyn was asked to do in her composition course, although she took away many useful skills from that earlier course.

Moving from the Individual Case to the Larger Situation

Robyn decides to write on a subject of personal interest to her. She has two sons with strikingly different personalities. She would like to get at the possible causes of those differences. But she also keenly aware of the need to connect the particular case to a larger theme. As Chris Gilbert observed, research in psychology often draws larger lessons from localized cases. Robyn chooses to research the question, "Does birth order affect personality?" She is also interested in the age-old debate about nature and nurture, knowing full well that she may draw from a tremendous amount of research already done and published. Robyn begins her paper by setting forth the research question:

As far back as the origin of Cain and Abel, people have been aware of sibling rivalry and differences in the personalities of siblings. Despite commonalities such as the same parents and the same home environment,

> sibling personality differences can be
> great. But what factors affect personality
> the greatest? Researchers in psychology
> agree that siblings differ, but there is
> much discussion about the reasons for the
> differences. Variables such as age range,
> gender, birth order, and nonshared environ-
> mental factors have been studied as possi-
> ble causes. This study examined the extent
> to which birth order can affect personal-
> ity. It also attempted to show a correla-
> tion between birth order and personality.

Her review of the literature begins with Darwin's theory of evolutionary divergence but quickly moves to recent research done specifically on the development of children within the family unit and, even more specifically, on the variance of siblings' personalities. Based on her review of previous studies, Robyn reports that "characteristics of personality have been associated with birth order" and describes, in broad terms, what those characteristics are.

Being Comfortable with the Language and Methods of the Discipline

Having selected a topic and reviewed the relevant literature, Robyn begins to think about the *measurements* that she might employ to discover results. She will need instruments that will allow her to gather information as to both personality differences and birth order, since the correlation of the two is at the heart of her study. To measure personality, Robyn decides to use the reliably accurate Myers-Briggs Type Indicator to help her gauge differences of personality; she uses the MBTI's categories of extraversion, introversion, perceiving, judging, thinking, feeling, sensing, and intuitive. In addition, she designs her own questionnaire to gather information on birth order. The latter briefly elicits information such as date of birth, gender, number of siblings, birth order, years of separation between siblings.

"The biggest obstacles," wrote Robyn in an e-mail interview, "were figuring out how to collect my data reliably and how to evaluate the data." Her sample consisted of "70 randomly selected adolescents and adults, from whom 55 surveys were returned." Her final sampling (after the relatively few responses of children were eliminated) "consisted of 51 people ranging in age from 15 to 90 years of age."

Upon reflection, Robyn recognizes that this sampling can hardly be a "representation of the population as a whole," especially given the fact that all surveyed were Caucasian and middle-class. She recommends a cross-sectional study that cuts across various ethnic and class groups.

Even more daunting for Robyn is the need to test for independent variables. In other words, she needs to arrive at a statistical formulation that demonstrates that any correlation of personality and birth order is not attributable to factors external to those tested by the study. Upon consultation with a math professor, Robyn establishes a *null and alternate hypothesis,* respectively:

Null: *The personality trait . . . is independent of birth order.*

Alternate: *The personality is dependent on birth order.*

Robyn also needs to find the *critical value,* which aims at determining the reliability of results. Then she must calculate "the expected values for each cell" of her tables. If the null hypothesis is true, goes the logic, how many participants would be expected to show these particular traits? That number is juxtaposed with the figures signifying the number of participants who actually show the traits. (See the table below.)

	OLDEST	MIDDLE	YOUNGEST	
E(XTROVERT)	2(8)	10(8)	12(8)	24
I(NTROVERT)	14(8)	7(9)	6(10)	27
Totals	16	17	18	51

"When doing a research study," observed Robyn, "the data determine the outcome." This was quite a revelation to Robyn, who is usually confidence when writing papers for a course—but that confidence derives from a certain amount of control that she customarily feels about the outcome. In a research study, the writer needs to give up some of that control. A final draft of Robyn's paper follows.

Nature and Nurture 1

Nature and Nurture:
Does Birth Order Shape Personality?
Robyn Worthington
Psychology 52
Dr. Mary Zahm
December 7, 1999

Nature and Nurture 2

Nature versus Nurture:
Does Birth Order Shape Personality?

Introduction
As far back as the origin of the story of Cain
and Abel, people have been aware of sibling rivalry and differences in the personalities of
siblings. Despite commonalities such as the
same parents and the same home environment,
sibling personality differences can be great.
But what factors affect personality the greatest? Researchers in psychology agree that siblings differ, but there is much discussion
about the reasons for the differences. Variables such as age range, gender, birth order,
and nonshared environmental factors have been
studied as possible causes. This study examined
the extent to which birth order can affect personality. It also attempted to show a correlation between birth order and personality. This
paper will examine the extent to which birth
order can affect personality in siblings. Using a sample of randomly selected adolescents
and adults, the author uses the Myers-Briggs
Type Indicator, as well as a background questionnaire, to obtain data. While this study
demonstrates a significant relationship between birth order and the traits of extraversion and introversion, it cannot support the
initial claim that birth order can affect differences in personalities in siblings.

Statement of Reason
As the mother of three boys who share the same
family environment, I have always been struck

Nature and Nurture 3

by the differences in their personalities. In doing this study, I hope to have a better understanding of how and why these differences occur.

Literature Review

Darwin's theory of evolution and, more specifically, his principle of divergence, has been used as a possible explanation for the differences in sibling personality (Sulloway, 1996). Darwin theorized that "given enough time, species tend to evolve multiple forms that diverge in character, a process called adaptive radiation" (p. 85). Humans tend to diverge with their minds.

According to Sulloway (1996), the family environment is actually a collection of micro environments, or niches, and children within the same family use adaptive radiation to establish their own niches within the family. Children work to develop their own niche in order to receive the same amount of parental attention or investment. As each child is born into the family, the environment changes and the way that parents interact with each child can affect their personality (Leman, 1985). By diverging, younger siblings do not have to compete with older, bigger, more experienced siblings.

Certain characteristics of personality has been associated with birth order. Oldest, or firstborns, have been characterized as ambitious high achievers who are usually confident, organized, and conservative (Sulloway, 1996; Leman, 1985). Both Sulloway and Leman suggest that children born second tend to diverge as

Nature and Nurture 4

much as possible from the firstborn, taking on a totally different set of characteristics. They are noted as being more sociable, cooperative, and more open to experience than their conservative older siblings, who have a tendency to relate strongly with their parents.

Because of their position in the family, youngest children tend to be charming, affectionate, outgoing, and may use any means to get attention (Leman, 1985). In contrast, they can also be found to be spoiled and impatient, possibly due to the fact that they can be coddled by the rest of the family.

Gender, age range, and nonshared environment are also thought to be factors in personality differences in siblings. In a study of university psychology students, Tammy Mann (1993) predicted that nonshared environmental factors would account for personality differences more than other factors. However, the results showed that the family constellation variables of age, birth order and gender may be more firmly associated with personality differences in siblings than the nonshared environment. In fact, 27% of the correlations between constellation variables and sibling personality differences were statistically significant.

Present Study

As a model for this study, I used Darwin's theory of evolution as well as the theory proposed by Frank Sulloway concerning birth order and personality. I hypothesized that birth order would account for the differences in personality in siblings. Birth order was defined as ei-

Nature and Nurture 5

ther oldest, middle, youngest, or only child. Personality was assessed by the Myers-Briggs Type Indicator (Briggs & Myers, 1980), in the categories of extraversion/introversion, sensing/intuition, thinking/feeling, and judging/perceiving.

The initial sample consisted of 70 randomly selected adolescents and adults from whom 55 surveys were returned. For statistical calculations, only children were eliminated from the sample, as their number was too few. The revised sample consisted of 51 people ranging in age from 14 to 90 years of age. All were Caucasian and considered of middle class backgrounds. Of the 151, 16 reported being the oldest sibling, 17 reported as being middle born, 18 reported as being the youngest.

The Myers-Briggs Type Indicator was distributed to the participants along with a background questionnaire (see Appendix) on which was supplied personal data, including birth order. The surveys were collected, scored and each assessment was labeled with four letters which corresponded to the participants personality type: E for extraversion, I for introversion, N for intuitive, S for sensing, F for feeling, T for thinking, J for judging, and P for perceiving. (See Tables 1-4.)

The information collected was statistically evaluated by establishing a null and an alternate hypothesis for each personality trait. The scores were placed in a Contingency Table and the calculations were performed and evaluated using the Chi-Square test for Goodness-of-Fit. (See Tables 1-4.)

Nature and Nurture 6

Summary of Results and Conclusions

A statistically significant relationship between birth order and personality traits was
found in one of the four areas. Calculations
revealed a significant relationship between ex-
traversion/introversion at the .005 (one half
of 1%) level of significance. Of the 16 oldest
children, 14 preferred introversion, 10 out of
17 middle born showed a preference for extraversion, and 12 out of 18 youngest also showed
a preference for extraversion. In all other areas the calculations fell short of a reliable
level of significance. In the traits of sens-
ing/intuition, thinking/feeling, and judging/
perceiving, the test values were below 1, too
low for even a .05 (5%) level of significance.

While this study was able to demonstrate a
significant relationship between birth order and
the traits of extraversion/introversion, I do
not feel that my hypothesis, that birth order
would account for the differences in personality
in siblings, was supported. Although I still
suspect that birth order plays a role in personality development, the variables involved may be
too difficult to assess statistically. Gender,
number of children in the family, and the spac-
ing of siblings all influence the way that parents relate to their children and the way that
siblings relate to each other, which in turn affects personality. Genetics and nonshared environmental experiences such as playgroups and
nursery school/daycare, also have an impact on
personality. With so many variables, assessing
the causes of personality differences in siblings is extremely difficult. Based on the re-

Nature and Nurture 7

sults of this study, I have concluded that personality development is not likely the result of any one factor, but a combination of many.

Since this study included only middle-class Caucasians, it is not a representation of the population as a whole. In addition, the information concerning day care/nursery school was not considered in the results in any valid way. Future research might include a cross-sectional study of various ethnic and socioeconomic groups as a better representation of the population. Furthermore, utilizing information on day care/nursery school may help to demonstrate the impact of non-shared environment on the differences in sibling personalities.

An interesting result of the study was that, when the personality traits were divided by gender, 24 out of 31 females demonstrated a preference for the trait of feeling to that of thinking. Future research might include a study of gender on personality differences and/or personality differences among siblings based on gender.

Nature and Nurture 8

References

Briggs, K. C., & Myers, I. B. (1980). *Myers-Briggs Type Indicator*. Palo Alto, CA: Consulting Psychologists Press.

Leman, K. (1985). *The Birth Order Book*. Old Tappan, NJ: Revell.

Mann, T. L. (1993). A failure of nonshared environmental factors in predicting sibling personality differences. *The Journal of Psychology*, 127, 79-86.

Sulloway, F. J. 91996). *Born to Rebel: Birth Order, Family Dynamics, and Creative Lives*. New York, NY: Random House.

Nature and Nurture 9

Appendix

Table 1

	Oldest	Middle	Youngest	
E	2(8)	10(8)	12(8)	24
I	14(8)	7(9)	6(10)	27
Totals	16	17	18	51

$$\frac{(16)(24)}{51} = 7.529 \quad \frac{(16)(27)}{51} = 8.47$$

$$\frac{(17)(24)}{51} = 8 \quad \frac{(17)(27)}{51} = 9$$

$$\frac{(24)(18)}{51} = 8.471 \quad \frac{(18)(27)}{51} = 9.52$$

$$\frac{(2-8)^2}{8} + \frac{(10-8)^2}{8} + \frac{(12-8)^2}{8} + \frac{(14-8)^2}{8} + \frac{(7-9)^2}{8} + \frac{(6-10)^2}{8} = 13.5$$

13.5 > 10.597

(critical value at .005 level of significance)

Table 2

	Oldest	Middle	Youngest	
J	11(11)	11(12)	13(12)	35
P	5(5)	6(5)	5(6)	16
Totals	16	17	18	51

$$\frac{(16)(35)}{51} = 11 \quad \frac{(17)(35)}{51} = 12$$

$$\frac{(18)(35)}{51} = 12 \quad \frac{(16)(16)}{51} = 5$$

$$\frac{(17)(16)}{51} = 5 \quad \frac{(18)(16)}{51} = 6$$

$$\frac{(11-11)^2}{11} + \frac{(11-12)^2}{12} + \frac{(13-12)^2}{12} + \frac{(5-5)^2}{10} + \frac{(6-5)^2}{5} + \frac{(5-6)^2}{6} = .56$$

.56 < 5.991

(critical value at .05 level of significance)

Nature and Nurture 10

Table 3

	Oldest	Middle	Youngest	
T	6(6)	7(6)	6(7)	19
F	10(10)	10(11)	12(11)	32
Totals	16	17	18	51

$$\frac{(19)(16)}{51} = 6 \qquad \frac{(17)(19)}{51} = 6$$

$$\frac{(18)(19)}{51} = 7 \qquad \frac{(16)(32)}{51} = 10$$

$$\frac{(17)(32)}{51} = 11 \qquad \frac{(18)(32)}{51} = 11$$

$$\frac{(6-6)^2}{6} + \frac{(7-6)^2}{6} + \frac{(6-7)^2}{7} + \frac{(10-10)^2}{10} + \frac{(10-11)^2}{11} + \frac{(12-11)^2}{11} = .48$$

.48 < 5.991

(critical value at .05 level of significance)

Table 4

	Oldest	Middle	Youngest	
N	6(6)	6(7)	8(7)	20
S	10(10)	11(10)	10(11)	31
Totals	16	17	18	51

$$\frac{(16)(20)}{51} = 6 \qquad \frac{(20)(17)}{51} = 6$$

$$\frac{(20)(18)}{51} = 7 \qquad \frac{(16)(31)}{51} = 10$$

$$\frac{(17)(31)}{51} = 11 \qquad \frac{(18)(31)}{51} = 11$$

$$\frac{(6-6)^2}{6} + \frac{(6-7)^2}{7} + \frac{(8-7)^2}{7} + \frac{(10-10)^2}{10} + \frac{(11-10)^2}{10} + \frac{(10-11)^2}{11} = .476$$

.476 < 5.991

(critical value at .05 level of significance)

Nature and Nurture 11

Background Questions

Date of birth: _____   Sex: M   F

How many siblings do you have?
  brothers _____ sisters _____

What is your birth order?
  oldest   middle   youngest   only child

How many years separate you from the
siblings who were born just before
and/or just after you?
  a brother _____ years older
  a sister _____ years older
  a brother _____ years younger
  a sister _____ years younger

As a young child, did you attend day care
or nursery school?   Y   N

If yes, how old were you when you first
attended? _____ How many years did you
attend? _____

Grounding the Theory

1. Identify a question or frame a hypothesis drawn from one of the subjects that you are currently taking. Design a study to test that hypothesis, and write up your findings in the format used in Robyn's paper. To locate relevant sources, consult one or more of the indexes listed in Chapter 3.

2. Imagine that you have identified a cross section of people for research on a particular consumer trend (for example, online shopping) or issue of public concern (whether school vouchers should be used toward private school funding). Design a survey that will elicit pertinent data.

For Extended Writing

1. Using one of your courses as a focus, write a detailed description of the procedural knowledge expected in that course. Begin with the most basic kind of information (knowing what kinds of safety precautions to take, in the case of lab procedure) and then move on to the more complex (methods of dissection, for example).

2. Locate two research articles in professional journals, each drawn from subjects that you are currently taking. Contrast the two articles on the basis of the methods used in each experiment: How were experiments designed and data collected in each case?

Conducting Research in the Extra-Curriculum: Oral History

Research is not merely an academic pursuit. In other words, research is being done not just in universities but on the pages of newspapers, in magazines, and bestsellers. The work of Studs Terkel, for example, attests to the popular appeal of oral history as a research method. An oral history attempts to reconstruct the past through individual testimony as gathered through personal interviews. Like the case study, the *oral history* provides rich detail of an individual life in the hope of representing the lives of the group or the whole. As Chris Gilbert (borrowing from the poet William Blake) puts it, the oral history is yet another attempt to view the world in a grain of sand. Creating effective oral history is a challenging and daunting task, requiring more than simply putting a tape recorder in front of an interview subject. The task involves the following, critical steps.

Choosing a Worthwhile Topic

An oral history that has consequence must spring from a belief that your subject can provide an important glimpse into the past. If we acknowledge that people see the world through the lens of their own experience, we must be ready to provide important *context*. That means we need to define, validate, or evaluate an individual experience by conducting multiple interviews, and examining a diverse combination of printed and photographic sources. The point is to discover something important about the past and to note the intersection of local history with larger public events.

Researching the Historical Record

In no way is an oral history meant to be the first or last word about the past. When you begin an oral history project of your own, you must supplement your knowledge of your subject by relying on the historical record. Doing so makes you a more informed and more effective interviewer, of course. But beyond that, such research gives you a sense of perspective on your project, a sense of its historic significance.

It may seem odd to you that a member of your family, or your neighborhood, might have connections to more public historic events, but keep in mind that all history is rooted in the lives of individuals and communities. Take a walk down your street and you might notice that the sidewalk—the very same sidewalk that you've used to ride your bicycle as a child or to walk your own child—has a plaque embedded in it that reads, "WPA 1937." With additional research you will discover the nature and importance of the Works Progress Administration during the Great Depression. Or imagine that in your gathering of important family documents you discover your father's original Social Security card. You would do well to inquire what "social security" really means and how it came about (again turning to the history of the Depression). And when you do such research, don't restrict yourself to written materials like journal articles or book-length studies. Photographs, recordings, and other media can help in very important ways to fill in the background that you'll need going into this project.

The *American Historical Association Guide to Historical Literature* might be a place to begin your search, since it will guide you toward articles in professional journals. But you may also want to engage in genuine "field research" and check out primary documents like court records, government documents, and firsthand testimonials. You may discover, for example, oral histories of workers who built roads and bridges under the WPA and photographs of their efforts, samples of which are accessible through the Library of Congress's *American Memory* project (http://www.loc.gov/).

Creating a Time Line

As you do some preliminary research on your subject, consider composing a time line of significant related events. At its simplest, a time line consists of a straight line drawn across a page labeled with important years and brief descriptions of what occurred in those years. A time line renders in visual form the passing of time and provides a frame of reference for your own research.

Interviewing

Locating Informants and Arranging the Interview

Once you have completed some preliminary research, you face the challenging task of deciding whom to interview. Obviously, if you are preparing a family history, you have ready access to sources within your family. But if you are preparing an oral history of a battle in Vietnam (and have not personally met veterans) you face the difficult prospect of locating informants who fought that battle or, more generally, served in the war. A variety of organizations and speakers' bureaus are available to provide such sources, if you know where to look for them (the World Wide Web and the old-fashioned yellow pages may be the places to start looking). It is especially important that your oral history project incorporate as wide a range of perspectives as possible among your sources.

Obtaining Informed Consent

As noted earlier, you must obtain *informed consent* from your subjects before proceeding with your research. "Informed" consent is the key here: when you arrange an interview with a potential informant, you are ethically bound to inform that person *before* beginning the interview as to the nature of the project and her role in it. You should obtain permission from your subject in writing, using a standard consent form that includes not only a description of the project but a statement of how it is to be used (whether it will be published, in other words) and authorization to use the informant's own name or a pseudonym. Of course, your informant must be told ahead of time if you are going to use a recording device.

Sample Consent Form

"I, ____ have been informed of the nature of this research project and consent to allow ____ to use my name and the content of our interview as material for this project."

Signature of Subject   _____

Address   _____

Telephone   _____

E-mail   _____

Date   _____

Taping and Transcribing the Interview

If you are to closely study the interview record, you must naturally have access to that record. You should, if at all possible, tape-record your sessions. Given the degree to which you will be engaged in asking questions, listening patiently, and making important eye contact with your informant, you will hardly be able to take notes in any great detail (assuming you *could* reproduce what was said accurately for the written record).

Transcribing the interview and doing so accurately are crucial requirements for an effective oral history. Transcriptions provide a text for close and steady analysis (speech is ephemeral and hard to recall). Accuracy ensures that the document has credibility and authenticity.

Asking the Right Questions

Although you will have prepared questions prior to the interview, it is important that you be a good listener and follow up on pertinent comments made during the interview. Accord-

---

Writing Up and Analyzing Your Findings: A Checklist

Oral historians do more than simply interview, transcribe, and publish raw transcripts. They must find a way to report back what they have learned—to offer important context, and to reflect critically on their subject's stories. Here are some questions worth considering:

- ✓ What hypothesis about the subject did I formulate before the interview(s)?
- ✓ How does the hypothesis fare against my sources' perspective?
- ✓ How do my sources confirm on another's account of the past?
- ✓ How do they diverge?
- ✓ How do I account for any divergence?
- ✓ What, finally, is the perspective that I wish to highlight?

---

ing to criteria established by the Oral History Association, interviewers should explain the purpose of the interview, treat the subject with respect, explore "pertinent lines of thought," challenge where appropriate, and follow up on "significant clues" (Oral History Association, 1992, *Oral History: Evaluation Guidelines*, Los Angeles, Oral History Association, 10).

The Power of Oral History

The most powerful oral histories express the authority of their informants' voices but also provide a window into the public past. Consider the following oral history of a woman packinghouse worker, Marge Paca, from the 1930s:

> The meat specialties, that is about the coldest place in the yards. That's where they prepare medicinal extracts from meats, for hospitals, I guess. Anyway, they have a

room there that's 60 degrees below zero. Nobody is supposed to stay there longer than 3 minutes, but some of the men go in there for 15 minutes at a time.

I used to have to pack the brains in cans. They would be frozen stiff and my nails would lift right up off my fingers handling them. It's always wet there and very, very cold. I had to wear two and three pairs of woolen stockings, two pairs of underwear, a couple of woolen skirts and all the sweaters I had, and on top of that I had to wear a white uniform. My own. But I couldn't stand it there, it was so cold. It's easy to get pneumonia in a place like that.

In cleaning brains you have to keep your hands in ice cold water and pick out the blood clots. They have the most sickening odor. Cleaning tripe, though, that's the limit. Rotten, yellow stuff, all decayed, it just stank like hell! I did that for a few weeks.

Then I worked in the sausage department. In the domestic sausage. We'd have to do the pork sausages in the cooler. Sometimes we wouldn't be told what kind of sausage we'd have to work on and then when we'd come to work they'd say "pork for you" and we'd have to throw any dirty old rags we could pick up around our shoulders and go to work in that ice-box. If they had any sense or consideration for the girls they could let them know ahead of time so that girls could come prepared with enough clothes.

In summer sausage, they stuff very big sausages there. That's very heavy work. A stick of sausage weighs 200 pounds, five or six sausages on a stick. They have women doing that. It's a strong man's job and no woman should be doing that work. The young girls just can't, so they have the older ladies, and it's a crime to see the way they struggle with it. On that job I lost 27 pounds in 3 months. That was enough for me. It's a strain on your heart, too. Women got ruptured.

They pick the strongest women, big husky ones, you should see the muscles on them, but they can't keep it up. It's horses' labor.

In chipped beef the work in much easier. You can make better money, too, but the rate has to be topped, and it's very, very fast work.

"Working Women in the 1930s." 1939. American Memory. <http:// lcweb2.loc.gov/ammem/ndlpedu/lessons/oralhist/workers.html>. Date visited 28 May 1999.

Collected as part of the Federal Writers' Project, this excerpt shows us a glimpse of an industry before federal regulation. It also enriches our understanding of women's role in the workplace.

Taking a Closer Look

1. Compose an oral history that examines the role of altruism in the psychology of a particular community at a particular point in history. We have heard much, in recent years, about "The Greatest Generation," the generation that fought in World War II out of democratic ideals and, some have argued, the principle of self-sacrifice. Identify a representative of that generation or of a generation of your own choosing and determine the significance of self-sacrifice for that group.

2. *Web Follow-Up.* Access and read more oral histories that are part of the online collection "Working Women in the 1930s": http://lcweb2.loc.gov/ammem/ndlpedu/lessons/oralhist/workers. htmlhttp://lcweb2.loc.gov/ammem/ndlpedu/lessons/oralhist/ workers.html. Conduct an oral history of a cross section of women working today, with the intent of focusing on the questions, "What are the working conditions of women in the new millennium? What have been the gains since the 1930s?"

Chapter 5

Reflection: What Does It All Mean?

Seeing the Big Picture

Once you have collected data for your research project, the challenge then becomes finding significance in the data. What meanings and patterns can you derive from the wealth of materials that you have gathered? What is the "big picture"?

These are not easy questions since answering them requires *knowing* in a mode distinctly different from the ways we have been discussing to this point. Up to now, your focus has been on such matters as (1) identifying a workable question, (2) working with available scholarship, and (3) collecting new information on your subject. You've been attending to detail, to the minutia of survey design and the location of subject indexes. Now you need to stand back and gain distance from your project.

One way of looking at this process of reflection and evaluation is to think of it as *recursive;* it involves your going back to the criteria with which you began to work. For example, among the stated goals for a lab report on the fuel efficiency of "gasohol" (a combination of gasoline and alcohol derived from grain products) are determining the practical uses of such fuel (costs, both to use and produce) and to consider its implication for industries as well as for environmental quality. Naturally, you might then be guided in your reflection by the questions, "What are the practical uses of "gasohol"? and "What is its impact on the environment?" Or, let's say that you have conducted research on attitudes toward Jews in the period when Shakespeare composed his play *The Merchant of Venice,* in which the character of Shylock, a Jew, plays a key part. Your research has informed you that Jews had been banished from England since the year 1290, three hundred years prior to the performance of the play. You may then ask, "To what extent does Shakespeare's Shylock express anti-Semitism?" But even more intriguing, especially considering the fact that Shakespeare would have few if any encounters with Jews, would be the question, "How does Shakespeare work against prevailing attitudes at the time?" In other words, you will have created a baseline of opinion about Jews (they remained banished and unwelcome), but next to that baseline you might infer whether Shakespeare resisted (or not) the easy bigotry of his times.

Essentially, reflection requires you to ask, What does all this data mean? Why is it important? Perhaps another way to put it is, What are the implications of my study? The last question suggests that facts rarely speak for themselves. Rather, their significance needs to be articulated. In the example given above, you may ask, Why study the uses of "gasohol"? Upon reflection, the answer may be that alternative fuels like "gasohol" may prevent additional damage to our environment. In reference to the other example given, you may ask, Why study attitudes toward Jews in Shakespeare's time? Perhaps in asking that question you can arrive at ways to recognize such attitudes in existence today and work to eradicate them.

Reflection is also prompted by discrepancies between the intended outcomes of your work and the results actually found. If you intended to discover that "gasohol" was far more efficient than gasoline, but your results showed otherwise, you might be led to reexamine your earlier assumptions. Similarly, you might have begun your research into Shakespeare's attitude toward Jews by assuming that the character of Shylock is punished merely for his actions rather than his religion. But your research might steer you to discover societal prejudice toward Jews and to surmise Shakespeare's own expression of that prejudice.

The Difference Between Deductive and Inductive Reasoning

How do you actually determine the significance of your data? What kinds of thinking are involved? The answer to each question varies, depending on the nature of the reasoning used. It is useful to distinguish between two kinds of reasoning:

Laying the Groundwork for Reflection: Questions to Ask

✓ What results had you expected?

✓ What results did you actually have?

✓ What were the discrepancies between what you expected and what you in fact produced?

✓ What is the significance of your results?

---

deductive and inductive. Your awareness of the difference will allow you to monitor your use of data as evidence.

Deductive reasoning holds that some particular piece of data is true because it conforms to a general principle. We begin with the principle and determine if that principle is supported by the data at hand. For example, because we know that the yeast ingredient in a loaf of bread causes the loaf to rise when reaching a certain temperature, we can assume that the yeast in a particular loaf will act the same way if that temperature is achieved. Or, because we know that a right angle measures 90°, we can assume that the right angle before us also measures 90°. Many of the sciences—including mathematics and the laboratory sciences—favor such reasoning. *Hypothesis-driven research* offers a theory that attempts to predict particular cases. Darwin's theory of natural selection, for example, predicts that species adapt to their environment as a way to survive. Such a theory would explain specific adaptations that humans have experienced over the millennia, such as the ability to develop a language system or hunt for and gather food. Of course, if the cases do not bear out the theory, then the theory needs to be reexamined, as do many other factors that might have influenced the outcome (including variables, measurements followed, state of the equipment, and so forth).

Inductive reasoning works quite differently: Specific cases *produce* a general principle. If we have discovered in our case study of gang activity (see Chapter 4), for example, that every gang member studied came from a single-parent household, we might be led to assume that divorce and out-of-wedlock pregnancies have a role in driving young people to join gangs. A word of caution: Such reasoning may lead to faulty assumptions if samples are not representative of a larger group, or if additional variables are not considered. In fact, such reasoning could be considered illogical.

Nevertheless, several disciplines employ this way of thinking. In the social sciences and in the humanities, for example, researchers often begin by studying a particular community or a specific text, and from it they articulate broad principles. Noted American psychologist Stanley Milgrim engaged in such reasoning in his study of obedience. In that study, subjects were told to administer increasingly potent electrical shocks to a "victim" in another room (whose shouts could be heard by the subject). From such observation, Milgram was able to induce the view that pressures to conform might lead any of us to engage in actions that we would otherwise abhor. Milgram was specifically attempting to understand how Germans could have permitted the execution of millions during the Second World War.

Grounding the Theory

1. Give one example each of inductive and deductive reasoning drawn from your own experience.
2. Read the following statements and identify each as either deductively or inductively reasoned. Explain.
    a. Judging from those that I have met, people with body piercings are rebels.
    b. Being a triangle, that shape contains 180°.

Knowing When the Evidence Is Good Enough

In practical terms, knowing the difference between the two kinds of reasoning won't mean much unless you can evaluate the claims that you have made next to the evidence provided. In other words, when it comes time for you to make sense of your data, you will need to be able to distinguish convincing claims and the evidence brought in their support on the one hand from weak claims and insubstantial evidence on the other. For example, if a claim was made for gasohol's fuel efficiency on the basis of rural road tests, rather than city driving, you might question the claim itself, until stronger evidence is presented.

How do you know if the evidence you've brought forth is strong enough? How do you know if you've proven something to be true? The issue is quite problematic, especially if you consider that in some disciplines the challenge is not to "prove" the truth nor simply to provide facts but to offer the best *available* evidence to support a claim. Here is how one specialist—a genealogist—describes the challenge:

> Often the test of genealogical conclusions are compared with legal concepts such as "beyond a reasonable doubt" (BARD) or "preponderance of evidence" (POE). The former is generally applied in criminal cases, while the latter is a test in civil cases.
>
> Conviction in a criminal case requires that 12 people unanimously believe that there is *no* reasonable doubt that the accused committed the crime he or she is charged with. While you may aspire to this level of certainty, it is generally a level above what can usually be attained in genealogy.
>
> On the other hand, "preponderance of evidence" (POE) in a civil case can mean that evidence on the side of the plaintiff only slightly outweighs the evi-

---

Discerning the Shape of the Evidence: Questions to Ask

✓ Around what point or points has the evidence gathered? In other words, where is the evidence converging, for the most part?

✓ What claim does the evidence seem to be supporting?

✓ How does that claim fit with your previous knowledge of the subject?

✓ What claims have not received sufficient evidence?

✓ What extraneous evidence is left?

✓ What claims might such evidence support?

---

dence on behalf of the defendant. A jury in a civil case can vote by a majority of one in favor of one side or the other. This is a test that is generally below that sought in genealogy.

Whether the standard is "preponderance of evidence" or the lack of "reasonable doubt," evidence can be brought to support the justness of a claim. Here are some questions to ask when determining the shape and significance of the evidence that you've presented.

Consider the claim that standardized testing will raise the achievement of school children. Among the evidence for this claim is the alarming rate of "social promotions," whereby students are promoted to higher grade levels without the skills required to do the work in those levels. However, your own research into the matter of social promotion has produced evidence that teacher-student ratios continue to be high, that inner-city schools lack the level of support given in affluent suburban schools, and that students who don't do well in school are likely to have parents who lack high school degrees themselves. The shape of the evidence seems to point not toward the use of standardized testing but to the matter of how schools are funded and staffed as well as to the level of education within the students' family.

Grounding the Theory

1. Read the following quotations from Henry David Thoreau's *Civil Disobedience.*

   > I heartily accept the motto, "That government is best which governs least"; and I should like to see it acted up to more rapidly and systematically.

   > Under a government which imprisons any unjustly, the true place for a just man is also a prison.

   Write a claim about Thoreau for which the above statements might be used as evidence.

2. Pick one of the quotations above and use it as a claim that *you* are making. Provide two pieces of evidence in support of the claim.

Drawing Inferences

Chapter 3 discussed the importance of knowing how to paraphrase and summarize when working with sources. The point was not to minimize the importance of summary per se. On the contrary, it is a complex but useful task, especially when you are asked to capture the gist of a long and challenging argument. But it's important to distinguish the way of knowing associated with summary from the even more complex activity that is required when you draw inferences from your reading—an especially important tool if you are to make sense of the data that you have collected.

An *inference* is the meaning that readers are able to derive from the available facts or statements. Not explicitly contained in the facts themselves, inferences result from the active participation of the reader, who makes logical deductions from what is given. Here's an example, drawn from a case study of a tutoring session (which we will read in detail shortly) involving a writing tutor, Lynne, and a student named Chin. Lynne recounts Chin's struggle to "give the teacher what she wants":

> Chin continued her explanation by providing a wonderful example of a sentence from one of her essays, which read, "My husband decided to leave me, leaving a big dent on my heart." Unfortunately for her, the teacher felt that she needed to state more directly what she was trying to say, which was, "He hurt me." Chin stated to me that the indirect writing is a significant part of her culture, and that it is also the way she prefers to write. However, she also told me how teachers in Korea are revered and referred to them as "heroes," *so it is not surprising that when she could not resolve the dissonance between her teacher's expectations and her desire as a writer, that she decided to leave the entire paragraph related to her personal life, including the sentence about her husband leaving her, out of the essay.*

Note the italicized portion of Lynne's analysis. From the evidence provided, Lynne has drawn the inference that Chin fails to "resolve the dissonance" between her own expectations and her attitudes toward the authoritative figure of her teacher (and all teachers).

Let's look at another example of inference building. Consider this passage, taken from *Pedagogy of the Oppressed* by the Brazilian educator Paulo Freire, followed by a summary and then by an inference.

The Original
Education thus becomes an act of depositing, in which the students are the depositories and the teacher is the

---

Drawing Inferences: A Checklist

✓ **Summarize or recapitulate what has been explicitly given or observed.** This is ground zero, the place from which to draw inferences. Without a sure knowledge of what an author has stated explicitly, you will find it very challenging to dig deeper.

✓ **Consider what has not been stated or immediately observed.** In some sense, you are bringing a text with which to compare the reading. In other words, your previous experience and expectations may guide you in determining what has not been included. Inferences as to the author's credibility on a subject may be drawn from the gaps in the writing.

✓ **Draw out the implications.** What is the significance of what has been stated or seen? No data is innocent—that is, without consequence. If the claims and the evidence brought to support them are true, then what difference does that make to your understanding of the subject and to your connection with it?

✓ **Backtrack.** How has the data produced those implications? As a way to check or monitor your inferences, go back to trace the claims and evidence that produced them. You might spot gaps in your own reasoning as a result.

depositor. Instead of communicating, the teacher issues communiqués and makes deposits which the students patiently receive, memorize, and repeat. This is the "banking" concept of education, in which the scope of action allowed to the students extends only as a far as receiving, filing, and storing the deposits.

Summary
According to the "banking concept" of education, teachers deposit information into students, who receive and memorize that information until it is called forth by the teacher.

Inference
Freire reveals his distaste for teaching that does not foster independent thinking and problem-solving.

It might be useful to regard an inference as partly a matter of intuiting or sensing a writer's attitude about a subject, when that attitude is not given explicitly. However, the process is really much more complex than that. As a reader (even of your own writing) you need to bring a whole set of strategies for inference building. In addition, your own previously acquired knowledge of the subject at hand plays a role in the process. Consider, then, the preceding checklist box as a guide toward the building of inferences.

Grounding the Theory

1. Again drawing from Henry Thoreau's *Civil Disobedience,* read the following excerpt:

   > Governments show thus how successfully men can be imposed on, even impose on themselves, for their own advantage. It is excellent, we must all allow. Yet this government never of itself furthered any enterprise, but by the alacrity with which it got out of its way. *It* does

not keep the country free. *It* does not settle the West. *It* does not educate. The character inherent in the American people has done all that has been accomplished; and it would have done somewhat more, if the government had not sometimes got in its way.

Test out the process suggested above by writing your response to the passage (starting with summary). After you've stated the significant implications, remember to describe how you formed them.

2. Take a passage from one of your course textbooks and subject it to the same process.

Disciplinary Perspective: Reflective Practice in Education

An Interview with a Teacher of Education

Ron Weisberger, director of tutoring at Bristol Community College, holds his doctoral degree in education from the University of Massachusetts at Amherst, with an emphasis on ways of promoting the development of individual learners. His dissertation research traced the development of a group of men over a series of semesters beginning with their entry into a community college. He found a remarkable transformation in their attitude toward schooling and provided explanations for that change.

Q. How would you define the act of reflection?

Reflection as making sense of information

A. In my mind the act of reflection is crucial to understanding the educational process. It is not sufficient to memorize information; rather, a person needs to be able to make sense of it. In order to do so one has to ask questions and consider how what is being learned connects with previous learning; how it changes the way we understand things or amplifies what we already know. In essence the process of reflection allows us to take perspective on what we are learning by standing somewhat apart from it and trying to see what difference it makes in our lives.

Q. How is writing related to reflection?

A. I feel that writing is a wonderful way to reflect on what we have attempted to learn. Oftentimes we are not sure about what we really know or understand until we can see it laid out literally in front of us. Through the process of writing we can, in a somewhat more objective way, try to consider what in fact our thoughts and ideas really are about. After doing so we then have the opportunity to accept, revise, or discard what we have written down.

Writing as a form of reflection

Q. What is the relationship among learning, action, and reflection?

A. As I mentioned, learning can be seen as a process that enlarges our understanding of ourselves and the world. In order to do this we have to see how what we have learned plays out in the "real" world. This involves reflecting on our learning. It also involves, in some circumstances, actually acting in the world to see if there is a correspondence between what we think we know or understand and what we can actually experience in the world. In so doing we can then verify the validity of the ideas or go back and make needed changes. For example, our understanding of a particular religious practice could be validated, changed, or refuted by attending a service at a church, mosque, or synagogue in the community and discussing what we have seen with religious leaders and practitioners. Currently, the movement in higher education called "service learning" allows students to study a subject such as poverty and then go out and volunteer with an agency or community group that works with people living at or below the poverty line. This experience allows students to both gain an overall understanding of the causes of poverty, for example, and also see how it plays out "on the ground." This allows for a rich interaction between theory and practice that

"Real-world" connections

can help students come to a better understanding of the subject under consideration.

Q. In your experience, how do students view reflection?

Steps toward independent thinking

A. My experience with encouraging students to reflect on their learning is a mixed one. I have learned that asking students to reflect on a subject is part of a process that takes some time. Typically in the beginning of students' academic careers, the request to reflect is met with some bewilderment. They are used to the instructor being the source of information and they lack faith in their ability to come up with their own answers. Some students will even be hostile, feeling that the instructor is making an unfair demand on them. Answering what appear to be straightforward questions through so-called objective tests seems to them to be the way things are or should be. However, taking small steps in the direction toward independent thinking can help lead students to a new awareness about what constitutes learning.

Q. What assignment, as an example, have you designed that encourages students' written reflection?

What you think about what you read

A. An assignment that I give students in my history courses or in independent study projects is what I call "reflection papers." On a weekly basis I ask students to tell me something about the assignment that stimulated them in some way. I ask them not to tell me what they read but rather what they *thought* about what they have read. Often in the first assignments students will still repeat what they have read. While I don't penalize them, I respond to their papers by posing particular questions about their responses and ask them to elaborate. Eventually, a number of students get the idea and begin to discuss their own feeling or perspectives about the subject. Others never quite get it and continue to relate what they have read rather than reflect on it.

Q. What obstacles do students encounter when they are asked to write reflectively?

A. The major obstacle that students face in writing reflec- Fostering the
tively has to do with developing what psychologist Robert capacity to
Kegan calls a "capacity" to reflect. While most people have reflect
the potential to develop this reflective capacity, it generally
happens only through stimulation and practice. College is a
good place to begin this process if instructors intentionally
create an atmosphere in which this process is fostered. Even
so, it takes time, and might not necessarily occur through one
course or even one or two years. However, it is important to
begin the process, and ideally it would be optimal if all
courses had as one of their goals the development of the reflective process. In this way students would be challenged to
reflect on their learning and at the same time be supported as
they develop as reflective learners. To my knowledge there
are only a few schools that intentionally create this atmosphere. However, one of the important new movements in
higher education is the establishment of teaching and learning centers for faculty development. Hopefully, as this movement becomes more widely spread, instructors will learn
more about the process of student development and collabo-
rative programs can be established with one of [their] goals
being the fostering of reflection.

Case Study

REFLECTING ON A TUTORING SESSION

Lynne's Background

Although she had not yet declared a major, Lynne enjoys tutoring and learning "outside the 'standard' classroom" and is
clearly gravitating toward teaching. Lynne writes that she
"used to say that I wanted to become a teacher," but now she
declares that she "would like to teach." For her, the difference
is more than a matter of phrasing: "Becoming," she writes,
"sounds so permanent and restrictive." Lynne is especially in-
trigued by the new field of cognitive science, especially as it

traces the relationship between women's studies and developmental education.

The Assignment

In a course called "Tutoring in a Writing Center: A Practicum," Lynne and her classmates are asked to write an "Anatomy of a Tutoring Session." Here is the assignment.

Overview and Objective:

Please write up a case study of a particular tutoring session. The objective is to gain a clear understanding of the session and to draw from it lessons that might apply to other tutoring experiences. You are to profile a student whom you tutored during the semester, taking care to describe the student's background, his or her writing needs, the steps that you took to assist the student, and the outcome of your effort.

Format:

Your paper should be at least three pages long, typed, double-spaced. I see this "anatomy" as having the following elements, although, having said that, I want to make it clear that your paper should have a unity and a focus; it should read as a single paper and not as three distinct papers.

Part I: Background

For this element, I would like you to collect, through an interview, as much *relevant* information as you can about the student's experience as a writer. Remember that the key here is to research material that will aid you in understanding what happened (or will happen) in the tutoring session.

Part II: The Session

In this section, I expect you to provide a "thick description" of the tutoring session, in other words, a richly detailed rendering of the experience. Please show patience as you narrate your account of what happened. Include, with the student's consent, reference to the actual writing, if provided in the session.

Part III: Reflection

Finally, I would like you to reflect on the lessons that you learned from the tutoring session. I recommend that throughout this assignment you draw upon the list of reflections, which I am including here:

A PROCESS FOR REFLECTING ON TUTORING SESSIONS

(Adapted from Pamela M. Kiser, "The Integrative Processing Model: A Framework for Learning in the Field Experience.")

Gathering Data

What did I observe in the session?
What did I observe about my own behavior?

Reflecting

How did the session affect me?
What emotions and thoughts were triggered?
What assumptions did I bring to the session?
How do I evaluate my effectiveness?

Identifying Relevant Knowledge

What course work or reading is relevant to this session?
What principles have I learned which relate to the experience?
How did the experience contradict, challenge, or validate my classroom or academic knowledge?

Examining Dissonance

What, if anything, do I feel uncomfortable about in this situation?
What conflicting information do I have?

How does this experience contradict my previous
assumptions?

Articulating Learning
What are the major lessons I learned from this ses-
sion?
What skills did I acquire?

Developing a Plan
Based on what I have learned, how might I modify
my own approach, methods, or behavior?

These questions will guide you in your reflection on
the session. Importantly, they will lead you to integrate what you have previously known with the new
knowledge that you are acquiring as a result of the
session and your analysis.

Part IV: List of Works Cited
Since I expect that you will be citing sources (from
among our class readings), I am asking that you prepare a list of Works Cited, following the Modern Languages Association (MLA) format.

Part V: Written Consent
Please make certain to inform the participating
student thoroughly about the scope and purpose of
the project. You must obtain written informed consent
to conduct this research. A sample form might include the statement, "I have been informed of the nature of this research project and consent to allow
[name of researcher] to use my name, my writing, and
the content of our interview as material for this project." Include the written consent with your paper.

Making Sense of the Tutoring Session
This assignment is particularly challenging. Lynne needs to
describe in considerable detail the substance of her tutoring
session with Chin, an international student from South Ko-

rea, as well as whatever relevant information about Chin as a writer can be gathered from an interview. But, beyond the narrative and descriptive requirements of the assignment, Lynne needs to offer a reflective portion in which she considers the lessons that she has learned from the tutoring experience. She is also expected to reflect on the ways that her classroom readings and discussion have application to the practical matter of tutoring.

For Lynne, the assignment poses another challenge—in part because of a tendency that she herself sees displayed in her tutoring to become lost in the "details" of a session. Often she would approach a student's writing by examining each error as it came along, rather than trying to discern both the "big picture" concerns (Is there a thesis in the piece? Is there logical development?) and patterns of grammatical and mechanical errors (Are the tenses consistently used? Do subjects and verbs typically agree?). This particular assignment requires that Lynne not only account for the *local detail* of a session and of a piece of writing but also reflect on large-scale issues to try to get at the *why of things*, in the student's writing and Lynne's own tutoring behavior.

Anatomy of a Tutoring Session 1

Anatomy of a Tutoring Session

Lynne Bernier

English 62

Dr. H. Tinberg

November 27, 2000

Anatomy of a Tutoring Session 2

Anatomy of a Tutoring Session

Although I have been tutoring at the college for over a year, my experience as a writing tutor has been limited to just a little over a month. In that time, I have enjoyed tutoring students from all over the world, including Cape Verde, Puerto Rico, Korea, and Africa. However, the sessions with these students were so interesting that it became difficult for me to choose just one student as a case study for my paper. While trying to decide which student's tutoring session to focus on, I thought about what Kenneth Bruffee says, "Reflective thinking is something we learn to do, and we learn to do it from and with other people" (129). As I thought about this quote, it reminded me of some of the professors whose encouragement and insight has helped in my development as a learner. Then I thought about one woman: her passionate essays; our insightful and inspiring conversations; a mirror of an entire culture I knew nothing about, placed gently in my hands. We talked and I learned.

She is a young Korean woman named Chin, whom I have tutored in the writing center, as well as at the tutoring and academic support center (TASC) at Bristol Community College. Although her parents both live in Korea, Chin, now thirty-six, has lived in America for seventeen years. She is divorced, with two boys. At home, she speaks and writes in both Korean and English, and her sons are fluent in both languages.

Since starting college, Chin has completed all of the required ESL courses and is now taking a basic writing course. Her writing focuses

Anatomy of a Tutoring Session 3

primarily on issues that are very close to her, such as her family, her sons, and the differences between her native country of Korea, and the United States. One strength in her writing that I have noticed is her ability to write so passionately across so many disciplines. For example, regardless of whether she is writing a psychology, history, or English paper, her voice is strong and her passion flows throughout each piece of writing, which makes our conversations pursuant to her writing very enjoyable. For instance, we have discussed divorce, raising children, pursuing a college education, and even sexual abuse, as well as differences in the educational systems of Korea and the United States. Through our conversations, I have come to admire not only her writing, but also the courage she shows by raising a family, as well as pursuing her education in a foreign land.

Nevertheless, my ability to see Chin as a strong writer results from an earlier experience I had with another ESL student, who I thought was a "slower learner" because of the difficulties the students was having in understanding the English language. However, I was very surprised to find out that this student had obtained a master's degree in art from her own country. This lesson taught me that discrimination can be so discreet that the person discriminating doesn't even realize s/he is doing it, and that as tutors we need to be careful of our preconceived and often mistaken views of culturally diverse people. I am grateful for these types of tutoring sessions with wonderfully articulate and compassionate peo-

Anatomy of a Tutoring Session 4

ple, because they help me to break down the prejudices concerning culturally diverse people, some of which I don't even realize I have.

Certainly, when working with ESL students, tutor prejudices are just some of the challenges that the tutor must confront, because as the tutee struggles to learn the English language with all of its rules, and the many exceptions to those rules, the tutor must struggle to understand how the student's language, as well as culture contributes to her writing. Caposella addresses this problem by saying, "In other cultures, explicitly stating the point anywhere in the essay is considered an insult to the reader's intelligence" (93). This directly relates to a point that Chin mentioned while being interviewed by me, in which she beautifully illustrated how ignorance regarding other cultures can affect our ability to help people with their writing. She said, "In Korea, good writing means trying to extend the reader's imagination." In other words, a writer's job is to be as indirect as possible, which conflicts with the expectations of many teachers who expect the students to be very direct and to the point.

Chin continued her explanation by providing a wonderful example of a sentence from one of her essays, which read, "My husband decided to leave me, leaving a big dent on my heart." Unfortunately for her, the teacher felt that she needed to state more directly what she was trying to say, which was, "He hurt me." Chin stated to me that indirect writing is a significant part of her culture, and that it is also

Anatomy of a Tutoring Session 5

the way she prefers to write. However, she also told me how teachers in Korea are revered and referred to them as "heroes," so it is not surprising that when she could not resolve the dissonance between her teacher's expectations and her desire as a writer, she decided to leave the entire paragraph related to her personal life, including the sentence about her husband leaving her, out of the essay.

Nevertheless, she was not happy about it, but again the high status of teachers in her country makes it difficult for her to approach them regarding these types of misunderstandings. Now I understand why it is so important, as Brannon and Knoblauch point out, "The focus will be, not on the distance between text and some teacher's personal notion of its most ideal version, but rather on the disparity between what the writer wanted to communicate and what the choices residing in the text actually cause readers to understand" (217). I think that in this case, the teacher was eventually given what she wanted, but it was not how Chin intended to convey the information. Fortunately, Chin and I have become friends during the two semesters that I have tutored her, so she felt comfortable sharing this type of information with me. Although I did not challenge the teacher's authority to make comments and suggestions on her paper, I did let her know that many people do not understand the cultural differences and the impact they can have on writing. In addition, I told her that I appreciated her explaining these cultural differences to me, and that I not only understood why

Anatomy of a Tutoring Session 6

she wrote the sentence the way she did, but that I liked it, and that I was sorry she had to change it. She was sorry too.

Surely, there must be more students who come into the writing lab with similar problems, and I see cultural diversity as it relates to writing as a critical issue that needs to be addressed in education. However, at this point we start by helping one student at a time, so I was pleased when I saw Chin enter the writing lab. Unfortunately, I had not had a chance to talk with her all summer, but we greeted each other as old friends, and I could tell that she was excited to show me her paper. She quickly pulled it out of her backpack, along with the instructions from her teacher. The assignment was to write a paragraph about anything, and she chose to write her paper about getting her son to eat properly; she called it, "My Little Fussy Eater." What a wonderful idea for a paragraph, and her writing was just what I have come to expect, a passionate piece that elicited my empathy as a mother and a friend. Of course, as so many of us do, I could sense in her paper that she was searching for the "right" answer. She wrote about how her friends, as well as society, were trying to get her to feed her son "proper nutrition," while her son, on the other hand, was fighting for the "it tastes good" side of things. She went on to explain her struggle in reconciling the different views regarding good nutrition.

After she finished reading her paper, I told her how well written I thought it was, and how much I enjoyed it. Then, we began to look at

Anatomy of a Tutoring Session 7

some minor grammatical errors, which she had
started to correct on her own while reading her
paper. I pointed out a few verb tense errors
that she had overlooked, which she easily corrected by herself. In addition to the verb
tense errors, she also had a few errors concerning articles. For example, she wrote, "the
Parent magazine" instead of "*Parent* magazine,"
and "an hamburger" instead of "a hamburger."
She also used "is impossible task" instead of
"is an impossible task." However, she corrected
all these errors except the first one I mentioned, and after thinking about it, I think
she may have wanted to express it as a magazine
for parents, and not just name the magazine.
Although, she did capitalize the word "Parent,"
so I think my recommendation to take out the
"the" was correct. But the teacher did not correct it on the final draft, so I'm not sure
about that error. Fortunately, since last semester I have seen the number of verb tense and
article errors on her papers decrease, which
tells me she is becoming more skilled in
adhering to the grammatically rules of the
English language. In addition to these minor
grammatical errors, we also worked on a frag-
ment sentence that read, "In addition, stressful comments from friends, You are creating a
monster," which she later changed to "In addition, I received stressful comments from
friends." Certainly, the interview we had was
very informative as to the types of errors she
was making. For example, she explained to me
that in her language nouns are not pluralized,

Anatomy of a Tutoring Session 8

verb tenses do not change, and articles are not used. This helps to clarify for me the reason that she may be having difficulties with these types of errors.

In addition to the errors, I felt the paper was too long for the assignment, and that this needed to be addressed in the session. As I mentioned earlier, the teacher's assignment asked for a paragraph, but she had almost one and a half pages double spaced, so I explained that although her paper was well written, she needed to shorten it in order to meet the teacher's expectations. This problem directly relates to one of the five "primary traits" mentioned by Dr. Tinberg, wherein he describes criteria that can be used to evaluate different forms of writing. One of these "primary traits" that he mentions refers to the writer's audience, which he explains by saying, "Good writing is appropriate to the reader, the purpose, and the occasion" (Tinberg 63). It is interesting to me that I often see students, including Chin, who are not following the teacher's instructions, not because they don't want to, but because they feel an attachment to what they are writing about, and feel so strongly that the information they are giving is relevant, that they are torn between "writer-based" and "reader-based" modes of writing (qtd. in Caposella 37). Hopefully what we do in the lab is help the student compromise in order to meet the teacher's expectations and receive a good grade, while at the same time keeping their voice and point of view in their paper.

Anatomy of a Tutoring Session 9

In fact, this is what I tried to do with Chin during this tutoring session. I talked to her about the importance of following the teacher's instructions and how the length of a paragraph usually extends anywhere from about four to five sentences to as long as three-quarters of a page. At first, she expressed difficulty in shortening the paper because she felt that everything she wrote was relevant to her thesis, and I agreed. However, I started rereading her paper in order to find parts that could possibly be taken out, when it occurred to me that maybe instead of taking something out, she could simplify it and restate it instead. For example, I noticed that she used a chronological order to organize her paper, so when she wrote about her son's eating habits, she stopped at each meal to discuss the problems she was having with him. I asked her to think about whether she needed to stop at each meal in order to discuss the problems that occurred there, or could she just state the problems without using the chronological pattern of organization? We discussed that by editing the paper in this way, she would be able to keep the main points that supported her thesis in the paper. She agreed that this would be a good way to shorten her paper.

As a result of our discussions, I think the student felt able to revise her paper, while at the same time keeping what was truly important to her in it. I might add that our discussions, or conversations, easily connected to a single, yet critical point that many of the authors

Anatomy of a Tutoring Session 10

from our class readings make. For example, Stephen North defines the purpose of a writing center by saying, "We are here to talk to writers" (30). Similarly, Kenneth Bruffee states the purpose of peer tutors in the writing center is to "not write or edit, or least of all proofread. What they do together is converse" (133). I like these models better than the "fix it shop" models because of their emphasis on communication and co-learning. For example, when we focus on communication rather than simple editing, it extends the limitations of a tutoring session by focusing on what the student, who is also the writer, knows, instead of just working from what we as tutors know or understand about their writing. Brannon and Knoblauch state this rather nicely by saying, "Writers know what they intended to communicate. Readers know what a text has actually said to them" (218). Thankfully, not only did Chin know what she intended to convey in her writing, but as an articulate and intellectual person, she was able to use her verbal skills to help me understand her essay. Even though her essay was pretty clear, I find that having the student explain what the sentence or paragraph is about can give the student more word choices, which sometimes is all they need to correct the problem.

In addition to the importance of communication, understanding the connection between tutoring and co-learning is also important. For example, when I think of myself as a co-learner, it is easier to put aside some of the

Anatomy of a Tutoring Session 11

anxiety that I have about needing to have all the "right" answers. I have also found support for the co-learning method in a book that uses midwifery as a metaphor for the co-learning teaching method by stating, "While the bankers deposit knowledge in the learner's head, the midwives draw it out. They assist the students in giving birth to their own ideas, in making their own tacit knowledge explicit and elaborating on it" (Belenky et al. 217). Certainly, this is one of the best metaphors for co-learning that I have read about as of yet, and I think it reflects beautifully the purpose of writing tutors, as well as being an important element for teaching in general.

However, this model can be difficult for the inexperienced writing tutor. For example, Caposella states two roles to avoid when tutoring, and I have difficulty avoiding them both. The first is that "A peer consultant isn't a surrogate teacher," and the other is "A peer consultant isn't the author this time around (Caposella 2). I am thankful that I remembered this information, because it allowed me to have the student correct her own grammatical errors, which helped me pull back from the surrogate teacher role, a role that I am not comfortable with anyway. As for keeping myself from becoming the author of this paper, I am fortunate because this particular tutee is such a strong and passionate writer that it is almost impossible for me to insert my own voice into her writing. Unfortunately, I think that when I work with more tentative writers, it is much easier to infiltrate their writing with my own

Anatomy of a Tutoring Session 12

voices, as unintentional as that might be. However, I must say that due to the information I am learning in class, as well as the experience at the writing lab, I am finding myself much more adept at keeping my voice out of other students' writings.

Certainly, as I reflect on this tutoring session with Chin, the first thing that comes to mind is that I should have started with the appropriateness to the assignment or the organization of it, which luckily didn't need any work, but instead I started with what was most comfortable for me, the grammar. This is something that I struggle with at every session, not to evaluate the writing from a sentence level. When I do this, I find that I get lost and often miss the "big picture," such as paragraphs not supporting thesis statements, and focus and organization difficulties. Caposella gives some great ideas, such as "using a technique called glossing, which can help identify several different types of problems with paragraphs, such as having more than one idea in a paragraph or having one idea spread over several paragraphs" (39-40; 5). It is interesting that before reading about grouping surface errors and using some of them as models, I would have thought glossing would be difficult to do. However, now I feel that I could help a student gloss one or two paragraphs, explaining the significance, and then he/she could do the rest on their own.

Of course, I was very pleased with the entire tutoring session with Chin. She left with a paper that she felt she could revise in order

Anatomy of a Tutoring Session 13

to meet the teacher's expectations without having to leave out parts that she felt were relevant to the paper. Certainly, the student was
not the only one to benefit from this tutoring
session; I too gained a lot from her, as I do
with all our sessions. For example, not only do
I enjoy reading her papers, but also they provide me with knowledge about the ways that culturally diverse people think, as it relates to
writing. In this particular essay, I especially
liked how she ended it by saying, "With exhaus-
tion and feeling failure, I threw myself down
on the couch and swear the words that I am so
familiar with, I am not cooking again. Nevertheless, my mind is already miles way searching
for what to cook for him for the next day."
What a wonderful way to end such a beautiful
piece of writing. I know that writing will always be an important way for her to express
herself, and I hope that the help and encouragement I have given here will in some way pos-
itively affect her development as a writer.

As a result of this tutoring session, I
think both of us benefited from the conversation that we had together regarding her writing. For example, we talked about the frustra-
tion of getting our children to eat the "right"
foods, and the guilt that accompanies us when
we break down and let them eat "junk" food,
both of which were illustrated beautifully in
her paper. As compassionate women, we reached
out and comforted each other because we both
sensed that this was an issue of guilt and
uncertainty for both of us; the conversation

Anatomy of a Tutoring Session 14

helped each of us support the other as we both try to live up to the role of "good mothers."

In addition to benefiting from the conversation regarding her writing, I have also benefited by becoming more aware of my own strengths and weaknesses as a writer. For example, if I ever need to shorten something I have written, I can draw on my experience from this session and use the same techniques that I thought of for shortening Chin's paper. In addition, by having to explain to her how different grammatical rules apply to her writing, I have expanded my knowledge regarding these rules. Chin also helps me practice not becoming a co-author of the essays that I read with students, because she is such a strong writer herself.

Without a doubt, the most surprising part of the session came much later, when I had a chance to read her final draft, for which she received an "A." She kept the same chronological order that she started with: Her son eating breakfast; then lunch; then dinner! This was not how I had envisioned the paper to look. I thought she would take out the chronological schedule of meals, and replace it with something else. Obviously, she liked what she had written, and she wasn't willing to give it up. I am so pleased that she is a strong writer and followed her own mind when revising this piece. She definitely has a sense of what good writing entails, and it was a joy to read the finished draft. This also teaches me to focus on the writer's intentions instead of just my own preconceived notions of what essay writing should entail.

Anatomy of a Tutoring Session 15

Certainly, knowledge comes in many forms, such as books, television, and magazines, as well as through lectures. However, I think the most important vehicle for the transference of knowledge comes from our interactions with other people, especially when that interaction is based on a co-learning or connected teaching style. For example, as Belenky and her colleagues state, "Objectivity in connected teaching, as in connected knowing, means seeing the other, the student, in the student's own terms" (224). They see that "The connected class constructs truth not through conflict, but through consensus" (223). Bruffee seems to agree with this method of teaching, thus relating it to peer tutoring by saying, "Education is not a process of assimilating the truth" (135). He also relates it to writing by saying, "writing is temporally and functionally related to conversation" (130). And it is exactly in these "conversations" with other compassionate people like Chin that a critical element of my education takes place.

Anatomy of a Tutoring Session 16

Works Cited

Belenky, Mary Field, Blythe McVicker Clinch, Nancy Rule Goldberger, and Jill Mattuck Tarule. *Women's Ways of Knowing: The Development of Self, Voice, and Mind.* New York: Basic, 1986.

Brannon, Lil and C. H. Knoblauch. "On Students' Rights to Their Own Texts: A Model of Teacher Response." Caposella 213-22.

Bruffee, Kenneth A. "Peer Tutoring and the Conversation of Mankind." Caposella 127-38.

Caposella, Toni-Lee, ed. *The Harcourt Brace Guide to Peer Tutoring.* Fort Worth: Harcourt, 1998.

Flower, Linda and John R. Hayes. "The Cognition of Discovery: Defining a Rhetorical Problem." Caposella 155-66.

North, Steven. "The Idea of a Writing Center." In Christina Murphy and Steve Sherwood, eds. *The St. Martin's Sourcebook for Writing Tutors.* New York: St. Martin's, 1995: 22-36.

Robinson, Chin. Personal Interview. 10 Nov. 2000.

Tinberg, Howard. *Border Talk: Writing and Knowing in the Two-Year College.* Urbana, IL: National Council of Teachers of English, 1997.

Early in her paper, Lynne comes to realize that reflection does not arrive magically and in isolation. It is, rather, a result of methodically watching and listening to others. Quoting from the composition teacher and educational theorist Kenneth Bruffee, Lynne observes, "Reflective thinking is something we learn to do, and we learn to do from and with other people." A case in point might be the experience Lynne describes prior to her tutoring of Chin. Lynne had tutored another student whose native language was not English and admits to thinking that the student was a "slow learner" because of her language difficulties:

> However, I was very surprised to find out that this student had obtained a master's degree in art from her own country. This lesson taught me that discrimination can be so discreet that the person discriminating doesn't realize they are doing it.

Here Lynne engages in the practice of reflection.

In the session with Chin, Lynne comes to an important realization after re-reading Chin's paragraph, which, to Lynne, seemed at first to be overly long and in need of serious cutting:

> At first, [Chin] expressed difficulty in shortening the paper because she felt that everything she wrote was relevant to her thesis, and I agreed. However, I started re-reading her paper in order to find parts that could possibly be taken out, when it occurred to me that maybe instead of taking something out, she could simplify it and restate it instead.

Specifically, Lynne noted the repetition caused by the strict attention to chronological order and wondered whether Chin's decision to stay with strict chronology was necessary.

Chin would, however, continue to hold to the original structure and to her own purpose. Lynne comes to see this act as affirming important points raised in her class readings:

(1) In writing centers, students and tutors need to be regarded as writers, and (2) Knowledge gained during tutoring sessions is the product of "conversation" between student and tutor and not something dictated by the tutor.

Beyond the Midwife: Making "Real World" Connections

Lynne goes even further in defining her role as tutor, based on her experience with Chin. Drawing upon her reading in women's studies, Lynne is taken by the metaphor of the tutor as "midwife" (as opposed to "depositor" of information), whose role is "assisting" the creative work of the writer. But Lynne senses the dangers of that metaphor in practice, distinctively different though it may be from imagining the tutor as lecturer/authoritative teacher. Keeping in mind class readings that warn the tutor not to be a "surrogate teacher" or to write the paper "this time around," Lynne checks herself during the session:

I am thankful that I remembered this information, because it allowed me to have the student correct her own grammatical errors, which helped me pull back from the surrogate teacher role, a role that I am not comfortable with anyway.

By her own admission Lynne is more comfortable with a focus on grammar and mechanics than with a consideration of the broader writing concerns. She realizes, in the writing of the paper, that once again the session centered on grammatical issues:

Certainly, as I reflect on this tutoring session with Chin, the first thing [that]

comes to mind is that I should have
started with the appropriateness to the
assignment or the organization ...,
which luckily didn't need any work, but
instead I started with what was most comfortable for me, the grammar. This is
something that I struggle with at every
session, not to evaluate the writing from
a sentence level. When I do this, I find
that I get lost and often miss the "big
picture," such as paragraphs not supporting thesis statements, and focus and organization difficulties.

Lynne seems ready to move beyond the narrow frame of
grammar.

The case study receives closure when Chin brings the paper, graded, back to Lynne, who is surprised. What surprises
Lynne is not so much the grade (the "A") but the fact that Chin
decided to stay with the original structure. This serves as a
fresh reminder—and, later, the product of reflection—that
writers do have the final say in how their writing turns out.
Lynne has also come to view tutoring as another form of "connected teaching," in which the aim is to produce collaboration and consensus, not intimidation or perfect unanimity.

Grounding the Theory

1. Read the following passage from an essay called "Women's Place
    in Everyday Talk: Reflections on a Parent-Child Interaction" by
    Candace West and Don H. Zimmerman. What inferences can you
    draw from the passage?

    Fishman (1975) observed that in fifty-two hours of tape-
    recorded conversation collected from three couples the
    women employed the "D'ya know what?" opening
    twice as frequently as men. Overall, the women asked
    almost three times as many questions as the men. The

implication is, of course, that the greater reliance on such question forms by women stems from *their* limited rights as co-conversationalists with men.

2. Read the following passage, taken from Theodore Sizer's *Horace's Compromise*. Draw as many inferences as you can from it, taking care to think about the larger implications of Sizer's view:

> Schools that always insist on the right answer, with no concern as to how a student reaches it, smother the student's efforts to become an effective intuitive thinker. A person who is groping to understand, and is on a fruitful but somewhat misdirected track, needs to learn how to redirect his thoughts and to try a parallel but somewhat different scheme. Simply telling that person that he is wrong throws away the opportunity to engage him in questions about his logic and approach (105).

3. Read the following excerpt from Ira Shor's *Empowering Education*. Reflect, in writing, on the implications for the hiring and training of teachers:

> On the job, urban and rural teachers are especially burdened by the size of their classes, the number of classes they are assigned, the short class hour, the many academic and personal needs of the students, the oppressive paperwork and bureaucracy, the absence of resources and support services, and the restrictions of required tests, texts, and syllabi. Teachers themselves lack power in their institutions, which are run from the top down (102).

4. Read Lynne's paper, paying special attention to her closing. What relationship does Lynne infer between tutoring and the idea of consensus-building?

For Extended Writing

1. Selecting one of the courses that you are currently taking, write an "anatomy" of a single class. Be certain to follow both the

structural format and the list of reflective questions given with the assignment.

2. Review what Ron Weisberger has to say about a "reaction paper." Then write your own reaction paper about any reading drawn from your current course work. Remember the key distinction made in that interview between summarizing what you have read and offering your own thinking about the reading. In your reaction paper, you should be describing your reaction, rather than restating the author's points.

Reflective Writing in the Extra-Curriculum: The Electronic Bulletin Board

How often have you dashed off an e-mail or electronic bulletin board posting wishing that you could somehow delete or unsend what you had written? If your experience is like mine, it has probably happened more often that you would wish. As pressure mounts to respond to more and more information in electronic modes, the need to write reflectively increases. How can we become that kind of reflective writer in the digital age?

Given the inherently social nature of electronic bulletin boards, the writing on such sites can demonstrate the power of reflection as a tool for teaching and learning. Here, as an example, is a series of postings on an electronic bulletin board set up for writing tutors. The group is discussing the complex challenge of tutoring students whose first language is not English (L2 writers).

Strategies for tutoring L2 writers

Previous   Next

Displaying message 43 of 329 messages

12/4/2000 9:02:10 AM   Respond

From:

Subject: Strategies for tutoring L2 writers

Message: Hello English 62:

I've just received this message on WCenter, a listserv for writing center folks. Based on our readings for this week, can you offer any advice or strategies for addressing the needs of writers whose first language is not English?

<English (is not) a Simple Language even for those whose job is to give advice about the application and specific mechanics of the language. It is a prevailing problem for the growing body of foreign students at the Salt Lake Community College. As a writing consultant, one is faced with a number of questions regarding how to best serve these students with such issues ranging from simple grammatical errors, to an adverse inability to think critically in their OWN language, let alone in a language with which they are not comfortable>.

Displaying message **44** of **329** messages

12/4/2000 3:51:42 PM

From:

Subject: Re: Strategies for tutoring L2 writers

Message:

I think the best way we can help a student is to honor their intentions as a writer. If everything we do extends from there, it should be a positive session. (Honoring their intentions may also include asking them about their culture as it directly relates to their writing style, etc.)

I think the first thing tutors should do when reviewing their papers is to make sure that we understand what they are trying to say, and if there are any areas in their text that we are unclear of, we start there. This is because if there are points in the text that we don't understand, it will be difficult to see if the bigger issues are being met, such as if the student understands and is responding to the assignment, etc. For example, if the student is having difficulty responding to the assignment, we need to talk with them and help them understand. Then, we need to draw out what they, as writers, want to say. As for grammatical errors, these can be addressed (to some degree) at the same time we are reviewing sentences that don't make much sense, and the rest can be addressed after we have made sure that what they want to say is actually what they are saying.

Displaying message **45** of **329** messages.
12/5/2000 8:46:09 AM

From:

Subject: Re: Strategies for tutoring L2 writers

Message:

I agree with Lynne that having an understanding with the writer is the first step in establishing an effective situation. Sometimes an understanding will not be met by reading the paper, so I think this level can be achieved through conversation with the student. The intent of the student should be put on the table. Also, the issue of whether or not they understand the assignment should be addressed right away.

After this basis of information is set, I think the paper can be read over. This is the time in which structure and grammar can be addressed in patterns at the same time (if that really is possible).

Lastly, I think the most important part to the session, as in any session, is patience. Even if things are not going exactly the way it was planned to, patience and perseverance will eventually bring the session to the desired level.

Thanks,

Displaying message **46** of **329** messages.

12/5/2000 3:41:46 PM

From:

Subject: Re: Strategies for tutoring L2 writers

Message:

Dear Dr. Tinberg:

An ideal situation would be to have a diverse group of tutors available at the Writing Lab to help with consulting; remember I said "ideal." English is one of the most difficult languages to learn and also to EXPLAIN to someone else. This was evident when I tutored the young Asian student at Durfee [a neighboring high school] and found myself having to explain verb tenses. Sometimes for us as tutors there is a point that we must send them back to the English Teacher for a better understanding. Still as stated in Border Talk, ". . . it might be that effective tutoring sessions have to acknowledge the complex web of intentions behind a piece of writing[. . . .] We need, in our protocol, to allow opportunity for writers to provide that context" (Tinberg 67).

Getting at the heart of their intent is first and foremost and dealing with the grammatical comes next. There is a web site according to Rafoth's book on page 138. Perhaps we could suggest that as an additional avenue to pursue.

Displaying message **47** of **329** messages.

12/6/2000 12:07:26 AM

From:

Subject: Re: Strategies for tutoring L2 writers

Message:

>Hi Everyone:

>The subject of L2 writers seems to be causing a bit of dissonance with me. I understand the problems that the L2 writers have with the prose of the English language, but I'm not sure that I agree with the tutoring methods suggested in our readings.

>Each case has to be considered on its own merit, since there are so many different and complex problems associated with L2 writers (Powers 239). Having writers read their papers aloud may not help at all (Powers 239). Without the familiarity of the English language, they may not catch problems with diction.

>Having to read over the L2 writer's paper and discuss what they are trying to say sounds good in theory, but what if the

writer accepts everything you have to say, thinking that you are an expert? This seems to be crossing the line in the tutor, tutee relationship. This area is very gray. Are we creating a loophole when we let down our guard as tutors? Will some L2 writers take advantage of this type of tutoring just to have their paper edited? Are we in fact peer tutors if we are not L2 writers ourselves?

>Again, each case must be considered on its own merit, and we are there to help students with their writing, but we must make sure that we are not creating a loophole that we would not ordinarily afford our other non-L2 peers. Integrity of the writing must stay with the writer.

>Having stated these precautionary pitfalls, I do believe we can help most of our L2 tutees if we are afforded the necessary time, and we possess the patience required to work with L2 writers. Letting them keep writer's integrity, and not losing patience with editing must be difficult tasks for a tutor. It seems that the situation with an L2 writer calls for a tutor with either a lot of experience tutoring or a specialty in tutoring L2 writers.

In this exchange, a problem is set forth to the group (in this case from me, as an instructor, although in response to a posting on an electronic listserv devoted to writing center work). Each writer attempts, either indirectly or directly, to offer suggestions to resolve the problem by turning to a series of precepts and practices gathered in the course. Some even quote from a particular reading or summarize a reading. They adopt language from the original message in their response—

Effective Communication on Electronic Listservs and Bullentin Boards: A Checklist

✓ **An awareness of beliefs that you bring to your subject.** In an integrative model of reflection, it is important to establish what you know now so as to sharpen what you will soon learn.

✓ **A thorough reading and understanding of the original thread or message.** As is the case with the set of beliefs prior to coming to the bulletin board, this knowledge may serve as counter-balance to the knowledge to come.

✓ **A recognition of the "dissonance" between what you have read and what you already believe.** In becoming aware of such difference, you lay the groundwork for inference- and knowledge-making.

✓ **A restatement of that thread, or its significant parts.** The process of selecting pertinent aspects of the initial posting not only grounds or positions your own reflections but begins the process of inference building.

✓ **A "talking back" in dialogue with previous messages.** Establishing connections with the larger world beyond your own experience is an important prelude to productive reflection.

✓ **A review of the writer's own response to determine its effect on the bulletin board community.** When you post a response to a message, consequences ensue. Take time to see what effect your words have had on the bulletin board community.

as well as language from the readings—in their reflection. There is, in other words, a turning back toward what is already known as a means of solving the problem. Interestingly, the writer of the final posting notices a "dissonance" between what he has been taught in class and the experience described (echoing an earlier writer who had tutored an L2 writer and from that experience) wonders whether teachers should get involved in such matters.

It follows then that reflective writing in such electronic bulletin boards should include these practices shown in the checklist on the page 250.

Taking a Closer Look

1. Access *Peer Centered* (http://www.slcc.edu/wc/peercentered/index.html), an online resource for peer tutors in writing and a site for online interaction among peer tutors. Read and review various messages along a number of threads. Write your own account of the ways in which tutors reflect on each other's postings, using the guidelines above.

2. Locate an electronic bulletin board whose mission is to address a significant public issue (such as environmental or medical concerns). Read recent messages to get a sense of key threads. With the group's consent, send postings in response to a thread of your own interest. Separately, write down your reflection as to how participants responded to your assertions and how you yourself expressed your concerns.

Chapter 6

Presentation: What to Write? For Whom? Why?

Understanding Genre, Audience, and Purpose

Framing a question, surveying the available literature on your subject, gathering new data, and reflecting on the significance of those results—all these ways of knowing contribute to *writing with consequence.* But now it is time to present your findings in writing. How do you go about doing that? What do you need to know? Answering these questions calls upon yet another way of knowing: *presentation.*

An effective presentation requires an awareness of genre, audience, and purpose—in other words, a knowledge of what you are writing, for whom, and why:

- First, you need to know a good deal about the kind of writing that you are being asked to write: whether a lab report, an annotated bibliography, or a film review. Each kind of writing depends on a certain set of *conventions* and rules unique to that kind, as you will see shortly.

- Second, you need to have an awareness of your audience's expectations. If your writing is truly to have consequence, then it must meet and perhaps exceed those expectations; it must not only inform your audience but also change it in some way.

- Third, your writing must have a purpose. The consequences that your writing achieves are to be purposeful: you intend your writing to have impact.

All three considerations—genre, audience, and purpose—converge and are dependent on one another. After all, a knowledge of genre necessarily involves a sense of what your audience needs to know as well as an expressed purpose. The overlap is especially obvious in a classroom setting, in which meeting your teacher's expectations is tightly interconnected with a knowledge of the kind of writing assigned by that teacher and your purpose in writing at all.

To highlight each of these distinct concerns, let us examine an example of writing. You will see that it points to the interrelatedness of one concern to the other as well as differentiating them. Consider this letter, written to the Secretary of Agriculture, about the treatment of circus animals:

February 14, 2000

The Honorable Daniel Glickman
Secretary of Agriculture
U.S. Department of Agriculture
14th St. and Independence Ave., SW
Washington, DC 20250

Dear Secretary Glickman:

The circus is coming to town . . . your town. The Ringling Bros. and Barnum & Bailey Circus is scheduled to perform at MCI Center, March 23–26, 2000 and at D.C. Armory, March 28–April 9, 2000.

I have written countless, mostly unanswered, letters to various local and state legislators to make them aware of, and to editors of newspapers asking them to publicize, the cruelty of wild animals forced to entertain us in circus acts. I have written to sponsors and organizers asking them to withdraw their support in light of this same cruelty. I am now shooting straight for the top. I am asking for your help, Mr. Glickman, to *change* the animal protection laws.

As more and more people are becoming aware of the suffering and the cruelty involved in forcing animals to perform, circuses are finding fewer locations to set up their big tops. The use of animals in entertainment has been banned, or at least radically restricted, in several countries, including Denmark, Finland, Sweden, Switzerland, and India. In England, circuses with animal acts are often denied public space. Several cities in our country enacted ordinances regulating the treatment of wild animals in circuses. Revere, Massachusetts allows no display of wild animals for public entertainment on city property and prohibits animals from being either forced to live separated from their own species, or publicly exploited. Quincy, Massachusetts prohibits the use of wild animals in circuses, carnivals, and competitive races. Hollywood, Florida forbids the display of vertebrate animals for entertainment on public property, and regulates their display on private property. They all do this, sir, because it's simply the right thing to do.

In many locations, fresh drinking water is unavailable, and, therefore, cleaning the animals and their cages takes a very low priority. This is a hardship for some animals, like elephants, which normally bathe often. Food is often limited as well. The climate is also a hardship to most of the animals. Hot weather is especially hard on bears, while lions and tigers suffer most from the cold. Veterinarians qualified to treat wild animals are usually not readily available, and many of the animals have suffered and even died due to improper medical attention. Clever comic acts, such as elephants balancing on balls, and bears riding bicycles, are physically uncomfortable and behaviorally unnatural to these animals. Endless hours with whips, harsh words, and drugs are used to coerce wild creatures to cavort for us. This is how it has been done for hundreds of years, and this is how it is still done today.

Please review and amend the Animal Welfare Act. Let's stop the barbaric exploitation of these beautiful wild animals now, in our lifetime.

Sincerely,

A letter, whether of a public nature (as in a letter to an editor or a letter to a cabinet secretary) or private (a letter to a friend or family member), carries certain expectations as to form (letters need to begin with some greeting, for example) and content (letters don't normally "get to the point" immediately but offer some "ice breaker" or salutation). While a letter needs to have a purpose, that purpose may not be stated at the very beginning, as you might expect in another genre, such as a thesis-driven academic essay. In this case, however, the writer's intent, while not stated in the very first paragraph, is nevertheless clearly stated in the second paragraph: the animal protection laws need to be changed. The statement is followed by supportive evidence, drawn from international and national settings. Notice as well the writer's sense of her audience. The secretary of agriculture would be most interested to read about relevant legislation currently on the books. Because the writer and the writing are informed, the intended reader is likely to grant the letter credibility.

The Dictates of Genre

In the workplace and at home, you are likely to encounter a variety of written genres: a business memo, a news story, or an editorial. Each is distinctively different in form from the other, and, in each case, form affects content. A business memo, for example, typically begins with the name of the person to whom the memo is addressed, the name of the writer, and a brief phrase describing the subject:

MEMO

To: Robert E. McCormick

From: Julius Jones

Subject: ABC Company, January 1995

I have examined the *Wall Street Journal Index* for references concerning ABC Company in January 1995 and uncovered the following items of interest:

- The CEO committed suicide on January 9, 1995.

- The company announced an aggressive plant expansion in their Six Mile, SC facility.

- The company announced that it would hire an addition 1,200 workers over the next year.

The common stock of the company opened the month at $5.50 per share. The highest closing price in the month was $6.25 on January 19th, and the stock price closed at $6.00 per share. The dividend is paid quarterly and is currently $0.50 per share.

The tone is formal and the language efficient. Items of importance receive bullets for ease and economy of reading. The memo does not, in an explicit way, convey the writer's opinion about the subject. The memo stays focused on its subject.

Quite different in form is this news account from the *Boston Globe*:

House Votes for Human Cloning Ban
Sets $1m fine, prison term up to 10 years
By Susan Milligan, Globe Staff

WASHINGTON—The House of Representatives voted yesterday to ban all human cloning, making a statement about the sanctity of life but threatening medical research that one day could lead to cures of painful or deadly illnesses.

In a 265-to-162 vote, the House approved legislation that would impose a fine of at least $1 million and a prison sentence of up to 10 years on anyone who participates in human cloning. The measure also prohibits importation of a cloned human embryo or its "product"—an undefined provision that the ban's opponents fear could keep Americans from benefiting from possible cures developed overseas.

The bill, supported by 200 Republicans, 63 Democrats, and two Independents, is backed by President Bush, but faces shakier prospects in the Democrat-controlled Senate.

Members of the House were in virtual agreement that cloning human cells for the purposes of reproducing whole human beings should be outlawed. But in an anguished debate that encompassed questions of religion, science, and the origin of human life, the House fought bitterly over whether regulated cloning to obtain specific types of human cells—which may someday prove useful in the battle against such ailments as Parkinson's, Alzheimer's, or heart disease—should be allowed as research.

"Human beings should not be cloned to stock a medical junkyard of spare parts for medical experimentation," said House majority whip Tom DeLay, Republican of Texas. Cloning, even for research purposes alone, is "no better than medical strip mining. The preservation of life is what's being lost here," DeLay said on the House floor.

As a matter of convention, newspaper stories offer a headline (and, as in the case of a front-page story, a brief statement stating an important detail from the story), followed by the byline (the writer's name and position) and the place from which the story was reported. But note in the example how form affects content. Like a memo (but unlike a letter), a news account must get to the point immediately (newspaper space is at a premium). In this story, the writer gets to the point in the very first paragraph. She offers details of the vote and of the legislation itself in the following paragraph. Only later do we learn about the complex factors behind the vote and only at the very end are we given testimony from one of the participants in the vote. Nowhere do we see evidence of the writer's own view of the matter. Commonly referred to as an inverted pyramid, the structure used in news writing typically begins with the most newsworthy information and ends with less significant details.

The situation is quite different when we turn to an editorial in the same newspaper. The genre of an editorial allows presentation of the writer's perspective (or the editor's opinion) on a significant issue of the day. The intent is not primarily to provide factual material (that would have been done elsewhere in the paper). In fact, the writer assumes that you have already been given the facts of the matter, offering only a quick reference to the subject. That is certainly the case in the following editorial, also from the *Boston Globe*:

Face to Face on Race

The Bush administration's disdain for international treaties is on display again this week as US officials raise the possibility of boycotting a United Nations conference on racism to be held next month in Durban, South Africa. The administration objects to two items on the agenda: a call for reparations to African countries by colonial slave-trading powers and an attempt by some Arab governments to adopt language equating Zionism with racism.

These two contentious issues do threaten to derail the conference from its main agenda, which is to renew the global commitment to eradicating racism that was expressed in the UN Declaration of Human Rights in 1948. The Zionism question in particular was settled by the United Nations 10 years ago when it repealed a resolution condemning Zionism. Reopening the issue now would be a divisive mistake. But for the United States to avoid the conference outright would be high-handed and unproductive. It is far better to work toward removing the offending items or, should diplomacy fail, refuse to sign the final protocol.

The writer's viewpoint is clear and unequivocal. Notice that no name is given. Editorials, although written by an individual (who may or may not be an editor), appear to represent the positions of the newspapers themselves.

As a practical matter, writers probably know the form in which they are to write as they begin to compose their work. An avid reader of a newspaper, stirred by an editorial, sits down to write an impassioned letter to the editor, knowing something of the demands of the form. Such a reader probably knows the importance of beginning the letter with a reference to the editorial in question, including the date of the newspaper in which it appeared. That reader also knows full well the need to be concise and economical, since space is so much of a concern in any newspaper.

Similarly, a would-be contributor to a scientific journal must be acutely aware of the requirements or conventions dictated by the form of the scientific article included in such a journal. That knowledge includes a whole host of considerations, from including an abstract that begins the article to assembling, in the appropriate form, a bibliography that ends it. Within the body of the article, the writer must take care to provide the conventional sections that comprise work in such a journal: a survey of current and relevant studies, a description of the current project and its aims, an account of methodology, a record of results, discussion of those results, and a concluding section that explores the implications of the research (see Chapter 4). Knowledge of the genre assumes as well a familiarity with the sometimes-specialized language of the discipline. When considering the genre in which you plan to write, it will be useful to ask questions, such as those in the checklist on the following page.

Considering Genre: A Checklist

✓ Have you determined the form in which you intend to write?

✓ Have you researched and discovered models or examples of writing in that form?

✓ What guidelines or expectations come with the genre?

Grounding the Theory

1. Research examples of genres within your own home (such as movie reviews or editorials). What makes each genre distinctively different?

2. Review the genres used in the Extra-Curriculum section of each of the preceding chapters. Summarize the rules governing two of the genres represented.

Thinking about Academic Genres

You may think of the writing that you do in school as being of one kind—the academic essay. In fact, you are likely to write in a variety of genres. You may be asked, for example, to write an *annotated bibliography,* which is a summary and evaluation of source material. Or your teacher might insist that you include with your research paper a *survey of the literature* on your subject as well as an *abstract* of your complete paper. The study of genres puts into focus the distinctive nature of individual acts of writing, calling into consideration matters of form, intended audience, and purpose.

Let's take a look at a sampling of academic genres.

Components of an Abstract: A Checklist

✓ **A statement of purpose**   What is the purpose of your project? Why did you undertake the project?

✓ **A description of methods used**   What techniques did you use to gather information? What sources did you use? In what way was your study limited?

✓ **A discussion of results**   What did you learn? What new facts or lessons did you discover?

✓ **A set of conclusions**   Why do your results matter? What future studies do you recommend?

The Abstract

Articles in scientific journals are often accompanied by a brief synopsis, or abstract, of the article's content. Meant as an aid to readers, an abstract offers the gist of the article. The abstract is usually a paragraph in length and appears just under the article title and author's name. An abstract of a research article typically provides the information in the checklist above.

Abstracts often duplicate the technical language and the scientific style used in the full text of an article, as we see in this example, published in the research-focused *Journal of Clinical Child Psychology:*

Coregulation of balance between children's prosocial approaches and acts of compliance: a pathway to mother-child cooperation

Examined the free-field interaction of 32 mother-child dyads who volunteered to participate in a 1-hr home observation. Observers coded mother instructions, child compliance, and child prosocial approaches plus mothers' social attention as potential reinforcers for the children's compliance and social approaches. Herrnstein's matching law was used to analyze covariations between mothers' attention and the children's 2 responses. This analysis was followed by correlational and sequential probability analyses to determine linkages between these 2 child responses and the children's willingness to obey their mothers' instructions. Results showed consistent matching between mothers' social attention and the children's production of prosocial approaches and acts of compliance. An index of the proportions of these 2 responses also covaried with the children's compliance probabilities, and the prosocial approach component was the direct covariate. These findings are discussed within an interactional synchrony framework in which children's willingness to obey their mothers is influenced by opportunities for the dyad to engage each other in specific forms of social interaction.

It's important to emphasize, again, that abstracts express the content and style of particular disciplines and of particular occasions. As contrast to the example above, this abstract of an editorial appeared in the *British Medical Journal*. The subject is less specialized than that of the abstract that we've just read.

Psychological Implications of chemical and biological weapons: Long-term social and psychological effects may be worse than acute ones.

Biological weapons may be used mostly to cause fear and terror rather than disease outbreaks. This could cause mass psychosomatic illnesses in populations. Since the September 11 attack in the US, this has happened in a middle school in Washington State, and a subway station in Maryland.

The Critical Annotated Bibliography

A critical annotated bibliography is a list of sources in a particular area of study. For each source listed, this kind of bibliography includes a very brief summary and an evaluation of the source. These annotations are meant as a guide for readers, who may then determine whether the source seems useful for their purposes. While some annotated bibliographies provide only a summary of each source, the critical annotated bibliography attempts to offer answers to questions such as these:

- **What are the writer's main points?**
- **How credible is the author?**
- **How accurate and useful is the information provided?**

Here is an example of an annotated listing, drawn from a bibliography of Holocaust-related teaching materials:

Hilberg, Raul. The Destruction of the European Jews [3 vols.]. New York: Holmes and Meier, 1985.

This authoritative reconstruction of the Holocaust remains the standard text to which all others are compared. Hilberg's primary focus is on the methods of the Nazi murder process, including the organizational and bureaucratic machinery of destruction. Hilberg's explanation of the role of Jews themselves in their destruction and of the lack of resistance has been criticized.

It is worth noting, as we did regarding abstracts, that annotated bibliographies can differ significantly, depending on the discipline and subject covered. Here is another example (note that it follows the APA bibliography style).

Flanagan, O. J. 1992. *Consciousness Reconsidered.* MIT Press.

Argues that consciousness can be accounted for in a naturalistic framework. With arguments against eliminativism and epiphenomenalism, evidence from neuroscience and psychology, and discussions of the stream and the self.

In addition to the terms specific to the discipline (the science of human consciousness), this annotation directly expresses the stylistic choices and values of the natural sciences: It provides a brief summary only, leaving out the subjects of sentences. The latter quality is especially revealing in that it suggests an attempt to be "objective," still a goal in many of the laboratory sciences.

The Essay Exam

Writing under the pressure of time requires that you be efficient both in your use of time and your utilization of genre. Typically, you will be asked to write essay exams for at least some of your courses. As a genre, the essay exam can be conveniently divided in this way:

Introduction
a. An acknowledgment of the question that you are attempting to answer
b. A claim or statement of thesis, which will serve as the core of your paper
c. A brief listing of the evidence to support your claim

Body
a. A description of a piece of evidence or reason, made concrete by reference to classroom materials
b. A description of a second piece of evidence, made concrete by reference to classroom discussions
c. A description of a third piece of evidence, again buttressed by reference to readings or classroom materials

[you may of course offer more than three grounds for support, depending on time constraints and your own purposes]

Conclusion

a. Summary of claim

b. Description, if time allows, of the implications of that claim: why it matters

Consider this example from a political science exam.

The Question:

In the past 30 years, members of Congress who seek re-election generally win. Based on class notes and your readings, how do you explain this? *Be specific.*

The Student Wrote:

One of the biggest worries for a congress-person after being elected is re-election. Even though it is more of a problem for senators than the House representatives, it is still a major concern and something that they focus their attention on from day one. Although it seems that a challenger has a fair shot at taking down the incumbent, the incumbent does have some advantages that can help him or her win. Among these advantages are the "in-kind" advantages, the "home-style," and the campaign finance aspect.

The "in-kind" advantages are those that are available to congresspersons strictly because they are in the office. None of these named are granted to the challengers. The first is the enormous staff that a congressperson has at his or her disposal. Manpower is very important for running a campaign and the extensive staff provided for the incumbent when in office can be utilized to keep up the re-election efforts all through the term. The most popular is to send a portion of them to the home state to take care of

any private matters so as to keep the constituency happy. The best part is that this huge
staff is paid for by taxpayer's money, not the
incumbent's wallet. Second, the incumbent can
fully utilize his or her role of ombudsman, cutting through bureaucratic red tape and doing fa-
vors for the constituents. This leads to happy
constituents and the word-of-mouth advertising
is an important part of obtaining votes. Third,
there is the ability of the incumbent to make
direct communication with the home state. The
congresspersons have access to extensive databases that can let them compile a mailing list
for their propaganda. Once the list is made, the
incumbents can now take advantage of their
franking privilege. This is their ability to
send out free mail to all of the names on the
list and write it off as public information so
that there is no cost to them personally.

Finally, there is the campaign committee
which doles out money every election year to
candidates in the running. This is a good resource for the incumbent to accumulate even
more wealth because the money that the committee hands out is only given to incumbents.

The "home-style" advantage, although it seems
somewhat insignificant, can be important to an
incumbent's re-election. This is referring to
the importance of the image of the incumbent
while in office. With coverage of Congress continuing to expand, congresspersons have better
chances of getting some publicity to promote
themselves and show they are doing a good job.
As the saying goes: "When in Rome, do like the
Romans." It is extremely beneficial to tailor

one's image, so that it is condusive to the constituency and not destructive.

The last advantage is that of campaign financing. It is far from inexpensive to run a re-election campaign, but the incumbents do have a slight advantage over the challengers. The ratio in the HOR is 4:1 and the ratio in the Senate is 2:1. After an election or re-election, the politician can keep any leftover money from the election for the re-election. This is called a class trust and it allows the incumbent to start from a sum of money, whereas the challenger starts at zero. Also, the Political Action Committees have been known to hand out money according to the "always bet on a winning horse" saying, and give the most to the incumbents because of their increased chances of winning.

In conclusion, the incumbents may have to worry about re-election, but there are certain advantages that they benefit from strictly because they are in office. These advantages have kept turnover rates from being too high, and it seems it will most likely stay that way.

Note that the writer has laid out an organization from the very first paragraph. Doing so allows her to visualize the entire response before it is fully written. Each section of the paper conforms to the structure that has been anticipated: a structure that makes it easier for the teacher/reader to follow the writer's points more easily.

As you take essay exams for particular courses, you will need to demonstrate a knowledge and facility with the terms and texts that you've studied in a course. While the genre remains fairly stable regardless of the course, your ability to perform well in an exam situation will depend on the extent to which you've internalized—and can apply—the concepts that your instructor and readings have provided.

The Survey of Literature

As we saw in Chapter 3, scholarship is integral to the making of knowledge. Acknowledging previous studies on a given subject confirms the idea that researchers are not pursuing their work alone, but, rather, that they depend on the work of others. A key component of writing involving research (defined earlier as the making of knowledge) is the literature survey. Appearing at the beginning of a research article, the literature survey offers a quick but significant glance at relevant previous studies. The following is a passage taken from the beginning of an article on student attitudes toward writing. The writer lays a foundation by referring to the work of others:

> Students' [. . .] comments frequently fall into one or more of the following areas: negative beliefs about learning (Thomas and Rohwer); problems regarding communication (or lack of it) with their writing educators (Murray); or a severe feeling of disappointment due to lack of control over the writing process (Rose, *Writer's* 78).

The in-text citations are keyed to the Works Cited section at the end of the paper:

Murray, Donald. "Teaching the Other Self." College Composition and Communication 33 (1982): 140-47.

Rose, Mike. Writer's Block: The Cognitive Dimension. Carbondale: Southern Illinois UP, 1984.

Thomas, J.W., and W.D. Rohwer. "Grade-Level and Course-Specific Differences in Academic Studying: Summary." Contemporary Educational Psychology 12 (1987): 381-85.

Referencing works does more than merely acknowledge previous studies. The author, in the body of the article excerpted above, extends the scholarship by providing ways for educators to meet students' concerns and anxieties about writing. In other words, previous scholarship serves as an anchor for the article's writer and also as a point of departure for her own research. As you might expect, the literature survey is most common in journals that promote research. For example, it should come as no surprise that an article in the journal *Bioscience* (on "Ecosystem Consequences of Changing Biodiversity") should provide a reference early on to relevant research:

> Current extinction rates are 100–1,000 times higher than prehuman levels, and the expected extinction of currently threatened species could increase this rate by a factor of 10 (Pimm et al. 1995).

No matter what the field, the in-text citation is linked to a bibliography that gives the complete publication information:

> Pimm SL, Russel GJ, Gittleman JL, Brooks TM. 1995. The future of biodiversity. *Science* 269: 347–350.

The Argument

You will find that many of your teachers will require you to produce writing for the purpose of mounting an "argument," yet another distinct genre. It is important not to confuse the colloquial use of that term with the academic convention. Outside of the classroom, you might consider an argument as a heated exchange with another person (we would say, euphemistically, "words were exchanged"). But inside the classroom, the word *argument* implies much more: For one thing, it is usually written—in the form of an essay. That fact alone implies a level of formality that you need to be aware of. But beyond that fact are some important components of an academic argument:

- A clear statement of a claim to be argued
- Objections to the claim
- Rebuttal to those differing views
- Detailed warrants or evidence to support your claim
- Affirmation or rejection of the claim in the light of the evidence provided

Academic "proof" must rely on more than personal knowledge. It is usually drawn from scholarly texts (as part of your literature review, for example) or the subject matter that comprises the focus of your course, such as lectures and readings.

Scholars of rhetoric (the ancient study of spoken persuasion) provide additional tools with which to mount an argument. They might, for example, point to the importance of *ethos* in fashioning a good argument—in other words, the character and credibility of the person arguing the case. Or they may point to *pathos*—the ability of an individual to empathize with the audience and to create feelings of support. But do note that written argumentation raises the bar, as it were. Appeals to an audience's feelings alone usually won't be sufficient for academic argument: reason must be employed.

Here is an example of an argument, together with annotations provided by its author, Daniel Kies, a professor of English. Note that, as happens so often in the humanities, the argument is a response to a written text.

English Language Metaphorical Thinking

Daniel Kies

Introduction: identification of the problem.

In "The English Language Is My Enemy," Ossie Davis argues that English is inherently racist by presenting the reader with two lists of synonyms for the words *white* and *black*. The lists present clearly divergent sets of meanings associated with the two words.

White is associated with purity, cleanliness, and goodness. *Black* is associated with evil, dirt, and death. The differences in meaning suggest to Davis that the language is inherently biased against blacks. While the differences in meaning are undeniable, I suggest that the differences are due to ability of humans to think metaphorically, not racism necessarily.

The suicide rate in the Scandinavian countries is comparatively higher than the rate in the rest of the world and highest in winter. Horror films are typically set at night; think of *Halloween* and *Night of the Living Dead* to name just two examples. In fact, Freddie, a popular horror villain of late, most often appears to people at night, while they dream.

These two different facts share one thing in common—darkness. Being as far north as they are (right on the Arctic Circle), the countries of Sweden, Norway, and Finland can experience up to twenty hours of darkness each day in midwinter. Seasonal depression is a common illness there, and its effects on the individual's will to survive can be catastrophic. However, the Scandinavian nations are not unusual in this regard: seasonal depression is common in all latitudes that experience long winter nights, and the fear of the dark is a common human trait, as parents of toddlers all around the world will readily attest.

These two facts support a single generalization about us humans generally and Western (European-oriented) culture particularly: darkness represents the UNKNOWN while light (and vision) represents KNOWLEDGE. In other words, the psychology and thought of most Westerners portray darkness as a metaphor for the unknown (therefore the dangerous) and light as a metaphor for the known. A metaphor, remember, is the process of employing one concept to represent another concept.

In fact, those two metaphors of light and dark organize (and possibly control) the way we Westerners think about knowledge or the lack of it. Our language (and other European languages as well) is filled with expressions that show how our thinking about knowledge is organized by those two metaphors of light (and vision) versus darkness. Consider the following examples of the LIGHT (AND VISION) IS KNOWING metaphor:

- I see what you're saying.
- It looks different from my point of view.
- What is your outlook on that?
- I view it differently.

Margin notes:

Thesis (claim): the last sentence in the opening paragraph.

Evidence: facts about human reactions to the dark.

Second set of evidence: the metaphoric meanings associated with light and dark.

- I've got the whole picture.
- That's an insightful idea.
- She is a brilliant woman.
- The argument was clear.
- Could you elucidate on that?
- It's a transparent argument.

Similarly, consider these few examples of the DARKNESS IS IGNORANCE (literally a 'lack of knowledge') metaphor:

- It was a murky discussion.
- The discussion was opaque.
- I didn't follow his thinking; I'm still in the dark.
- Let's see if we can't throw a little light on the subject.

What those expressions teach us is that we Westerners metaphorically link *thought* with *light*, ignorance (and fear) with *dark*.

Objection: note the acknowledgment of validity of the opposition's perspective.

Granted, Davis might feel that I am evading his point by shifting the attention from the reality of racist language to some esoteric discussion of the psychology underlying some metaphors in the English language. Davis could even point out that many racist words are related to color and vision. The notorious *n* word has its origins in the Spanish word for *black*.

I will grant too that the language may indeed be inherently racist (and sexist). It does seem that the language has far more derogatory terms for minority groups and women than for the majority group and men. Modesty forbids me from writing examples here, but a simple "thought experiment" will illustrate my point: make a mental list of all the words that are deliberately insulting to blacks, or women, or any other minority group. Make a similar list of derogatory words aimed at whites or men. I find that the lists are unequally long: there are far more derogatory words against any minority group. To my mind, that is stronger evidence to suggest that the language may have an inherent bias.

Rebuttal

Yet the fact of the matter is that racist and sexist language has more to do with unequal power than it has to do with the meanings associated with words like *white* and *black*. For example, if you want to find out whose manner of speech is the most admired and is the prestige dialect within a country, simply find out which social group has the highest prestige in that country. There is a direct correlation between social prestige and linguistic prestige.

So when Ossie Davis looks at the enormous number of unfavorable synonyms associated with the word darkness and concludes that "The English Language Is My Enemy!" I do not explain that fact on the inherent racism that Davis believes pervades our thoughts. To me, that explanation of racism is both too simple and unjustified when one looks at the language in a larger perspective. Instead, I see the enormous number of unfavorable synonyms as a result of the way our minds organize our feelings about issues like KNOWLEDGE & IGNORANCE and KNOWN & UNKNOWN (the unknown is also dangerous).

However, do not misread me. Racism is a real issue in both society and language. One need only read the newspapers to learn of the growing numbers of hate crimes. One need only listen to the media to hear racial and ethnic slurs used thoughtlessly. Although Davis and I disagree about the origins of the unfavorable meanings associated with the synonyms for words referring to darkness, we do agree on an even more important issue: we must learn to control our minds and our tongues if we ever wish to control our destiny.

Conclusion: re-interpreting the original position in light of the new evidence.

Document URL: http://papyr.com/hypertextbooks/
engl_102/critique.htm
Last revision: 12/27/2001 13:51:18

In contrast to the essay, written argumentation in the laboratory sciences is likely to find its proof not merely in previously published studies but also in empirical evidence—the evidence produced in the laboratory (whether in the literal sense of that word or out "in the field") itself.

Grounding the Theory

1. Review an essay exam that you have recently taken. Pay special attention to the instructions given you by your teacher. Describe the teacher's expectations as to the genre of the essay. Then, turning to your own writing, analyze the various sections and their purposes.

2. I've been saying that genres follow certain conventions or rules. Let's test this theory out by looking at the following example of an abstract, a relatively brief restatement of the key points in an

article or conference presentation. Using the guidelines that I provided on page 263, write an assessment as to how successful the writer is at drafting an abstract. Take care to specify your reasons for thinking so.

Effects of Health Diagnosis, Environment, and Social Interaction on Cognitive Development of a Pre-term Infant

When people think of a pre-term infant, they tend to picture a tiny person that will be severely lacking in cognitive ability throughout his or her life. Past research has found that these pre-term infants are developmentally slower in basic communication and language skills compared with their full-term peers. For example, many of them have greater difficulties in achieving skills such as word comprehension and production or in the rate of acquiring new words. More recently, researchers have found that factors such as infant's health, enriched environment, and social interaction affect the chances of a pre-term infant developing at the same pace as their full-term peers. This longitudinal case study used a combination of direct observation, literature review, and professional assessments to assess the effects of these factors on the cognitive development of a pre-term infant who is eleven months chronological age (nine months corrected age). Results indicate that the infant's cognitive development was consistent with that of a full-term infant of the same chronological age. When using corrected age, as experts suggest, the pre-term infant's development level was above the level of a full-term nine-month-old infant. One limitation of this study is that the infant who was observed was relatively healthy at birth, received positive social interaction (along with early intervention), and lives in an enriched environment. Future researchers should explore the effects of physical and ecological factors on the cognitive development of neonates born with poorer health and develop useful strategies to help parents of pre-term infants learn how to optimize their infant's communication and language skills.

Working with an Audience

Just as you should consider the genre in which you write, so should you be mindful of the reader or readers to whom you are writing. What do your readers already know about your subject? What do they need to know? The answers to those and other questions will undoubtedly shape your writing, as you work to adopt a tone and a message uniquely tailored to engage and change your readers in some way. For academic genres, your teachers typically are the audience. They are likely to expect a level of formality conducive to reasoned work and a familiarity with the materials covered in the course. On the other hand, if you were writing a message on the official web site of the Back Street Boys, intended for fans of the group, you might produce something like this sketch of band member Nick Carter, ever mindful of the band's fan profile (young girls between 5 and 15):

Full Name: Nickolas Gene Carter

Height: 6'2"

Weight: 190

Hair: Blond

Eyes: Blue

Ideal Girl:

Honest

Loyal

Romantic

Independent

Feisty with great personality

Good heart

Natural, confident in her looks, and doesn't wear too much makeup.

Dream Date: A moonlit walk along the beach

The kind of detail that you choose to produce is meant to appeal directly to your readers' interest.

Of course, it is one thing to write for an audience naturally predisposed toward your subject. But let's imagine that your readers might not agree with what you have to say or, at best, may be indifferent to your subject. How useful will an understanding of audience be in such circumstances? Of course, you can simply plow ahead and ignore the expected resistance or apathy of your audience. But if you choose to write with consequence, you will need to take into account not only *your* interests but also those of your readers. For example, if you were preparing to write on the medical benefits of marijuana use, you would do well to consider your intended audience and to consider the probability that there may be some in that group who feel strongly that marijuana should remain illegal, whatever the circumstance. If you work with your audience, rather than appear indifferent—or even hostile—to it, you may stand a greater chance of achieving your ends. In that case, you might at least acknowledge the possible abuse of the drug and offer strict regulations on its use for medical purposes.

Let me emphasize this point: Understanding audience is important not for its own sake but for the purpose of working with your readers to produce genuine *consequence*. That consequence might include the alteration or qualification of your own point of view. Perhaps you had not planned on introducing strict requirements for the medicinal use of marijuana, but in doing so you might satisfy the concerns of readers who are concerned about the abuse of marijuana.

The following questions in the checklist below may guide you as you work with your audience. The last question reinforces the point that working with an audience may affect the presentation of your writing—from the words that you use to the structure of your proposals. If your audience expects you to use specialized vocabulary in discussing the globalization of the marketplace (like *global stratification*), you would do well to meet that expectation. On the other hand, if your audience is a lay or general audience, you might strive for less specialized language.

But how do you get to know things about your audience? One approach is locating materials that you believe are currently being read by that audience and examine them closely both for both form and content. That is the process used by those who are new to a knowledge community and who intend to publish work to be ready by members of that community. Usually, they read currently published works in the field and glean from them a knowledge of the written conventions and subjects valued by the community. In addition, you'll find that most scholarly journals have information for authors, which typically includes guidelines for preparing a manuscript suitable to the journal's readers.

Considering Your Audience: A Checklist

- ✓ **Who is your intended audience?**
- ✓ **What does your audience already know about your subject?**
- ✓ **What does it need to know?**
- ✓ **How will the audience react to your purpose?** With agreement? With resistance? With indifference?
- ✓ **What adjustments to your purposes are you prepared to make in responding to your audience's anticipated reaction?**

Grounding the Theory

---

1. Write an audience analysis of an article in the journal *Science* that tries to answer these questions:

   a. Who is the intended audience?
   b. Specifically, what kinds of knowledge are expected of the reader? Include everything from a consideration of technical terms to background knowledge and conceptual knowledge

2. Analyze the level of knowledge expected in one of your own course textbooks.

Writing with Purpose

We have explored genre and audience. Remaining is purpose, a key ingredient in writing with consequence. As we saw at the beginning of this book, writing with consequence commences with *inquiry*, with a motive to discover knowledge. That motive lends purposefulness to your writing, a quality that fuels your engagement as a writer and helps shape your project. But it's important to see the purpose of your writing as involving your readers' interests as well. Remember the point throughout this textbook: Your writing should be useful to you and to others. The fact that the writing that you do in school has the express purpose of achieving a grade or passing some standard of assessment does not negate the proposition. Your writing can achieve other purposes as well, purposes tied to the impact of your writing on your readers. A research paper required for your biology class might become a pamphlet, distributed in the community, on the dangers posed by lead in local drinking water.

When considering the purpose of your writing, the important questions to consider are those shown in the checklist on the next page.

Let's say that you planned to write a paper arguing for continued governmental support of stem-cell research, the process of using the cells of embryos in order to develop ther-

---

Considering Your Purpose: A Checklist

✓ What, specifically, do you want your readers to believe about your project once they've read it?

✓ What do you want them to do with what they've learned?

✓ How will your readers react to your project?

✓ What adjustments to the writing do you intend, in the light of readers' reactions?

---

apies for a variety of diseases, including Alzheimer's and Parkinson's. You've done your research on the procedure involved. Now you are expected to share your findings with members of your class, in order for you to gauge the impact of your findings on your classmates. In small group discussion, some classmates have expressed deep misgivings about embryonic stem-cell research, chiefly on ethical grounds (they've taken the stance that embryos are human beings, deserving the right to be spared such experimentation). Might your original purpose—to argue all out for government sanctioning of such experimentation—be shaped in some way by what you've learned about your readers? Without ceding your own position, might you at least acknowledge the strongly held views of some of your readers? Might you be content, now, with just presenting the argument on behalf of your view without hoping to win converts to your view? These are not easy matters to resolve but they surely deserve your attention, given your own and your readers' investment in the writing.

Grounding the Theory

1. Review the advocacy pamphlets included in Chapter 3. Analyze the intended reader for each. Describe the purpose of each document as that purpose relates to the reader. In other words, what is the reader supposed to do with the information provided?

2. Write about an experience in which you tried to persuade someone to adopt a certain perspective on a subject. What was your purpose, exactly? Who was your audience? What was their reaction? How, if at all, did your plan change as a result of your exchange with others?

Disciplinary Perspective: Thinking about Genre in Nursing

An Interview with a Teacher of Nursing

Dr. Roz Seymour has been a teacher for thirty-six years. Holding both a masters in nursing and a doctorate in education, Dr. Seymour believes strongly in the need for nursing specialists to know "how to teach, or better yet how students learn." Much of Dr. Seymour's efforts in the classroom are devoted to helping students understand the role of new technologies in the health professions and acquire the thinking skills necessary in order to effectively use the information those technologies provide. In this interview, Dr. Seymour reflects on the knowledge of various written genres that nurses must write in once they are in the position of giving and recording care as well. She comments as well on the genres whose purpose is to train students to think and act like nurses.

Q. Specifically what kinds of writing tasks do you have your students do—both in the classroom and in the clinical or hospital setting? I understand, for example, that nursing students compose care maps. What are they, exactly?

The genre of care maps

A. A care map is a plan for management of care for an entire illness-to-wellness trajectory for a client. It includes a segment related to managing the illness, a segment on maintaining the wellness and a segment on family struggle during the illness as well. It is also called an algorithm and looks a lot like a tree.

Q. What are your expectations for students when they do one?

A. The expectation is that it is in-depth, which means [it] goes beyond the first question and answer; it does not focus only on problems but also on what is good and how to make that better or at least keep it good. The expectation is that the student can predict where the person will be on the care map trajectory based on interventions which evolve from the plan and are directed toward specific outcomes that are the end of the care map.

The purpose of care maps

Q. What particular content-specific skills or practices do students learn from doing it?

Thinking like a nurse

A. They learn how to base decisions on evidence rather than assumptions (critical thinking), how to make legitimate inferences, how to synthesize a trajectory of care, how to solve problems, how to assess, plan, and evaluate the care they are managing, in short how to think like a nurse.

Q. Do you ever draw up case studies or case histories for students to problem-solve with? Please describe what you might consider a typical case study or history and the questions that you might pose to your students.

A case study for evaluation

A. A typical case which appears on their next exam is this one:

This case is the script of a taped end-of-shift (7A to 3P) report by nurse Elie Norman.

Here is the case:

Hiya guys. This is Elie reporting on the new patient in 51. He was admitted before lunch but I'm just now getting his stuff together. I am so tired today, I am just dragging around. Ah, well, let's see, this patient was in the ER for a few hours before coming up here. His family is floating around the hospital somewhere. They are quite the tribe, watch out for them. Let's see, his diagnosis is diabetes insipidus and he soars to the bathroom every time you turn around. I think we are supposed to watch his intake and output really carefully but you know I believe in self-care. I am letting him record it himself. I started assessing him and got some things written on the intake form, but I only have a few hunches yet. No one knows why he has this disease; the docs from urology are working him up. They wrote some orders that I think were processed; the lab should be getting his blood by now. One thing I do know is that he is scared. I filled in one column of a care plan dealing with his fears, but I don't have it finished yet. I will try to get that done before I leave.

Questions about this relate to assumptions made about Elie, assumptions Elie has made about the family, which statements you identified about Elie are inferences and which are assumptions. [Other questions include:] How will you validate this? If you were responsible for further assessment of the patient and his family, what questions would you ask the patient, the family, Elie? What problem, specific facts, do you need to know about diabetes insipidous to assist you in this case? Where can you find such information? and many more [questions].

Informed reports vs. legal documents

Q. I'm guessing that this case study is a teaching case only, rather than a case meant to reproduce a nurse's notes. But I'm curious, would an actual nursing log or nurse note be so casual in language and inference? I guess I am thinking about all those cases that I have heard of in which nurses' notes are brought into court as significant legal documents. What do you tell your students about the legal ramifications of their writing—and the need to be aware of a potentially judgmental audience?

A. One of the things they are supposed to identify is the lackadaisical manner of the nurse who is taping the report. It is, however, a shift report and will be erased and is not written, so it is legally quite different. Students are told a great deal about the legalities of written documentation and instructed on how to do it. I was wanting them to see this one as poorly done so we could talk about the differences between verbal to be erased and written legal documents.

Case Study
MAPPING PATIENT CARE

Traditional nursing care plans, used mostly these days as teaching documents in nurse training programs, require that students engage in the following activities:

- Collecting data from patients
- Interpreting that data
- Identifying nursing diagnoses
- Prescribing interventions and priorities or goals
- Implementation
- Evaluation of patient response

As demands on nurses' time have increased (due in part to the shortage of nurses), so have pressures to streamline the writing that nurses do. Computerization of forms and standardization of diagnostic language have combined as well to alter the nursing plan. Nevertheless, as one nurse educator reminds us, "a well-written care plan is one of the best ways nurses have to talk to one another about patients and guarantee continuity of care" (Susan Oterman, "How to make care plans work for you," RN 54 (August 1991): 19-22). As such, the effective mapping of patient care relies on an acute awareness of audience as well as purpose. Each nurse who attends to a patient must be able to discern the patient's condition quickly and accurately, and the care that is the ultimately purpose of the plan is appropriately delivered as a result.

Matching Audience with Purpose: The Case of Derek
Derek, an advanced nursing student, can attest to the amount of work involved in preparing care plans. During an interview,

he informed me that the research phase at the hospital takes "anywhere from two to four hours" per patient and another six to eight hours of writing at home to design the care plan itself. A process of revision then begins, and a relatively brief worksheet is developed that reflects the evaluation of patient treatment and directions for future treatment. It is this more streamlined document that leads directly to patient care.

Derek admits that he writes his care plans as if his audience (other nursing students with whom he is working collaboratively) knows absolutely nothing about the patient. That quality, as it turns out, is double-edged. On the one hand, it allows for easier transfer of information from student to student (and later, care giver to care giver) and produces a more individualized record of treatment.

But Derek's attentiveness comes at a price as well. Because the care plan requires that the student be highly selective in the detail provided and eminently practical in the prioritizing of patient needs, Derek admits to being challenged as to what *not* to include in his plans. Given the integral nature of the plan, Derek must make certain that patient history and nursing priorities match. In fact, as we shall see, the problem of including too much detail will mar one of Derek's care plans. Since the assessment, diagnosis, and treatment of patient care drive the writing of a plan, trivial detail inevitably frustrates the purposes of the document.

Understanding the Genre of the Care Plan
In the context of a nursing education program, the primary purpose of the nursing care plan, in its full form, is to instruct students in the use of the nursing process. (In the clinical setting, of course, the care plan is designed to communicate to other health care professionals and family members the condition and care of patients.) In the classroom, it is the teacher who reviews students' plans, offers suggestions, and comments on the effectiveness of revisions. As a teaching

tool, the care plan compels students to break down the nursing process into its distinct parts and in a prescribed order: assessment, analysis, planning, implementation, and evaluation. As given to him, Derek's task is to complete a form requiring that students provide the following information:

- Patient's significant history
- Reason for current admission
- Significant events since admission
- Nursing priorities
- An evaluation of those priorities
- A second day's worth of nursing priorities
- Medications
- Rationales for such medication
- Pertinent lab results and interpretations
- Nursing interventions and rationale

All information must be filled out before care is given. To formulate his diagnoses, Derek must use the accepted list of nursing diagnoses as given by the North American Nursing Diagnosis Association.

A nursing diagnosis typically consists of three parts: the actual diagnosis, factors contributing to the problem, and key symptoms. Precision is essential: Simply stating a patient's need is not enough. Derek's diagnosis, while lacking precision in the diagnostic statement, does provide a list of causes and symptoms for the patient's deficit. In at least one case, however, Derek combines two separate nursing diagnoses, nutrition and fatigue. For purposes of clarity, Derrick will need to focus on one diagnosis at a time. Other errors to look out for when formulating a nursing diagnosis are: confusing medical diagnosis with a nursing diagnosis (defining a medical ailment as opposed to articulating a patient need), using legally inappropriate language (employing language that is sloppy and actionable in a court of law), and redundancy (restating as cause what has already been stated in the diagnosis).

The care plan assumes a thoroughness and selectivity in the collection of data, as well as the ability to draw reasonable inferences from that data. Highly formalized, the care plan requires students to number their diagnoses and to refer to those numbers throughout the document. As you can see, a knowledge of the nursing care plan as a genre is an essential ingredient for anyone who goes about writing an effective plan. What is required is not only an awareness to write about (patient diagnosis and treatment) but **how** to write it.

Grounding the Theory

In this chapter, we've been considering the ways in which genre, audience, and purpose shape presentation. The following exercises invite you to reflect on all three aspects.

1. Locate an advocacy pamphlet. Evaluate its effectiveness, using the checklist on page 136.

2. The following is taken from a visiting nurse's notes regarding the treatment of a one-year-old child named Lia Lee, who had been admitted at the age of eight months to the ER with severe epileptic seizures. Lee's parents, who are Hmong, require translators in all transactions with health care givers. A sample from the visiting nurse's log:

> Mother states she went to [hospital] as scheduled for blood test, but without interpreter was unable to explain reason for being there and could not locate the lab. Is willing to have another appt. rescheduled. States infant has not had any seizures. Have finished antibiotic. Are no longer giving Phenobarb because parents insist it causes diarrhea shortly after administration. Mother states she feels intimidated by [hospital] complex but is

willing to continue treatment there. . . . Reluctant to give meds but has been giving Phenobarb & Tegretol but refuses to give Dilantin. State it changes child's "spirit" & makes face look different. . . . Each drug is in small compartment with appropriate day & time but medications gone from wrong day. (Fadiman, A. <u>The Spirit Catches You and You Fall Down: A Hmong Child, Her American Doctors, and the Collision Of Two Cultures.</u> New York: Farrar, Strauss, and Giroux, 1997: 49)

    a. Regarding the log itself, what characterizes the way the nurse writes up her day's entry?

    b. What kinds of information does she include? What might she be leaving out?

    c. Who do you think is her intended reader? How does that fact affect the content and language of the entry?

3. Review the case study given in the interview with Dr. Seymour. Analyze the study by asking and answering the following questions:

    a. What is the purpose of the case study as a teaching tool?

    b. How well does the detail support that purpose?

    c. What do you think makes for an effective case study (you may refer to Chapter 4 for more information on the case study)?

4. Do a survey of the various genres that you are expected to produce in your various courses. What kinds are they? What are some of the conventions that define each? What do these genres have in common?

For Extended Writing

1. Using the letter to the Secretary of Agriculture as your model (see pages 255–256), write your own letter to a public official, expressing your concern over an issue of significance to you and your community.

2. Identify a written genre in the public domain (like a film review, a celebrity profile, even a tax return). Describe the formal requirements. Then discuss the social and public uses of that genre.

Presentation in the Extra-Curriculum: Writing a Press Release

As we have seen, presentation of writing matters, whether the writing occurs in the home, workplace, or school. In all such writing, a knowledge of the genre, an awareness of audience needs, and a sense of purpose interact to produce the most effective writing possible. A case in point is the press release, a document intended to publicize an event or achievement of significance to an organization or community. Knowing how to write an effective press release requires in part a knowledge of the form itself, a fairly standardized set of features that includes:

- The name and address of the organization producing the release
- The date of the release
- A clear and bold headline announcing the product released or event publicized, followed by the phrase, "For Immediate Release"
- The text of the release itself, about which I will say more shortly
- Name, address, phone number, and e-mail of a contact person

The name of the group producing the release may be presented in the form of the organization's logo, which creates easy recognition in the reader. The date is essential because press releases are usually time-sensitive, with currency being essential. Headlines must engage the reader quickly. The content of the release follows the same conventions as newspaper stories. You need to cut to the chase quickly, providing details as you go. The general rule of writing a news story and writing a press release is this: Provide the most important information early and the less important material later (see pages 259–260).

Of course, the story that you have selected to publicize must be seen as worthy and interesting to your readers. As I have said often in this chapter, the purpose of a presentation is shaped to a considerable degree by considerations of audience as well as genre. In preparing a news release, you must not only have a grasp of the genre's required format; you must also ask, How will people respond to this release? What change will this release produce in them?

Here's a sample release:

FOR IMMEDIATE RELEASE

'Lil' Black Releases New Album On the Road Again with Willie Nelson Duet

Austin, TX—January 30, 2001 —'Lil' Black is back on the chart path with his second album released by Big Baby Records, Texas' hot new indie label. The Texas rapper, raised on the streets of Elgin, infuses his raw talent with a polished vocal style befitting a western rapper. The small cow town outside of Austin endowed this preacher's son with all the musical passion of a gospel chorus and the macho energy of a Texas cowboy.

'Lil' Black, aka Nathan Mackey, Jr., reflects his talent as a singer-songwriter in every danceable track of On the Road Again. He raps with legendary Platinum country singer, Willie Nelson in a memorable duet for which the album is named. Such guest artists as Devin, ESG and Too $hort and Lifestyl join the foot-tapping infection of the tracks. Catch the magic with numbers like "Throw Em Up," "I'm Digging You," "What Time Is It?" and of course, the inspiration for the album, "On the Road Again."

No stranger to collaboration with seasoned performers, 'Lil' Black has taken the stage with such musical luminaries as Master P and the No Limit family, Mystical, Too $hort, MJG & Eightball and the Texas Hard hitters, (Scarface, Big Pokie, ESG, Lil Keke). Two

'Lil' Black records were featured on the Texas Artist Top 40 Countdown, one of which was Number One for five straight weeks.

One of the album's first singles, "Look at Me Now," captures the story of 'Lil' Black's life, sweetly dedicated to his mother. Destined to set a new trend in rap and country music, On the Road again will capture your ear and your heart at the same time.

For information on 'Lil' Black's touring schedule and On the Road Again, call 281-827-5347 or e-mail: diamondsent@aol.com.

ADDITIONAL CONTACT INFORMATION:
Freddy or Lisa Fletcher
Arlyn Recording Studio
200 Academy Dr # A
Austin, TX 78704
(512) 447-2337

Taking a Closer Look

1. Review the sample release above. Describe who the intended audience is and how you came to that conclusion.

2. Following the format given above, prepare a press release announcing an upcoming event on your campus. On a separate sheet, describe who your audience is and how you have pitched the release to those who you are trying to reach.

Chapter 7

Action: Drafting, Revising, Editing, and Distributing Writing

Writing as Production

The steps we have discussed so far—from framing a question and surveying the literature to gathering new data, reflecting on the significance of that data, and deciding on the most appropriate presentation—inevitably lead to the production of the writing itself. By no means does the writing begin only when steps one through five have been completed. Actually, the writing begins at the very point of inquiry, in listing or freewriting to discover a writing subject. And writing occurs every step of the way thereafter, as you summarize and critique your research sources, devise surveys and other research instruments, and reflect on the significance of your findings.

That said, all the work you've done to this point would have little significance to others unless it is acted upon—"written up" and distributed. We now turn, therefore, to the steps by which we extend our writing beyond ourselves, the steps that lead to publishing our efforts. I am using the word *publishing* to refer to a form of *extension*, rather than the more limited sense of select publication by a third party (a publishing "house"). How do we get to the point of sharing our work with others? Let's first consider the process by which you present your ideas in draft form.

Drafting

An Overview of the Process

A *draft* is a full and sustained piece of writing awaiting revision and editing. This chapter divides the process of drafting into the following steps, each of which raises some key questions:

- Beginning well (What is a statement of thesis and where do I need to place it in my writing?)

- Building connections (What are transitions and what purposes do they serve?)
- Ending well (What is the most effective way of ending a piece of writing? Do I merely summarize? Or do I reach for implications and suggest areas that haven't been discussed?)

Drafting takes time and a tolerance for the messy work of composing your ideas on the page. Although you may already have your own drafting style and method, I might suggest the following steps:

- Find a place to write that is most comfortable to you.
- Set aside a good deal of time in which to work.
- Don't expect to produce a complete draft in one sitting.
- Assemble all the writing that you have done so far, including notes, outlines, and any freewriting activities.
- Review your purpose (as expressed, for example, in guidelines drawn up by your teacher).
- Begin by blocking your draft, using an *outline* (to be discussed shortly) or a *list* (discussed in Chapter 2), or simply begin writing as a way to discover a structure and meaning.
- Amplify or develop the points made in your outline.
- Whether typing on a keyboard or using a pencil and paper, generate as much writing as you can at a single sitting, providing plenty of detail.
- Since the goal is to produce a draft and not a finished product, plow forward, resisting the temptation to revise or edit your writing.
- Avoid premature closure: End when you think you've achieved your purpose but not before.

Moving from notes to a draft can be challenging, especially given the preliminary nature of note taking. Let's see how one student accomplished the process. Writing a paper for her introductory literature course, on character and theme in Alice Walker's story "Everyday Use," the student began by listing the characteristics of two key characters in the story, Dee and her mother:

Major Character Static

Dee: attractive, willful, ashamed of her family & home, selfish, moves on with her life & and now wants "things" of her mothers that represent her heritage

Major Character Dynamic

Dee's Mother: Uneducated, but hard working, proud of her physical strength, knows Dee is ashamed of her, wishes to look like Dee wanted her to: lt. skin, thinner, feels sorry for Maggie [Dee's sister]

The notes, while sketchy, allowed the student to begin to attach qualities to each character, as well as to apply some of the more specialized terms used in the course (*static* and *dynamic*) to the story.

In an early draft, the student worked to amplify the character sketches. Moving beyond merely asserting character traits, she drew from the story for supportive detail.

Dee is a self-absorbed, black woman who is returning home to visit her mother & sister. As she was growing up she treated her family with scorn. She seldom brought her friends home because she was ashamed to have them see the house she lived in. When she returns home, she has become "Africanized." Her clothing, her hair, her speech, even her name has changed. She is full of a false pride in her heritage and suddenly seems interested in her fam-

ily's past and in particular handmade objects around the house that she wanted no
part of before. She wants these objects
for herself to display in her own home to
use as trophies of her heritage. . . .

Dee's mother is a large, heavy woman.
She can work as hard as a man and seems
proud of it. She envisions herself as she
thinks Dee would like her to be. She loves
her daughters although she seems in awe of
Dee and seems to feel sorry for Maggie.
She is very down to earth and seems to accept what life has given her. I feel that
she is a dynamic character in the story
because although she admires Dee for her
strength and style, she does not allow Dee
to take the quilts that she has promised
to Maggie. She realizes that they are more
important to Maggie in everyday use, than
to Dee as symbols of her heritage. . . .

There is no attempt here to provide a seamless, polished
piece of writing. As we shall see, that process will occur during the revision of this essay. Rather, the student is more concerned with developing fuller portraits of the two women
than her notes provided; now she is referring to elements of
the story's plot. The student is writing in paragraphs—an important step in the drafting process, since it indicates awareness of form and of the reader's need for such breaks. Nevertheless, you may find it sufficient simply to produce a rough
draft without attention to formal concern, which may be
taken up later in the revising stage.

Beginning Well: Five Examples

How you begin your writing depends to some extent on the
matters of presentation discussed in Chapter 6: the genre in

which you are writing, your reader's expectations, and your own purpose. For example, a conventional essay for a course might begin to state a broad, critical theme, as does this introduction from an essay on the function of American slave narratives:

> Most living things are born with the instinct to survive. In fact, it is a law of nature that if a species does not adapt, it will perish. The early American slave not only faced the problem how to escape slavery, but how to stay alive while enslaved.

A marketing plan might begin, on the other hand, with a description of a company's mission and target audience, as in this example of a plan written for a publishing firm:

> The Group Publishing, Inc. (Group Publishing) is the publisher of <u>Artists in Business</u> magazine. The magazine, which has already printed an initial issue in July/August 1996 is directed at artists at all levels of business throughout the United States. The management of Group Publishing is targeting a total combined circulation of "Artists in Business" of 206,000 in year one, increasing to 310,000 by the end of year three. The magazine will be published bimonthly with increased press runs throughout the first three years. Sample distribution, organizational sales, and direct mail to targeted lists of artists will be utilized to build subscriptions.

A lab report in physics might provide a brief statement of purpose:

> Purpose: To locate a value of *pi* by using measurements of the circumference (C) and the diameter (D), taken from several circular articles, in the following equation $C = (pi) \times D.$

And an article for an online magazine on the use of paper as an entry to the Internet might begin this way:

They're building something enormous at a research park outside of Lund, Sweden. Like any concept that eventually becomes the standard by which imagination is measured, it started out small and grew as its creators came to understand the scale of what they were making. Now it's half as big as the United States.

Each example speaks, as it were, to particular audiences. The last, from *Wired*, begins rather indirectly, hoping to create some suspense in its readers, who are likely to be hooked by the vagueness of the opening. In contrast, the terse, first sentence of the physics lab report no doubt reflects the clean efficiency demanded by its readers and by the genre itself.

And yet each of these examples is so obviously a beginning, a point of entry for writer and reader. None of these, including the rather vague opening in the *Wired* piece, simply thrusts its reader into the middle of things. Each provides a place to begin, a point of departure. In the checklist box below are some suggested strategies for beginning your own drafts.

Building Connections

As you draft your writing, you will need to do more than simply accumulate material. You will need to build a structure.

Beginning a Draft: A Checklist

✓ Consider the demands of genre in which you are writing, the needs of your intended reader, and the requirements of your overall purpose.

✓ Conform to the format of your chosen genre, while establishing a link to your purpose.

✓ Provide some kind of orientation for your reader.

✓ Avoid laboring over the opening in an attempt to compose the perfect introduction (save that for the revision stage).

Experienced writers view their work as organic, with each part contributing to the whole. It's not that less experienced writers don't appreciate the interconnectedness of good writing; it is just such a quality that these writers are referring to when they commonly say, "The writing here really flows." We can all appreciate, at some level, the sense of being carried along by skillfully crafted writing that resonates with meaning. In part, our reaction to such writing is a function of our own interests and what we bring to the work, but I have to believe that good writing builds *connections* in ways that sweep us along.

Such connections, in fact, start at the level of sentence and phrase. These building blocks make possible the deeper connections of meaning. Writers build connections through the adroit use of transitional phrases and meaningful juxtapositions. In other words, they establish relations among ideas by setting up signs on the road and through clever manipulations of the signs themselves.

Let's take a look at how one writer is able to make such connections. In the following paragraph, drawn from the essay on American slave narratives mentioned on page 298, the writer uses various connective techniques. The words that establish connections are italicized.

> As a means of survival, some slaves defied their masters, *especially when* faced with physical punishment. Occasionally *this* meant death for the slave, *but*, at other times, shock and fear kept the slaveholder from retaliating. Sometimes defiance was *more* subtle. A hungry slave might find a reason or excuse to visit a neighboring farm *where* the slaves were better fed in order to get a meal, even *if* it meant a whipping upon his return.

Each of these terms signifies a relationship of some kind, whether of space and time (*when* and *where*), difference (*but* and *more*), or condition (*if*).

To assist you in establishing connections in your draft, consider using some of these terms to establish relations among ideas:

Causation: because, since, as a result

Time: then, after, while, finally

Similarity: like, similarly

Difference: but, however, yet, while, unlike

Condition: if . . . then, unless

Of course, it isn't sufficient simply to insert these terms. You must be able to bring ideas together in some meaningful and logical way. Take this paragraph, for example, from an article on the matter of why planets are round. Again, note the italicized words.

> A planet is round *because* its gravitational field acts *as though* it originates from the center of the body and pulls everything toward *it*. With *its* large body and internal heating from radioactive elements, a planet behaves like a fluid, and over long periods of time succumbs to the gravitational pull from its center of gravity. The only way to get all the mass as close to [a] planet's center of gravity as possible is to form a sphere. The technical name for *this* process is "isostatic adjustment."

The first sentence, like the gravitational pull of the planet being described, "pulls everything toward it." Certainly, connective words such as *because* and *like* and pronouns such as *it* and *this* enable the writer to express relationships among the ideas in this paragraph, but it's important to note that the thinking follows through on the promise of those words. Thought is structured, in other words. The same is true in this excerpt from an essay on the human genome project.

> The ultimate map of any organism is the complete sequence of *its* genome. Over the past several years, an international consortium of scientists has taken advantage of technical improvements in DNA sequencing and mapping technologies to generate a working

302 Chapter 7 Action: Drafting, Revising, Editing, and Distributing Writing

draft of the human genome sequence. The first step in *this* effort involved the construction of bacterial artificial chromosomes (BACs), *each* containing a stable segment of approximately 160 kilobase pairs (kbp) of the human genome.

Notice the progression of ideas from a general definition of the genome project to a detailing, in sequence, of the process itself.

Depending on the genre, you may be given a rather explicit structure to follow, a structure that will make it relatively easy for you to build connections. A lab report, for example, may require you to set up separate subheadings, such as

- Theory or hypothesis
- Methods or materials
- Results
- Discussion of results
- Conclusion

Of course, you will still need to understand what each section is calling for and to establish connections within each (for example, "The calibration involved dropping the ball from a known height and measuring the time it took to travel the designated distance. Doing this yielded two new pieces of information: travel time and the average velocity").

Ending Well

What should an ending do? All readers expect to be brought to an end of some kind, *with care*. No one wants to be taken on a journey and simply left hanging. Although the effect is not intentional, the work of inexperienced writers may often leave us hanging or, to use another metaphor, panting for

✓ What are the implications of the points that you have made?

✓ What can or should be done with the knowledge that you have provided?

✓ What has *not* been said in this paper?

breath: The piece is ended prematurely. The reasons are many: an inability to see things from the reader's perspective (what teachers call a "reader-based" perspective), a lack of interest in the subject, a loss of control over the work itself.

Ending a piece of writing well is surely as much of a challenge as establishing connections within the writing. In fact, the two activities are clearly related. In order to design an effective closing, you must have a sense of how it all works—how the pieces fit to form a whole.

That final question in the checklist box above points to a set of paradoxes behind all conclusions: The last word always belongs to others, and the search for truth is always complex and difficult (requiring a variety of perspectives, ongoing research, and thorough reflection). What this means for practical purposes is this: You should end your discussion with some confidence but with a certain degree of humility as well.

An effective closing, following naturally from all that precedes it, reflects the thinking done previously, while providing a reflection on the implications of what has come before. Many of us have been told in the past that a closing should repeat the major points raised in the piece. That advice is especially useful if your writing requires *refocusing*—the act of reviewing your main points could help sharpen your piece. But if we assume that your writing is farther along and nearer the point of distribution, you might view your conclusion as both summary and reflection. In the essay on American slave narratives mentioned earlier, the writer uses her final paragraph to meet both ends:

> In these ways and many others, slaves managed to survive. Thrown into an intolerable situation not of their choosing, they used their wits, instincts, and sometimes their faith in God to deliver them. They bore the yoke of inhumane treatment while managing to hold to their human qualities.

The conclusion certainly distills the argument made earlier in the paper (the slaves' situation was "intolerable," but they were able to rely on "their wits ... and sometimes their faith"). But it also speculates, although very briefly, on this profound truth: Despite being treated as less than human, the slaves held on to their "human qualities."

But what if you are writing in a genre other than an essay? How do you bring things to a satisfying end? If you are writing a lab report, the chances are that your conclusion will need to follow the accepted conventions for concluding a report:

- Restate the objective of the experiment and your hypothesis
- Describe the results
- Account for any unexpected variations in your data
- Indicate any uncertainties
- Assess the validity of your hypothesis in the light of the data
- Suggest areas for future experimentation

The following is drawn from the concluding section of a lab report:

> The random errors in the times and distances measured in the present experiments were about ± 1%. We used the range of possible straight lines that could be

drawn to fit the data in order obtain the errors given in equations 13 and 14. In other cases, we used the standard rules for combining errors. As noted previously, the measured values of P are systematically about 1% too high when P has values near P min. This result is probably due to friction at the bearing and not due to any fundamental limitations of the theory. Therefore, we can reasonably assert that this experiment demonstrates that the behaviour of a compound pendulum is in accord with Newton's laws of rotation.

Endings should teach us something. When writing with consequence, your conclusion should make clear the impact, both expected and unexpected, of your work.

Grounding the Theory

1. Describe your own drafting process. As if you are telling a story, write an account of what you do when you draft a piece of writing—step by step, including a description of where and when you write and your materials. How does your method compare with the approach described in this chapter?

2. Read the excerpt, which is the beginning of a marketing plan, given below. Evaluate the effectiveness of the writing as an introduction, using the guidelines suggested in this chapter. Remember to discuss what the writing is doing rather than what it is saying. In other words, spend some time discussing the writer's purposes early in the plan.

JavaNet Internet Cafe

1.0 Executive Summary

The goal of this marketing plan is to outline the strategies, tactics, and programs that will make the sales goals outlined in the JavaNet business plan a reality in the year 1999.

JavaNet, unlike a typical cafe, provides a unique forum for communication and entertainment through the medium of the Internet. JavaNet is the answer to an increasing demand. The public wants: (1) access to the methods of communication and volumes of information now available on the Internet, and (2) a place to socialize and share these experiences with friends and colleagues.

Marketing will play a vital role in the success of JavaNet. JavaNet must build a brand around the services it offers by heavily promoting itself through local television, radio, and print advertising. Marketing efforts are just beginning by the time a potential customer enters JavaNet for the first time. A strong emphasis will be put on keeping customers and building brand loyalty through programs focused on staffing, experience, and customer satisfaction.

Our target markets include:

- Students from nearby housing centers
- Business people from the downtown business centers and professional buildings
- Seniors from nearby retirement facilities

Focusing Your Draft

It's important to adopt a "reader-based" perspective when reviewing your own writing. Try to develop the ability to imagine being in someone else's shoes when reading your work. When you are in the process of drafting—actively generating words on the page or screen—it is terribly difficult to be able to achieve distance from the writing. Essentially, you are in the writer-based mode. Experienced writers manage to achieve both perspectives with a good deal of certainty and control, sometimes shifting back and forth throughout the composing process. This much applies to all writers, experienced or otherwise, when preparing a manuscript for distribution: We all need to make certain that the writing is focused, expressing the writer's intention, the demands of the rhetorical task (the assignment that prompted the writing), and the reader's expectations.

To acquire added perspective on your writing, try one of two approaches: (1) constructing a descriptive outline, or (2) composing a succinct and accurate abstract. Let's consider the outline first. While an *outline* can be extremely useful in jumpstarting a piece of writing (for example, in the case of blocked writers who put too much pressure on themselves to get it right the first time) or in planning to write under time pressure (mapping out an in-class exam), it serves its most useful purpose in helping to focus what you already have written. A descriptive outline, as the phrase implies, merely describes what is already written down; it does not attempt to add information to your work. It lays bare the relationships between and among the ideas presented, and it reveals the terrain of your argument by distinguishing between main headings and subordinate headings or points.

Constructing an Outline

Outlines, when constructed methodically and conventionally, are exceedingly logical. They operate on the principles of *parallelism, subordination, coordination,* and *division.* In other words, outlines typically present headings that are expressed in parallel form, with less significant subheadings placed beneath; items of equal quality and content are placed in comparable positions. All headings and subheadings must be divided in a logical way.

Outlines may be done in topic or in sentence form and may be relatively complex (with a variety of subcategories) or fairly thin, depending on your own requirements. Examples of a sentence and a topic outline follow; each is drawn from the notes and draft of the paper on Alice Walker's story mentioned earlier.

Sentence Outline

I. Dee is a static character.
   A. Dee has always treated her family with scorn.
   B. She is full of false pride, showing an interest in her family's past only for "show."

II. The mother is a dynamic character.
   A. The mother admires Dee for her strength and style.
   B. The mother eventually refuses Dee's request for the quilt, realizing that Maggie's own quiet strength makes her the appropriate owner of the quilt.

Topic Outline

I. Dee
   A. beautiful and confident
   B. selfish

II. The Mother
   A. Envious of Dee's confidence and beauty
   B. Recognizes Maggie's quiet strength

While useful (especially when little time is available to draw up a more developed outline), a topic outline often lacks the detail of a sentence outline and, as such, may not carry the benefits of a more extensive, sentence outline. Nevertheless, the writer of the above examples learns something important in either case. She learned that she had not yet brought together the various strands of her draft to form an integrated whole. Each section is discrete, without transitions and connective phrases. How might she improve the current structure of the paper? She might revise the outline to look like this:

I. Dee values the past as a fashion statement.
   A. She has pride in her family's heritage.
   B. But she does not see the usefulness of the past other than as a showpiece.

II. Maggie embodies the past.
   A. Less attractive than her sister, Maggie seems to have little going for her.
   B. Yet, in her quilt making ability and in her appreciation of the quilt's uses, Maggie has a closer link to her family's heritage and a selflessness worth rewarding.

III. The mother must decide whose view of the past is to be rewarded.
   A. The mother is at first charmed by Dee's confidence and beauty.
   B. Although uneducated, the mother sees through Dee's selfishness and rightly recognizes Maggie's selflessness

This new structure lays the groundwork for a more cohesive version of the draft. The writer can now go back to the writing and supply needed transitional sentences, using main headings as her guides.

Distilling a Draft into an Abstract

Equally useful as a means of focusing a draft is the abstract, which, as we have seen, is a distillation of a long work (see pages 263–264). Abstracts can alert us if we are verging off topic or assure us that we have, in fact, stayed on course. Like outlines, abstracts may vary in the level of detail and specificity provided, but, unlike outlines, abstracts ultimately must provide only the gist of an argument. It cannot reproduce the argument itself.

One way of composing an abstract is to take the topic sentences of all the paragraphs (containing the core ideas of those paragraphs) and move them into a brief paragraph abstract. Let's see what kind of abstract the paper on "Everyday Use" might produce.

```
There are three main characters in Alice
Walker's "Everyday Use." Dee, a young, at-
```

> tractive, self-absorbed black woman who is returning home to visit her mother and sister, is full of false pride about her heritage. Maggie, Dee's sister, is thin and shy, and feels her lot in life is God's will. Dee and Maggie's mother, a large, heavy, uneducated woman, admires Dee but does not allow her to take the quilts that had been promised to Maggie.

As we saw in the outline of this paper, the abstract lays bare the central problem with the draft: the lack of an over-arching and unifying idea. Each element of the abstract is only tangentially related to the other. Now, let's try to revise the abstract with the purpose of unifying the paper's argument.

> In Alice Walker's story, we are taught that, when put to everyday use, our heritage can help us understand and appreciate the past. Dee, selfish and willful, values the past as a trophy to be displayed. Maggie, thin and lacking confidence, appreciates nevertheless the everyday nature of her heritage—a quality that her mother honors by giving her the family quilt.

With this abstract in hand, the writer can return to her draft and begin to establish key connections among its parts.

Briefly, then, composing an abstract depends on your being able to answer these questions:

- What is the larger point that I wish to make?
- What evidence or subsidiary points have I brought to support that view?

■ Which of those subsidiary points carries the most weight and therefore ought to be represented in the abstract?

By their very nature, abstracts need to be succinct and cogent. When used for the purpose of focusing your writing, abstracts require you to strip your message to its essentials. In doing so, you may be better able to recognize any divergence from your theme and to foreground the essential aspects of your argument.

Sharing Your Writing with Others

Constructing an outline and composing an abstract allow you to gain perspective on your writing. Of course, sharing your work with constructive readers provides a similar shift in perspective. Writing with consequence, by definition, calls upon others to play a role in your written production. When you are comfortable sharing your work, seek out safe and helpful readers, giving them the necessary context with which to understand your purpose but also allowing your writing to stand on its own.

Sharing Your Writing: The Writer's Role

✓ Provide a clear and clean copy for your reader's viewing.

✓ Include the writing prompt or question that you are answering with your draft.

✓ Prepare to be flexible and, above all, to listen well.

✓ Ask for clarification, if necessary, from your reader.

✓ After your reader has completed her response, comment on what you have heard or read.

✓ Decide on whether to make changes, if any are suggested.

Sharing Your Writing: The Reader's Role

✓ Read both the prompt and the draft completely through before commenting. Grasp the effect of the writing as a whole before attending to localized aspects.

✓ Ask for clarification, if necessary, about either the prompt or any aspect of the draft.

✓ Listen attentively to whatever context and clarification the writer offers.

✓ Respond honestly and constructively to the writing, starting with the strengths of the writing.

✓ Respond in a precise way to any weakness in the work, taking special care to point to particular passages as examples.

✓ Respect the writer's purpose in writing and her ownership of the work.

✓ Conclude by recapping your assessment of the writing.

Grounding the Theory

1. Compose a sentence outline of the "Focusing Your Draft" section that you've just read. Then describe the process that you used in putting together the outline. For example, how did you arrive at the major headings? In other words, how were you able to distinguish the main points of the section from the less significant portions?

2. Write an abstract of a paper that you've already done for this or another class (preferably a draft, rather than a finished product). Describe what you learned about the paper from constructing the abstract.

3. Show a paper that you're working on to someone whom you can trust. Review with your reader the guidelines given above about sharing your work. Write a commentary on how the process of sharing worked. Was it successful? How do you know? If it didn't work, why not?

Revising

An Overview of the Process

Now that you have generated a draft and begun to sharpen its focus, it is time to revise. The word *revision*, from the Latin, literally means to "see again" or "look back." The process involves taking another look—a fresh perspective—on your writing and adapting the writing in order to achieve your purpose effectively. Most important, revision requires an attention to the shape of the writing, to the contours of the argument, as well as to the "deep structure" within the work.

Your choice of language—the very words that you use—and the tone that your language produces are connected with more global concerns: the point that you wish to make, the proper development of your ideas, and so forth. Think big and small when it comes to revising your drafts. For example, take time to consider both whether a particular word is exactly what you want and what logical relationship exists between two paragraphs. And try to regard your writing as organic: Like the various organs and tissue of a living creature, the components of your writing are dependent on each other for the success of the whole. With that in mind, I suggest a variety of strategies when revising.

- **Think metaphorically.** As you set out to revise, create an image in your mind of what the process involves. Is it like peeling an onion? Is it like sculpting a figure out of stone? You need a metaphor that will guide your efforts to revise. This may seem like a trivial matter, but actually it goes right to the heart of the matter. If you are unable to conceive of the process as a whole, you will likely be left picking randomly at the edges of your writing, changing a word here, a mark of punctuation there.

- **Review your purpose, your audience, and the genre in which you are writing.** Much may have changed in the drafting of your paper. Perhaps you've even changed your original purpose or an earlier emphasis. Perhaps you more fully understand the needs of your audience and the expectations that come from the genre in which you are writing.

- **Take the paper apart**. Try rearranging sections of your paper, from paragraphs to sentences and even to the words themselves.

- **Put it back together**. Did you come up with a new and more powerful structure? You may have reproduced what you started out with, and that is useful as validation of that earlier attempt.

- **Think proportionally**. How much space do you actually spend on the key points of your draft? Perhaps you need to reapportion the elements of your paper to accurately reflect your emphases.

- **Think structurally**. How effective is your opening? Have you established meaningful transitions between the sections of your draft? What do you really want to achieve in your closing?

- **Think syntactically**. The word *syntax* refers to the function and order of words within a sentence. Review your word choice. Do your words fit within the sentences that you've constructed?

Restructuring and Reconnecting

If revision becomes more than a matter of changing a word here or there—if, in other words, revision is seen as *restructuring* writing—it can produce ideas in powerful combination. A case in point might be the essay on Alice Walker's "Everyday Use." As we saw in her notes and in her draft, the writer failed to connect the various strands of her paper in a unified and meaningful way. We were left with discrete pieces of fabric rather than a whole quilt, as it were. But we have already seen, through a revised outline and abstract, the possibility of powerfully restructuring the paper to achieve

an effective purpose. Let's see how a portion of the same paper might read when subjected to the kind of revision that
I've been describing.

> In Alice Walker's story, we are taught
> that, when put to everyday use, our her-
> itage can help us understand and appre-
> ciate the past. Dee, selfish and will-
> ful, values the past as a trophy to be
> displayed. Maggie, thin and lacking con-
> fidence, appreciates nevertheless the ev-
> eryday nature of her heritage—a quality
> that her mother honors by giving her the
> family quilt.
>
> As she was growing up, Dee treated her
> family with scorn and thought little of
> its history or heritage. She was so
> ashamed of her house that she seldom
> brought friends home. In fact, when their
> first home was burned down her mother felt
> that Dee was so happy she could have
> danced around the flames. Now, when she
> returns home, Dee has become "African-
> ized." She seems interested in her fam-
> ily's heritage and, in particular, objects
> around the house that were made by her
> ancestors—objects that she had wanted no
> part of before.
>
> In contrast, Maggie had never rejected
> the family's past. In fact, pale and
> slight though she was, Maggie was known
> as a skillful quilt maker, carrying
> on through her practice the ways of her
> ancestors. . . .

What has actually happened here? What do the changes
in the draft signify? If we think of revision as attending to
"deep structure" and to the making of meaning, then what we

have here is a significant shift of thought. Instead of simply keeping Dee and Maggie separate (representing two types of characters, static and dynamic) and presenting a rather flat style, the writer, through juxtaposition of ideas (placing them next to each other), through subordination (inserting modifying phrases within the body of a sentence), and skillful use of transitional phrases (words and expressions that link the various ideas of the paper), the writer creates a sense of wholeness. We also have writing whose consequence is a product of its whole vision and whose energy is no longer dissipated by a lack of a coherent structure. This writer, in short, sees far more now—and has accessed, in a far more effective way, the power of Walker's story—than she had in an earlier draft.

Grounding the Theory

1. Review the progress of the Walker paper from notes to draft to revision. Describe the various changes that have occurred to the writing and to the writer's original purpose.

2. Revise a paper of your own from one of your classes. Describe the changes that you have made and the reasons why you have made them.

Editing

Once you have worked to focus your drafts, you will need to turn your attention to *editing* your writing, to identifying and correcting surface errors. But in doing so, you will need to take with you an understanding about error. Here are some important principles to consider:

- Not all errors are equal in their level of complexity and in their impact on the reader's ability to understand your writing.

- Errors often occur in patterns and, if they do, can most effectively be addressed as errors in kind. For example, you might notice a habit of using a comma as if it were a period (an error called "comma splice"). Recognizing such patterns allows you to focus on correcting such errors efficiently and effectively.

- Errors of grammar, mechanics, and spelling have a social consequence, serving for some (incorrectly, I believe) as indicators of a writer's general literacy and, even, intelligence.

- Errors of grammar, mechanics, and even spelling may occur in response to a writer's struggle to understand a complex rhetorical and cognitive task. In other words, a difficult topic might cause you to make sentence level errors (like spelling or punctuation errors) because you are concentrating on the difficult task before you. For less challenging assignments, such errors may be less likely, given that you are not "distracted" by the demands of the topic.

- Errors may reflect a lack of experience and knowledge of conventions rather than a lack of intelligence or insight.

When applying these principles, try using these strategies:

- Give yourself some time to focus only on editing for surface errors (punctuation, capitalization, spelling, and grammar).

- That said, keep in mind that editing such errors may change your meaning and may require that you revisit your intention in a particular phrase or sentence.

- Try to identify patterns of error (shifting or inconsistent use of verb tenses, for example, or confusion between "loose" and "lose").

- Prioritize the errors, putting most of your energies into those that are the most complex and, potentially, have the most impact on getting your message out.

Error and Writerly Intention

Errors of grammar, mechanics, and punctuation can be seen as distracting a reader from a writer's intentions. In other words, when errors do occur, they not only tell a reader that certain rules are not being followed (rules of spelling, for example) but they also have the potential of misinforming the reader as to the meaning and purpose of the writing itself. For example, among the most common errors of grammar (by both native and non-native speakers/writers in English) is an inconsistent use of verb tenses. The issue is more than grammatical since it goes to the logical or temporal connection between or among events—in other words, to the meaning that we intend to convey.

Grounding the Theory

---

1. Using a handbook as reference and paying special attention to matters of punctuation, describe the errors that you see in this passage and make the necessary editing changes:

   > I enjoyed reading the poem ballad of Birmingham, it was very touching to me. I can feel the mothers happiness and then her ultimate pain in the way it were portrayed. How life must have been in the year 1963 and how much pain and suffering those people must have endured and continued to cope with through the following years.

2. Edit a paper that you're currently working on in one of your classes. Start by doing an inventory of the kinds of errors that you've discovered.

Distribution

Preparing a Reflective Portfolio

It has become quite common in a variety of professions and disciplines for individuals to collect their writing within a

Composing a Reflective Cover Letter: A Checklist

✓ What are my intentions in each of the pieces represented?

✓ What challenges or difficulties did I face in expressing those intended meanings?

✓ Who are my readers? What do they need to know about my subjects?

✓ What patterns of error did I discern in working out my intentions?

✓ What significant changes did I make to my writing over time?

✓ What are my strengths as a writer? In what areas do I need to improve?

portfolio—as a prelude to distribution and presentation. Usually the creators of the portfolios highlight particularly strong pieces in such a sampling of their work. I recommend keeping such a collection of your own work, perhaps for distribution within a course or as part of a job application.

Something called a *reflective portfolio* is expecially useful. Chapter 5 described the challenges and rewards of reflective thinking, of being able to discern meaning through reflection. A reflective portfolio incorporates the meaning-making power of that process as you "recollect" the writing that you have done. A key component of such a portfolio is the inclusion of a cover letter (not unlike a cover letter you might send out to a prospective employer, glossing the work listed in your résumé). In that letter, you reflect on the items in the checklist above.

There is something so powerful in the retrospective gaze, the glance back over the work that we have done—from the perspective of having struggled to make meaning on the page. There is something powerful as well in capturing that struggle in language. For example, naming our errors is an important step toward eliminating them. The following letter, written to accompany a student's portfolio, illustrates the point:

December 12, 2000

Dr. Tinberg,

I was very happy with the draft of my letter. The topic I chose was one that I deal with everyday at work. I see how difficult it is to pay bills at the facility and how the residents at the facility become affected by this. When revising my final draft, I added a solution that may help the financial situation at the facility. Since Mass Health supports most of the residents at this facility, I suggested that the rates of support should increase. By increasing the rates of support for each resident, the additional monies could be used to better the situation indicated in the letter.

The next writing assignment that I chose to include in my writing portfolio was the class charter. I was very pleased with the outcome of my class charter. This was one assignment that I thought would be a breeze to write, but instead I had a very difficult time getting started. It took me a couple of days before I could think of a proper introduction. Once I got started, though, it came together very nicely. I did not have to make many changes for my final draft. I reworded some of the titles in the body of the charter and I also added a student right component to the section titled "Student Rights & Student Responsibilities to the Teacher."

The profile was my third choice in my writing portfolio. When I started writing the profile, I thought it would be an easy task. How wrong I was. I did not have a difficult time writing about my subject's life, but, rather, I had a difficult time incorporating details about her when she told me about herself. Trying to add more details in the final draft was also very difficult for me. I tried to add certain details in the profile, but I still am not satisfied with the results. I have a very hard time writing in detail, which is a weakness of mine and it is evident in this profile.

Lastly, the proposal is the last writing piece in my writing portfolio. I enjoyed writing the proposal. I think that many people are unaware of the terrible wages paid to childcare workers. When researching this topic, I could not believe the number of articles addressing this subject. I did have a hard time with the solution portion of my proposal. I think that the United Child Care Union may be a solid solution in resolving the problem with poor wages, but I am not sure how the general public could get involved in this. I tried to look into this by reading the various articles I found on the different web sites. The majority of the articles addressed only the roles of the childcare centers' workers, the centers' owners and their role in the union. I was unable to incorporate anything further in

```
my final draft other than what I had writ-
ten. I did make some changes, though, in
the Works Cited section. Regarding the
three sources that I used, I was able to
get only one of the authors' names. I also
followed our textbook's section on the
MLA format with on-line and electronic
sources.

Sincerely,
```

In her next writing course, or in situations that call upon her to write, this student may well acquire even greater control over her writing, since she is acquiring a vocabulary with which to talk about the writing ("incorporating details," for example, and thinking through the relevance of her writing for the "general public").

Preparing a Paper for Distribution

The process of bringing your paper to this point has been a complex one. From finding a question to editing your draft, you've been asked to engage in diverse ways of thinking and to acquire a considerable body of knowledge. Now comes the time to prepare your writing for distribution. Of course you've already given considerable thought to such matters as your purpose, audience, and genre (which are part of your presentation), all of which will work to enable your purpose. But what about such mundane matters as size of margins, the need for a title page, size and type of font? Those are considerations that call upon your attention as well.

With your specific subject area in mind, consult one of the various reference guides adhered to by particular disciplines and work areas. The American Psychological Association (for example) will guide you on where to put an abstract of your paper, if one is required. The APA will also suggest ways of labeling tables and providing captions for them. The

Modern Language Association (MLA) will offer guidance as to setting up margins, space, and indentations (the latter used for quoted material). Of course, both guides (as well as the Council of Science Editors' (CSE) format) will assist you in setting up a bibliographical list. (See Chapter 3 for more information.)

For professional writers, preparing a paper for distribution involves more than attending to matters of form. They need to have considered where the appropriate "home" for their article or book might be, a consideration largely tied to the subject, purpose, and intended audience of the piece. A writer may well ask: How large a readership do I wish to have? Who do I really want to reach? How much control will I have in shaping the final product? This last matter is highly complex, since it brings into play the relationship between the writer's purpose, the intended readership, and the economy of the marketplace (efficiently producing a work that will sell).

Disciplinary Perspective: Composing and Distributing a Paper in English Studies

An Interview with a Teacher of Composition

Richard E. Miller, an associate director of the Writing Program and associate professor of English at Rutgers University, has taught since 1987. He currently teaches a first-year writing course as well as a graduate seminar for teachers in training. He describes the trajectory of his research interests in this way: "I started out interested in popular culture and its use in the writing classroom; then I began to focus on critical and radical pedagogies; now I'm interested in administrative systems and humane practices for managing the labor of others."

Q. Please describe for me your "usual" composing process when writing a paper in your field. Describe the writing "scene," if possible, from the initial point of composing to revision and editing (and back again).

Revising extensively

A. My composing process has changed considerably over the course of my career. When I was in graduate school, I made extensive notes while reading, transcribed these into my word processor, created notebooks where I developed connections across the readings, drafted and revised, re-drafted and re-revised.

It's a different story now. As an administrator of a very large writing program, I now have much less time to spend on drafting and crafting my articles. And, too, the main writing I do is no longer research essays in the field, but rather memos, e-mails, grant proposals, pleas for help, letters to prospective donors, studies of and reports on how the writing program has changed as it has grown.

Writing to start conversations

Now, when I am preparing to speak at a conference or during an invited visit, I no longer work on getting all the words down on the page. I also don't think of an essay as a place to make a seamless argument. I think of my speaking, and of the writing that my speaking rests on, as the occasion to raise issues and start conversations (if not fights!) rather than close down such moments of exchange.

Talking points

My writing for talks, thus, now takes the form of an outline typed out in a big font and I just talk my way from point to point. I'm not tied down to a specific formulation or to getting every word read in the time allowed. Instead, I use the writing to help me shape my remarks to the audience and I respond to their reactions. For what it's worth, the response is usually quite positive: I'm repeatedly praised for how polished my presentation was, praise I never received when I actually had spent hours poring over every word. So, one way my writing has changed as I moved through the profession is that I've come to realize that I've become a better public speaker by reducing my reliance on the written word.

My writing of articles has changed in similar ways. I'm working on an article now that started out like this:

Princeton

Rutgers

Social entrepreneurialism

Writing the piece has involved moving the cursor under each section head and writing up mini-essays. As each section develops, the outline changes and the direction of the essay evolves. The piece moves between exposition of a problem, articulation of a polemic, and discussion of how to move in other directions.

Because of my time constraints, the product of my efforts is usually pretty disjointed. I then go back through and work on the transitions and on the overall shape of the piece. A third trip through is for cutting the piece down—they always need to be shorter—and cutting many of my sentences in half—since they are always too long. *Shaping and pruning*

Q. At what point do you solicit feedback, from whom do you receive that feedback, and what process do you follow in working with feedback?

A. I never seek feedback to what I'm writing until I've gone through at least the first two stages of the process I've described above. Usually, I wait till after I've gone through the whole process and can pass an essentially finished piece of work. I relied on feedback much more earlier in my career. Now, because of time constraints, I'm usually just finishing the piece before a deadline and end up just pressing the send button without having anyone read it ahead of time. *Seeking feedback*

The actual feedback that I get are on the ideas that most concern me now—program management, fund-raising, working conditions. I'm able to discuss these issues with some trusted colleagues; it is in the endless flow of this conversation that I find my ideas forming and that I can listen to the responses to these formulations.

The feedback that is most useful to me is less centrally concerned with my writing than with how I've organized my argument; feedback that seeks to direct me to other conclusions or to abandon my position doesn't tend to have much influence on what I'm doing. That is, I'm more interested in feedback that reads "with the grain" of my work; since I tend to be reading and writing against the grain of the profession, I feel that I can pretty much anticipate the objections to my argument.

I rely most heavily on my wife for feedback about my style and organization. She's got a very good ear and, since she's not in the field, she offers advice that leaves my ideas and my argument intact.

Q. What is the process by which you distribute your writing professionally? What I mean by that is, how do you determine who receives your writing, for feedback and for eventual publication?

Distribution

A. Since I am employed by a Research I institution, my early decisions about where to publish were made for me: My book had to be placed at a first tier university press and my articles had to appear in the field's two flagship journals—*College English* and *College Composition and Communication*. While I was initially troubled by these requirements, I am now glad that I had to work within them, as this forced me to get my writing before less familiar audiences than I was accustomed to writing for.

Q. What should novice writers know about the action of composing and distributing writing in your discipline?

Genre

A. I've taught a writing seminar for graduate students twice, and each time the members and I have been struck by how little preparation future members of the profession receive for doing the kind of writing that their professional careers will depend on. The students I've worked with are unfailingly intelligent, generous, hardworking; they all write beautiful seminar papers that demonstrate their abilities to close-read a text and to work with the dominant paradigms of the day. What we spend the seminar doing is studying writing that is powerful in the academy and what we discover is that this writing rarely subscribes to the form of a seminar paper. We then work together to generate a formula that describes the writing they most admire. Inevitably, this writing assumes some version of the following form:

- It defines a conflict.

Rather than resolve this conflict, the writing seeks to reframe it, thereby providing other ways of seeing the problem.

- The writing makes new thoughts possible.

The standard form of the seminar essay, on the other hand, and of most scholarship, involves exposing the failures of some established position. In other words, most of the writing is largely adversarial. My students readily admit that they don't learn much by producing such writing and most of them don't much enjoy reading such writing.

I would say that even though the pressures to publish are constant, there's good reason to spend time on thinking about how to publish material that will get read. The way to do this, I believe, is to use your writing to teach you what you don't know rather than as a soapbox for espousing your insights or a window into your classroom. There are a lot of classrooms out there and a lot of teachers: you share much in common with your readers in the field. How can you present them with something they don't already know? That's the challenge, and the way to meet that challenge is to allow yourself to question your own pieties throughout the writing process.

Writing as learning

Taking a Closer Look

1. Ask a classmate if you can read his or her paper for the purpose of peer review. Establish a rubric (a scale for evaluation and a list of

criteria), creating your own template to be used with your review. Finally, write a letter to the classmate offering feedback and advice.

2. Ask your school's reference librarian for the titles of three to five professional journals. Perusing a sample issue from each journal, try to answer the following questions: How many use peer review? How many use "blind" or anonymous reviews? Finally, write down your own thoughts as to the purpose of peer review.

Case Study

REVISION AS MEANING MAKING

Kathy's Background

Kathy, a fifth-semester speech and language pathology major with a minor in English, didn't know what to expect when she enrolled in an introduction to literature course, although she knew that she had a "passion for writing." She quickly discovered, however, that she had entered unfamiliar terrain. Her first assignment in the course was to write a "500-word essay on a short story" of her own choosing. Up to this point, Kathy had written papers focusing on her own experience. Although she had written a research paper for the required composition course, she had apparently little experience engaging a work of literature and felt unprepared. What is an essay exactly? she asked herself. In any event, she chose to write about Isaac Singer's story "Gimpel the Fool," which she enjoyed very much. She proceeded to draft her paper.

The Draft

The draft begins in this way:

> Gimpel the Fool by Isaac Bashevis Singer
>
> This is a story written by Isaac Bashevis Singer. He was born in 1904, was born in Poland, is a son of a rabbi and grows up in the Jewish ghetto in Warsaw. In

```
1935, he went to New York and became a
journalist. He wrote Yiddish soap opera
on a radio station. He is known as the au-
thor of many volumes of short stories,
children books, the play Yentl and three
volumes of autobiographies. He died in
Florida in 1991.
     Gimpel the Fool takes place in Frampol
and is told in the first person. This
story is about a man who, in his younger
years, is taken advantage of by his
peers. . . .
```

Kathy goes on to retell the plot of the story in considerable detail.

It is only at the very end of the paper that Kathy begins to move beyond summary, finding a moment when she enters the paper: "To try to understand how someone can be made a fool of all his life and not judge those who ridicule him is difficult. He must be a very rare and special person." And yet nothing is made of this insight. In effect, she is not able to carve out a thematic approach or to focus the paper around a central idea (her teacher's feedback read "some editing and clearer central idea needed").

Confusing Revising with Editing

Not helped by the vagueness of her teacher's initial instructions and subsequent feedback, Kathy proceeds to work on her piece. Unfortunately, most of the changes that Kathy makes to the writing are at the level of words (editing), when her most pressing need is to reconceptualize the paper and think structurally (revising). Here is a sampling of the changes Kathy makes:

```
In the morning, he decides deciding not to
go through with it, and takes he took the
loafs of bread and digs dug a hole and
buries buried them. As he is burying the
```

~~loafs~~ ~~h~~<u>H</u>is apprentice appear~~s~~<u>ed</u>, and asked~~s~~<u>ed</u>, "What are you doing, boss~~?~~" ~~Gimpel indicates never mind~~<u>He stated, I know what I am doing.</u> ~~and he knows what he is doing.~~

The changes represent some skillful editing, including the inclusion of a subordinated phrase ("deciding not to go through with it"), and an appropriate use of direct speech ("He stated, I know what I am doing"). To this extent, Kathy is responding to the teacher's suggestion to edit her paper more carefully.

The problem, however, is that Kathy apparently regards such local changes as sufficient. Her revised draft is full of such editing changes but does not begin to address the conceptual problem in the paper: the lack of an organizing or controlling idea.

Thinking Structurally

With additional guidance (seeking the feedback of tutors at the college's writing center and from friends), Kathy might have begun to think structurally, a key ingredient of effective revision. The checklist box on the next page explains the process Kathy needed to follow.

The most significant change that Kathy made to her draft was to import a *thesis* into her essay early and to recast the title of her paper (her nondescriptive title from the early draft became, in the later draft, "Appearance of Reality of Being a Fool"). Most of the other changes made were at the level of word and phrase, perhaps suggesting the order of concern in the teacher's terminal comments. The paper's thesis, which Kathy moves to the second paragraph of the new draft at the urging of her teacher, remained embedded in the following:

You cannot help but feel sympathy as well as empathy for Gimpel. To try to understand how someone can be made a fool all his life and not judge those who are the one's [sic] who ridicule him is diffi-

Revising: A Checklist

✓ **Think conceptually.** What important lesson about the human condition did you take from this story?

✓ **Take the paper apart.** What sections of your draft seem to teach or confirm that lesson? What sections have little relationship to that controlling idea?

✓ **Put the paper together again.** How does the new arrangement read, now that you have eliminated the extraneous material? What needs to be included that isn't yet in the paper?

✓ **Think structurally.** How successfully are the sections of the paper connected to each other? Where and what kind of transition do you need to build?

```
cult. He must be a very rare and special
person. He never chastises any one of the
people who have mistreated him through
the years.
```

Kathy does not quite grasp the paradox implicit in the title of her new draft and Singer's own concern in the short story— that a "fool" may indeed be a wise man. She is close in that second paragraph and in the first sentence of her final paragraph ("He is a very remarkable person to be able to give forgiveness to the people who had mistreated him throughout his life"). Revision calls upon a writer to *make meaning*, which is at the heart of interpretation. Kathy, in the end, is unable to produce extended interpretative writing.

What might such a paper have looked like? The paper might well have begun in this way:

```
In his short story, "Gimpel the Fool,"
Isaac Bashevis Singer confirms two old
sayings: "things are not always what they
```

seem" and "people never change." In the
character of Gimpel, Singer presents us
with a man whom everyone regards as a fool
but who, in adversity, achieves a degree
of compassion and understanding that his
fellow villagers would do well to imitate.
He never chastises any one of the people
who have mistreated him through the years.
As a result, Gimpel becomes a moral barom-
eter of sorts: we judge others in the
story based on the ridicule that they heap
on him. He sets a standard that too often
they do not meet.

    Gimpel discovers, early on in the
story, that he can trust no one. Villagers deceive him for their own pleasure.
His wife, he discovers, has been unfaithful to him. A genuine fool would pay no
heed to these insults. However, Gimpel decides to take action: he will believe no
one. . . .

In shaping the essay in this way, Kathy would be saying
to her reader: I have something new to say about the text or
story at hand. As Richard Miller observes, that is a significant
hurdle to jump over. Rather than say, I have nothing to add to
a published author's work, and so I will merely recapitulate
the plot, she ought now to be saying, I have an interpretation
to share with others: in other words, I can make meaning and
not merely reproduce what others have given me.

Grounding the Theory

1. Interview two classmates to discover the process they use to draft,
    revise, and edit their work. Describe the similarities and differ-
    ences in the two accounts.

2. Using a database described in Chapter 3, locate and read an interview of a writer in which that writer discusses the drafting, revising, editing, and publication process. Describe what you have learned and, perhaps, note the difference between this account and your classmates' stories.

3. Create a portfolio of a selection of your best written work from the previous semester. Write a cover letter reflecting on the reasons that you have chosen those works.

4. Review Kathy's case study. Describe a writing experience that you've had in which you've struggled to understand the purpose or genre.

For Extended Writing

1. Using the Tracking Changes feature of Microsoft Word (use the Help index in Word to find out how to use this feature), keep tabs of the changes that you make in revising and editing your writing for a course. Describe the scope and purpose of the changes.

2. Write a sharply detailed description of your own "writing scene." Patiently lay out for your reader the setting in which you usually write and the modes or instruments you use.

Revision in the Extra-Curriculum: Peer Review

Writers who publish for professional journals (regardless of the discipline) must have their work undergo *peer review*, in other words, have their work read and evaluated by members of the profession to which they belong. Usually, reviewers are long-standing and respected members of a profession, whose experience both as contributors to journals and longtime readers give them strong qualifications with which to evaluate their peers' work. Reviews are often "blind," meaning that reviewers' names are withheld from the author in order to re-move the possibility of conflicts of interest and overly subjec-tive judgments. Editors of journals use reviewers' comments as the basis for their final judgments as to the quality of a sub-mission. Peer review typically carries a great deal of weight with those editors.

It is a mistake to view peer review as merely "gatekeep-ing" (deciding which manuscripts are worthy of publication and which are not). Peer review helps in significant ways to-ward shaping a manuscript, providing the author with in-valuable feedback. In other words, peer review implements, in the extra-curriculum, the view stated earlier in regards to your own writing: Writers require constructive feedback from real readers in order to write with consequence.

Guidelines for reviewers vary according to journals and disciplines. Nevertheless, the following example of a re-viewer's rubric gives you some idea of what is required of reviewers:

> Please rate the enclosed manuscript from one to five (five being the highest) in the following areas. Feel free to include a comment to explain your judgment. You may also write a letter directly to the author.
>
> - Style: Is the writing purposeful and clear?
> - Currency: Is the subject current?
> - Appropriateness: Is the writing appropriate in style and content for the journal's readers?
> - Significance: Will this manuscript add to what is already known about the subject?

Despite localized differences, reviews typically have these three components:

- A reference to the major points of manuscript
- An affirmation of what is useful in the piece
- Areas for further development

Sometimes reviewers (anonymously) take the time to write to authors directly. In those cases both authors and reviewers can clearly be seen working collaboratively. In this example of a letter to the writers of a manuscript, the reviewer takes pains to set the right tone for a collegial and constructive feedback:

> First of all, I want to thank you both for putting a spotlight on a neglected sector of higher education (the community college) and for providing a useful theoretical perspective from which to view the work done at the two-year college. Although more and more published scholarship and research on community colleges has become available (I'll recommend some works shortly), you are right when you observe that the "vast majority" of scholars in our field remain "blind" to work done at the community college. For many of us who teach at the community college, opening the field up to include such research is a work in progress.
>
> Let me also say that you've represented the rhythm of the two-year college quite accurately: students and (here I would disagree with you) and faculty are caught "between" places. You might revisit what you say about faculty, however, perhaps by looking at representations of community college faculty done by those faculty themselves: Given the course load (typically five sections a semester) and committee assignments and advisement responsibilities, faculty are rarely in their offices outside of office hours. Most faculty at the community college have chosen to work there and have embraced the mission of the institution (about which you need to say so much more). Most do not attempt to build shrines to the academy within those office spaces, as you suggest. I applaud you for interviewing faculty as part of your research but I am astonished that you have come away from

such interviews with what seems to be a view of faculty as privileged and distant.

Which brings me to another omission in your article. So much of what you say about the shifting roles of students at the community college applies to four-year institutions as well, especially state colleges and universities. In fact—and you are aware of this, I believe—the counter "space" throughout this essay seems to be the privileged space typified by prestigious private schools and colleges. Most students require more than four years to obtain a bachelor's degree and do so at public institutions.

I am very much appreciative of the view that you provide near the end of the article: positing a "third space." In fact, I would like to see that point highlighted much earlier in the piece, as a counter-weight to the skepticism regarding two-year college life and work. If I understand you properly, community colleges are compelling all of us to rethink the "situated" nature of learning. Our students belong to a variety of communities, as do we. The comprehensive mission of community colleges aims to map out that very space you mention: to import the academic to lives outside the classroom and to bring the world of work and play into the classroom. In my (admittedly, partial view), community colleges are expanding the borders of the academic (rather than, as stereotypically represented, diluting the academic with vocational and technical training).

Finally, let me suggest that you add to your list of references published works that focus directly on the spatial politics of the community college: Keith Kroll and Barry Alford, ed. *The Politics of Writing at the Two-Year College;* Mark Reynolds, ed. *Two-Year College English;* Nelson Grub and Associates, *Honored But Invisible;* Ira Shor, *Empowering Education,* as well as an issue of *College English,* which Shor edited in the 1970s and which focused on two-year college English instruction.

I want very much to see this essay published. Good luck.

The care and concern shown by the reviewer here toward the writing dramatize the central idea of this text: that writing matters. It matters a great deal to this reviewer; it is clear to what extent the reviewer has vested himself in the subject of the manuscript reviewed. Although we do not read the manuscript under review, we can nonetheless assume a similar investment on the part of the author to the task at hand. That, in the end, is my point. Writing is a serious business, capable of provoking serious consequences—for both readers and writers.

Taking a Closer Look

1. Take another look at the comment to the author given above. What objections does the reviewer raise about the article? What suggestions, if any, are given for revision? Finally, what do you think are the underlying reasons for peer review in the first place?

2. Share an example of your own writing with a classmate. Try to write a constructive review following the guidelines given for sharing writing on page 312.

CREDITS

Chapter One

Page 20   From S.I. Hayakawa, *Through the Communication Barrier.*
           © Estate of S.I. Hayakawa. Used with permission.
Page 21   From Sigmund Freud, "Libidinal Types." Reprinted by permission of Robert Bernheim, The Estate of A.A. Brill.
Page 24   "Disabled Golfer Casey Martin Wins Rights to Ride in Golf Cart at PGA Events." © 2001 Associated Press. Reprinted with permission.
Page 33   © 2000 Boy Scouts of America

Chapter Two

Page 51   "On Societies as Organisms," © 1971 by The Massachusetts Medical Society, from *The Lives of a Cell* by Lewis Thomas. Used by permission of Viking Penguin, a division of Penguin Putnam Inc.
Page 49   From Margaret Talbot, "The New Counterculture," *Atlantic Monthly*, (November 2001). Copyright by Margaret Talbot.
Page 60   Susanne Ziesmann, Enza McCauley, & Dr. Susan B. Piepho from www.curi-inc.org, "What's Under the Kitchen Sink?" © 2001. Reprinted by permission of the authors and The College University Resource Institute.

Chapter Three

Page 79   From I. Wilmut et al., "Viable Offspring Derived from Fetal and Adult Mammalian Cells" *Nature*, Vol. 385 (27 Febuary 1997): 810–813. © 1997 Macmillan Magazines Ltd. Reprinted by permission.
Page 93   From Steven Pinker, *How The Mind Works*, 284–287. © 1997 by Steven Pinker. Used by permission of W.W. Norton & Company, Inc.
Page 111   Daniel Collins & Robert Sutton, "Rhetoric as Commitment: Ethics and Everyday Life," *Teaching English in a Two-Year College*, Vol. 29 (2001): 45. © 2001 by The National Council of Teachers of English. Reprinted by permission.
Page 126   Kristen Leutwyler, "Protecting the Nation's Water Supply" *Scientific American*, (29 Oct. 2001). © 2001 by Scientific American, Inc. All rights reserved. Reprinted with permission from www.sciam.com/explorations.

Chapter Four

Page 143   Steven Spilatro, "Fermentation Rates in Presence of Different Types of Sugar" from a paper titled "Yeast on the Rise." Used with permission.

Page 143   Steve Spilatro, "Rate of Respiration and Presence in Different
            Amounts of Sugar" from a paper titled "Yeast on the Rise."
            Used with permission.
Page 144   Francine Garcia-Hallcom, "An Urban Ethnography of Latino
            Street Gangs" from www.csun.edu. Reprinted by permission
            of the author.
Page 145   From Harvey Blume, "Reverse-Engineering the Psyche" Steven
            Pinker. *Wired,* (March 1998). © 1998 Harvey Blume. Reprinted
            by permission of Conde Nast, Inc.
Page 151   Tom Barnwell, "Computer Enhanced Education Program"
            © 1994–1997. Reprinted by permission.
Page 157   D. Poole, "Student Participation in a Discussion-Oriented
            Online Course: A Case Study," *Journal of Research on Com-
            puting in Education,* Vol. 33, No. 2 (Winter 2000): 162. Copy-
            right © 2000 ISTE (International Society for Technology in
            Education), 800.336.5191 (U.S. & Canada) or 541.302.3777
            (int'l'). iste@iste.org, www.iste.org. All rights reserved.

Chapter Five
Page 210   From Richard A. Pence, "Understanding Sources, Citations,
            Documentation and Evaluating Evidence in Genealogy."
            © 1998 Richard A. Pence. Reprinted with permission

Chapter Six
Page 258   Susan Milligan, "House Votes for Human Cloning Ban" *Boston
            Globe,* 31 July 2001. © 2001 Globe Newspaper Co. Used by
            permission of the publisher via Copyright Clearance Center.
Page 260   "Face to Face on Race" *Boston Globe,* 1 Aug. 2001. © 2001
            Globe Newspaper Co. Used by permission of the publisher via
            Copyright Clearance Center.
Page 263   From Robert Wahler et al., "Coregulation of Balance Between
            Children's Prosocial Approaches and Acts of Compliance,"
            Journal of Clinical Child Psychology, Vol. 30, No. 4: 473–478.
            © *Journal of Clinical Child Psychology.* Used by permission of
            Lawrence Erlbaum Associates.
Page 272   Daniel Kies, "Metaphorical Thinking" © 1995, 2001 Daniel
            Kies. All rights reserved. Used with permission.

Chapter Seven
Page 305   Palo Alto Software, "Executive Summary." © 2000 Palo Alto
            Software, Inc. Used with permission.

Photographs
Page 41   From the Collections of Henry Ford Museum & Greenfield
            Village.
Pages   Reprinted by permission from *Nature* (Vol. 385): 810–812
81,83   copyright 1997. Macmillan Publishers Ltd.
Pages   Copyright Corbis Images.
133–134

INDEX

Abbott Laboratories Summer
  Internship Program, 141
ABI/Inform, 120
Abstract
  distilling draft into, 307,
    309–310
  of editorial, 264
  research paper, 180, 263–264
  scientific, 263–264, 261
Abstracts in Anthropology, 118
Academic essay, 17, 327
  thesis statement, 297–298
Academic genres, 262–277. *See also*
  Genres
  abstract, 180, 261, 263–264
  argument, 271–277
  audience in, 277–278
  critical annotated bibliography,
    265–266
  essay, 17, 297–298, 327
  essay exam, 266–270
  lab report, 17
  literature review/survey, 110–111,
    180, 182, 187–188, 261, 270–271
  nursing, 282–289
  scientific paper, 17
Academic proof, 271
Accreditation, 100
Accuracy, evaluating, 101
Achebe, Chinua, 38
Action, 9, 294–337
  distribution, 318–323
  drafting, 18–20, 294–305
  editing, 18–20, 316–318, 328–330
  in English studies, 332–333
  focusing your draft, 306–312
  learning, reflection and, 217–218
  peer review, 330–337

revising, 18–20, 312–316, 221,
  331, 328–333
writing as production, 294
Advocacy pamphlet, 2,
  129–137
  checklist, 136
Alford, Barry, 335
Algorithm, 283
Allied health, 8
  types of questions, 10
Alternate hypothesis, 183
"American Geographies, The," ex-
  cerpts, 104, 105
*American Historical Association
  Guide to Historical Literature,*
  196
American Memory project, 196
American Psychological Association
  (APA)
  citation style, 112, 113–114, 116,
    265–266
  informed consent guidelines,
    181
  paper format, 322–323
Americans with Disabilities Act
  (1990)
  Casey Martin and, 24–27, 78
  text of act, 28–32
American Water Works Association
  (AWWA), 126
American Water Works Association
  Research Foundation
  (AWWARF), 126
Analytical Abstracts, 119
Annotated bibliography, 17, 57, 58,
  265–266
Annotating, 49–54
Anthropological Index, 118

Anthropology
  bibliographic indexes, 118
  observation in, 153
Anti-Semitism, 206–207
Ants, 51–52
Appendix, 181
  sample, 193–195
Aquaculture, 8
Argument, 271–277
  parts of, 271
  understanding contours of, 89–98
Art
  bibliographic indexes, 116
  observation in, 153
Artificial intelligence, 145, 146
Arts, the, 7
Associated Press, 24
Astronomy and Astrophysics Abstracts, 119
ATP Tour, 24–27
Audience, 16–18, 19, 48
  in academic genres, 277–278
  checklist, 279
  credibility and, 99, 100
  matching with purpose, 285–288
  pathos and, 272
  presentation and, 278–279
  researching, 280
  reviewing, 313
  understanding, 231, 254–257
  working with, 277–280
  writing prompt and, 58
Author Index to Psychological Index and Psychological Abstracts, 118
Authority
  in biology, 120–129
  evaluating author's, 99, 272
  referring to key work and, 103
  of Web sources, 100
Author-year system of citation, 114, 125

Bar graph, 142–143
Barrow, Clyde, 41

Bees, 52–53
Belenky, Mary, 5
Bennett, John, 121–123, 124
Berthoff, Ann E., 75
Beyond a reasonable doubt (BARD), 210–211
Bias
  author, 66, 99, 101
  awareness of own, 62–63
  cultural, 100
Biased questions, 150
Bibliographic indexes, 116–120
Bibliography, 111, 261, 270–271
  annotated, 17, 57–58
  critical annotated, 265–266
Biography Index, 117
Biological Abstracts, 119
Biology, 8
  action in, 19
  bibliographic indexes, 119
  interview with teacher of, 121–123
  observation in, 153
  presentation in, 17–18
  referencing sources in, 112, 123–129
  reflection in, 15
  research in, 14
  sample essay, 51–54, 94–98
  scholarship and authority in, 12, 120–129
  student research report sample, 124–125
  types of questions, 9
BioScience, 121, 271
BIOSIS Previews, 119
Birth order, personality and, 179–196
Blake, William, 197
Blind peer review, 333–334
Blume, Harvey, 145, 148
Body, of essay exam, 266
Book, citation style
  American Psychological Association, 113–114

Council of Science Editors, 115
Modern Language Association,
    112
Book clubs, 2
Book review, 17
Book Review Digest, 117
Boston Globe, 258, 260
Boy Scouts of America, 32–35
Brackets, use of, 108–109
Brain, as neural computer, 145–146
British Medical Journal, 264
Bruffee, Kenneth, 225, 233, 240
Bruner, Jerome, 49
Bullets, use of, 258
Business, 8
    bibliographic indexes, 120
    types of questions, 9
    use of case study in, 156
    use of interview in research, 145
Business memo, 257–258
Business Periodicals Index, 120
Business plan, sample writing as-
    signment, 56–57
Business Software Database, 120
Buy.com Tour, 26
Byline, 255

Cambridge Ancient History, 11
Campaign finance, 269
Campbell, K. H. S., 79–88
Capitalization, 318
Captions, 323
Care map, 20, 282
    case study, 285–289
Care plan, 286–288
Case histories, 283–285
Case study(ies)
    business, 156
    computer science, 156
    designing, 155
    format, 159–160, 220–222
    history essay, 63–67
    management, 12
    mapping patient care, 285–289
    nursing, 283–285

psychological, 17, 156, 177–178,
    179–196
qualitative research and, 142
reflecting on tutoring session,
    219–244
as research method, 155–156
revision as meaning-making,
    328–333
student participation in online
    course, 157–176
student writing, 63–67
when to use, 157
Causation, terms of, 301
Cellular differentiation, 79–88
Chagnon, Napoleon, 95
Charter schools, 50
Charts, 142
Checklists
    analysis of oral history tran-
        scripts, 201
    beginning a draft, 299
    case study design, 155
    communication on listserv, 250
    conducting interview, 147–148
    considering audience, 279
    considering purpose, 281
    drawing inferences, 214
    endings, 303
    evaluating credibility of Web
        sources, 100–101
    evaluating source material, 99
    genre, 262
    narrowing your subject, 69
    producing advocacy pamphlet,
        136
    reflective cover list, 319
    reflective questions, 208
    revising, 331
    sharing writing with others,
        311–312
    summarizing, 93–94
    survey preparation, 150
    using quotations, 108–109
    writing prompt, 58–59
Chemical Abstracts, 119

Chemistry, 8
  bibliographic indexes, 119
Childcare workers, 130–132
Citations, 111–116
  in text, 22, 101–103, 270–271
Citation sequence style, 114
Civic consequence, of student writ-
    ing, 2
Civil Disobedience, 212, 215–216
Claim, 211, 271
Class, as community, 170–175
Class charter, 320
Class trust, 268–269
Clinchy, Blythe, 5
Cloning
  scientific article on, 79–88, 123
  news article on, 258–260
Closed response, 150
Closure, 302–306
  checklist, 303
Coffin, Thomas, 26
Cohorts, 149, 151
Co-learners, 233–238
*College Composition and Communi-
    cation*, 326
College English, 326, 335
Columbus, critical inquiry on,
    63–67
Columbus: His Enterprise, 64
Comma splice, 317
Commercialism, evaluating Web
    site's, 101
Community
  class as, 170–175
  knowledge, 6–7
Community colleges, 335–337
Composition
  case study, 328–333
  interview with teacher of,
    323–328
*Comprehensive Dissertation Ab-
    stracts*, 117
Computer conferencing, 158
Computer-mediated communica-
    tion, 158

Computer science, use of case study
    in, 156
Conceptual maps, 43
Conceptual thinking, 326
*Concise Encyclopedia of Western
    Philosophy and Philosophers,
    The*, 117
Conclusions, 302–306
  checklist, 303
  in essay exam, 267
  in lab report, 302, 304–305
  in sample argument, 274–275
Condition, terms of, 301
Conflict, writing and, 327
Connected teaching, 237, 242
Connections, building, 299–302
  techniques, 300–301
Conrad, Joseph, 38
Consequence
  audience and writing with, 2–3,
    254, 278
  of student writing, 2
Contact person, on press release,
    290–292
Contemporary Authors, 117
Content
  vs. form, 3
  of writing, 46
Context, 13, 62, 66, 69, 195
Controls, experimental, 122–123,
    140
Conversations
  scholarly, 72
  writing to start, 324
Coordination, 307
Cortical map, 97
Council of Science Editors (CSE)
  citation style, 112, 114–115, 125
  paper format, 323
Council on Undergraduate Re-
    search, 141
Cover letter, for reflective portfolio,
    318–322
Credentials, 99, 100
Credibility, 272

Crick, Francis, 96
Criminal justice, bibliographic indexes, 118
Criminal Justice Abstracts, 118
Criminal Justice Periodicals Index, 118
CRIS (Combined Retrospective Index to Journals in History), 117
Critical annotated bibliography, 265–266
Critical reader, 49
Critical thinking, 283
Critical value, 183
Cross-sectional study, 183
Cross-section surveys, 149
Cultural diversity, tutoring and, 226–229
Cultural values, influence on writing, 66, 100
Cumulative Subject Index to Psychological Abstracts, 118
Currency, evaluating, 101
Current Biography, 117
Curriculum, 7–8. *See also* Disciplines; Extra-curriculum

Danneels, Jeffrey, 126, 128
Darwin, Charles, 72, 208
Data
  collecting, 13, 160, 221
  evaluation of, 13, 210–212
  finding significance in, 206–207
  qualitative, 142–144
  quantitative, 142, 144
  selecting collection methods, 159
Davis, Ossie, 272, 274
Deductive reasoning, 207–208
Deep structure, 316
DeLay, Tom, 259
Dental hygiene, 8
Descriptive outline, 307
Design
  of case study, 155
  of surveys, 2, 151–152

Details
  discovering, 45–47
  local, 223
  supportive, 296
  using appropriate, 286
Diagnoses, 286–288
Dialectical notebook, 15, 75–77
Diary of A Young Girl, 73
Difference, terms of, 301
Direct observation, 39, 142, 152
Disciplinary writing, 3
Disciplines. *See also individual disciplines*
  knowing-in-action across, 20–35
    linguistics, 20–21
    management, 22–23
    news account, 24–32
    news release, 32–35
    psychology, 21–22
  knowledge distributed into, 7–8
  presentation in, 17–18
  reflection in, 15–16
  research in, 13–14
  scholarship in, 12
  types of questions, 9–11
  ways of knowing and, 6–7
Discrepancies, identifying, 208
Discussion of results, 302
Discussion-oriented courses, 157
Dissonance, 207, 221–222, 250
Distance learning, 158
Distribution, 18–20, 318–323
  preparing a paper, 322–323
  preparing reflective portfolio, 318–322
  of professional writing, 323
Division, 307
Documentation, in nursing, 20
Draft
  defined, 294
  distilling into abstract, 307, 309–310
  focusing, 306–312
Drafting, 18–20, 294–306
  beginning, 297–299

building connections, 299–302
checklist, 299
ending, 302–306
overview, 294–297
Drama, bibliographic indexes, 116

EBSCO's Academic Search Elite, 117
Editing, 18–20, 317–318
vs. revising, 329–330
Editorial, 257, 260–261
abstract, 264
Education
example of annotation, 49–50
interview with teacher of,
216–219
reflective practice in, 216–244
Einstein, Albert, 96
Elbow, Peter, 48
Electronic bulletin board, 244–251
communication checklist, 250
Ellipsis, 109
E-mail, 244, 324
Emoticons, 170
Emotions, imagery and, 96
Empirical evidence, 275
Empowering Education, 243, 335
Encyclopedia of Chemistry, 119
Encyclopedia of Philosophy, 117
Encyclopedia of Physics, 119
*Encyclopedia of the Biological Sci-
ences,* 119
Endings, 302–306
checklist, 303
Engagement with subject matter, 39
Engineering, bibliographic indexes,
119
Engineering Encyclopedia, 119
Engineering Index, 119
English studies, composing paper
in, 323–333
Environment Index, 119
Environmental issues, 137
Environmental Protection Agency
(EPA), 126
Environmental research, 14
Environmental Working Group, 137

ERIC, 118
Error
editing and, 317–318
writerly intention and, 317–318
ESL (English as a Second Language)
students, 225–228, 244–249
Essay
academic, 17, 297–298, 327
argument, 271
etymology, 38
mainstream, 21
seminar, 322
Essay and General Literature Index,
117
Essay exam, 266–270
sample, 267–270
Ethical guidelines for research with
human subjects, 147–148
Ethics research, 14
Ethos, 272
Evaluation. *See also* Reflection
of piece of writing, 229–231
of research methods, 156–176
of source material, 98–100
of Web sites, 98–101
Evans, Mariwyn, 22–23
"Everyday Use," 296, 315
Evidence
empirical, 275
evaluating, 99, 210–212
sample argument, 272–275
statistical, 142
using to support claim, 271
Experiment, 17
Experimental research, 12, 14,
177–178
Expertise, 40–42, 69, 99, 250. *See
also* Personal knowledge
Explicating text, 12
Extracurricular literacy instruction, 2
Extra-curriculum
advocacy pamphlet, 129–137
electronic bulletin board, 244–251
genre in, 23–35
inquiry in, 67–70
memoirs, 67–70

peer review, 333–337
    presentation in, 290–292
    reflective writing in, 244–251
    research in oral history, 196–203
    scholarship in, 129–137
    writing press release, 290–292

False identities, 171–172
Faraday, Michael, 96
Federal Writers' Project, 203
Feedback, 311–312, 334
    soliciting, 325–326
Feelings, way of knowing and, 5–6
Feminist scholarship, 5, 14
Field notes, 13, 153
Field research, 198
Film, bibliographic indexes, 116
Financial analysis, 57–58
Floating quotations, 107
Flocking birds, 53
Focus groups, 14, 142, 149
Follow the Dream, 66
Follow-up questions, 148, 200–201
Font, 322
Ford, Henry, 41
Form
    vs. content, 3
    for writing. See Genres
Format
    case study, 220–222
    research paper, 180–181
    understanding, 78–88
Freewriting, 47–48
Freire, Paulo, 214–215
Freud, Sigmund, 21–22

Gangs, study of, 142, 144
Gasohol, 206–207
Gender
    online learning and, 172–175
    personality differences and,
        190–191
Genealogy, evaluation of evidence
    in, 210–211
General science, bibliographic in-
    dexes, 119

General Science Index, 119
Generative questions, 46
Genetics, understanding format,
    79–88
Genres, 16, 19. See also Academic
    genres
    advocacy pamphlet, 2, 129–137
    business plan, 57–58
    care plan, 286–288
    checklist, 262
    composition, 322
    dictates of, 257–262
    drafting and, 297, 299
    in extra-curriculum, 23–35
    mainstream essay, 21
    marketing plan, 2, 12, 18
    memoir, 67–68
    news account, 24–27, 257–260
    news release, 33–34
    in public domain, 35
    reviewing, 309
    understanding, 254–257
    writing prompt and, 58
Geographical area, 100
Gilbert, Chris, 176–179, 181, 197
Gilligan, Carol, 5
"Gimpel the Fool," 328–332
Glossing, 235
Goals, research, 155
Goldberger, Nancy, 5
Grammar errors, 317–318
Grant proposals, 324
Graphs, 142–143
Greeting, in letter, 257
Grove's Dictionary of Music and Mu-
    sicians, 117
Grub, Nelson, and Associates,
    335
Guidelines
    audience and using, 279
    ethical, 147–148
    informed consent, 181
    oral history, 147, 201
Guidelines and Principles of the
    Oral History Association, 147
Guide to Critical Reviews, 116

Harvard Guide to American History,
  117
Hayakawa, S. I., 20–21, 89–93
Headline
  for newspaper story, 259
  for press release, 291
Heart of Darkness, 38–39
Hebb, D. O., 95
Hemingway, Ernest, 96
Herring, 53
Historical Abstracts, 117
Historical circumstances, 13, 62, 66,
  69, 197
History, 7. *See also* Oral history
  bibliographic indexes, 117
  etymology, 61–62
  as inquiry, 60–67
  research in, 142, 197–198
  student writing sample, 63–67
Ho, Cliff, 127
Holocaust, 72–73
Home-schooling, 50
Home-style, 267
Honored But Invisible, 335
Horace's Compromise, excerpt, 243
how, asking, 45–47
Howard Hughes Undergraduate Re-
  search Program at University of
  Illinois, 141
Hughes, Bob, 127
Human cloning, 258–260
Humanities, 7–8
  bibliographic indexes, 116–118
  inductive reasoning and, 209
  inquiry in, 38
  types of questions, 9
  use of interview in, 145
Humanities Index, 118
Human subjects, ethical guidelines
  for research, 147–148, 155, 181,
  199–200, 221, 222
Hypothesis
  alternate, 183
  analysis of, 201
  assessing, 19, 20
  identifying in sources, 121

  in lab report, 302
  null, 183
  psychological, 177
  scientific, 10, 15
Hypothesis-driven research, 208

Idea generation, reading and,
  49–54
Ideological framework, 13
"Image of Africa, An," 38
Imagine That! 94–98
Implications, discovering, 39
Independent study, 157
Independent thinking, 218
Independent variables, 183–184
Indexes, bibliographic, 116–120
Index Medicus, 119
Index to Mathematical Papers, 119
Inductive reasoning, 207, 209
Inferences
  defined, 213
  drawing, 212–216, 248
  in nursing, 283
Informants, 145, 147, 199
Informed consent, 147–148, 155,
  181, 199–200, 221, 222
  sample form, 200
Informed reports, vs. legal documents, 284
In-kind advantages, 267–268
Inquiry, 9–11, 38–70
  asking interesting questions,
  38–40
  detail, 45–47
  expertise, 40–42
  freewriting, 47–48
  history as, 60–67
  identifying gaps in knowledge,
  54–55
  limiting the subject, 68–69
  mapping and listing, 42–45
  memoir writing and, 67–69
  reading to generate ideas, 49–54
  starting to write and, 40
  writing prompt and, 56–60
Insects, social, 51–54

Institutional mission statement, 33–34
Interdisciplinary study, 8
International Council of Shopping Malls (ICSC), 22
Internet, 99–101, 158
Interpretation, making meaning and, 331–332
Interviews
  arranging, 199
  with biology teacher, 121–123
  case study, 220
  checklist, 147
  with composition teacher, 323–328
  with education teacher, 216–219
  with history teacher, 61–63
  with nursing teacher, 282–285
  oral history, 199–201
  with psychology teacher, 176–179
  research for, 145–146
  as research method, 57, 142, 145–148
  scheduling, 147
  taping, 200
  transcripts, 145, 148, 200
  when to use, 157
In-text citation, 270–271
Introduction, 65–66
  in essay exam, 266
  in research paper, 180
  sample, 186, 268
Inverted pyramid, 260

Journal. *See* Periodical
Journal of Advanced Composition, 145
Journal of Clinical Child Psychology, 263
Juxtapositions, 300, 316

Kegan, Robert, 219
Key points, 94
Key work, referring to, 102–103
Kies, Daniel, 272–275
Kind, A. J., 79–88

King Lear, 49
Kiser, Pamela M., 221
Knowing-in-action, 4
Knowledge
  building on work of others, 72
  distributed into disciplines, 7–8
  identifying gaps in, 54–55, 69
  identifying relevant, 221
  personal, 5, 13, 40–42, 250
  procedural, 57, 140
  received, 5, 11
  research and, 140
  scholarly, 11
  ways of knowing, 5–6, 8–9
    action, 18–20
    inquiry, 9–11
    presentation, 16–18
    in psychology, 178–179
    research, 12–14
    reflection, 14–16
    scholarship, 11–12
Knowledge communities, participating in, 6–7
Knowledge-making, 250
Koning, Hans, 64, 66
Kroll, Keith, 335

L2 writers, 225–228, 244–249
Laboratory experiment, 140
Laboratory results, 153
Laboratory sciences
  argumentation in, 275
  deductive reasoning and, 208
Lab report, 17
  building connections in, 302
  statement of purpose, 300
Ladies Professional Golf Association, 25
Lamarck, Jean Baptiste, 72
Lamontagne, Steve, 26
Language. *See also* Terminology
  bibliographic indexes, 117
  choice of, 314-315
  of discipline, 182–183
  psychological, 179
  technical, 59, 88

Learning
  action, reflection and, 217–218
  articulating, 222
  writing as, 327–328
Lee, Lia, 288–289
Legal documents, 287–288
  vs. informed report, 284–285
Legislative act, 28–32
Letter to an editor, 257
Letters, 255–257, 320
"Let Us Entertain You," excerpt,
  22–23
Leutwyler, Kristin, 126–128
Library of Congress, 198
Lifelines from Our Past, excerpt, 70
Life Sciences Collection, 119
"Libidinal Types," excerpt, 21–22
'Lil' Black, 291–292
Line graph, 142
Lines, Patricia, 50
Linguistics, 20–21
Listing, 43–45, 295
List of works cited. *See* Works cited
Listserv, 172, 250
Literature, 7
  action in, 19
  bibliographic indexes, 117
  presentation in, 17–18
  reflection in, 15
  research in 13, 140
  scholarship in, 12
  types of questions, 9
Literature review/survey, 110–111,
  180, 182, 261, 270–271
  sample, 187–188
Local detail, 223
Longitudinal surveys, 150–151
Loop writing, 48
Lopez, Barry, 104–106
Los Angeles gang member study,
  142, 144

MADD (Mothers Against Drunk Dri-
  ving), 132
Magazine article, 298–299
Mainstream essay, 21

Management
  action in, 20
  knowing-in-action and, 22–23
  presentation in, 18
  reflection in, 16
  research in, 14
  sample writing assignment, 56–57
  scholarship in, 12
  types of questions, 9
Mapping, 43–45
Margins, 317
Market analysis, 14
Marketing plan, 2, 12, 18, 57–58,
  298
  excerpt, 305–306
Marketing survey, 18, 57
Marketplace considerations, prepar-
  ing paper and, 318
Martin, Casey, 24–27, 77–78
Maternal social attention, 264
Mathematical Reviews, 119
Mathematics
  bibliographic indexes, 119
  deductive reasoning and, 208
Maxwell, 96
McWhir, J., 79–88
Meaning, making, 311, 322–328
Measurements, research, 182–183
Meat packinghouse worker, oral his-
  tory, 201–203
Mechanical engineering, 8
Mechanics, errors in, 312
Medical diagnosis, vs. nursing diag-
  nosis, 287–288
MEDLINE, 119
Memo, 257–258, 319
Memoirs, 67–70
  defined, 67–68
Mental imagery, 94–98
Merchant of Venice, The, 206–207
Metacognition, 6
Metaphorical thinking, 272–275,
  314
Method, description of research
  method, 159–160, 261, 302
Microsoft Word, 333

Milgrim, Stanley, 209
Miller, Richard E., 323–328, 332
Milligan, Susan, 258–260
Mind, computational theory of, 97
Mind maps, 43
Mission statement, 57, 58
MLA Bibliography, 118
MLA International Bibliography, 117
Modern Language Association
    (MLA)
  citation style, 112–113, 222, 237
  paper format, 323
*Modern World Drama: An Encyclo-
    pedia,* 116
Moody's Industry Review, 120
Murphy, Thomas Dowd, 62
Music, 7
  bibliographic indexes, 117
Music Index, 117
Myers-Briggs Type Indicator, 182,
    189

National Undergraduate Research
    Observatory at Northern Ari-
    zona University and Lowell Ob-
    servatory, 141
Natural philosophy, 7
Natural sciences, 7, 8
  annotated bibliography, 265–266
  bibliographic indexes, 119
  types of questions, 9
Nature, 54
Nelson, Willie, 291–292
Networked systems, 8
New Cambridge Modern History,
    117
"New Counterculture, The," ex-
    cerpt, 49–50
New Criticism, 13
*New Dictionary of Modern Sculp-
    ture,* 116
New York Times Film Reviews, 116
New York Times Theatre Reviews,
    116
News account, 24–27, 257–260,
    298–299

News release, 33–34
Nicklaus, Jack, 25
Nike Lakeland Classic, 26
Nike Tour, 26
Norman, Elie, 283–285
North, Stephen, 232
North American Nursing Diagnosis
    Association, 287–288
Note taking
  during interview, 148
  reflective, 75–77
Novell, 8
Null hypothesis, 183
Nursing, 8
  action in, 20
  care map, 20, 282, 285–288
  genre in, 282–288
  interview with teacher of,
    282–285
  presentation in, 18
  reflection in, 16
  research in, 14
  scholarship in, 12
  types of questions, 10
Nursing diagnoses, 286–288

Obedience study, 209
Objection, 272
  sample argument, 274
Objectivity, 101, 144
Observation, 39, 142, 152
Observational log, 54–55
Observational notebook, 15,
    152–155
  when to use, 157
Observer, impact on lab experimen-
    tation, 14
Occupational therapy, 8
Olinger, Ford, 25
Online assessment questionnaire,
    151–152
Online courses, case study of stu-
    dent participation, 157–176
Online databases
  business, 120
  humanities, 117–118

natural sciences, 119
social sciences, 118
Online magazine article, 298–299
Online source, citation style
    American Psychological Associa-
        tion, 114, 116
    Council of Science Editors, 115
    Modern Language Association,
        113
Open-ended response, 150
Oral history, 61
    analysis of transcripts, 201
    conducting research in, 196–203
    power of, 201–203
Oral History Association, 201
Oral History: Evaluation Guidelines,
    201
Organizational plan, 57
Outline, 295
    constructing, 307–309
    descriptive, 307
    history paper, 65–66
*Oxford Companion to American Lit-
    erature*, 117
Oxford Companion to Art, 116
*Oxford Companion to Classical Lit-
    erature*, 117
*Oxford Companion to English Liter-
    ature*, 117

Paca, Marge, 201
PAIS International, 118
Palmer, Arnold, 25
Paragraphs, drafting and, 297
Parallelism, 307
Paraphrasing, 101, 105–106, 212
Partially limited response, 150
Pathos, 272
Pedagogical moves, 168–169
Pedagogy of the Oppressed,
    214–215
Peer Centered, 251
Peer review, 333–336
    reviewer's rubric, 334
    sample, 335–337

Peer tutors, 230, 251
Periodical, citation style
    American Psychological Associa-
        tion, 114
    Council of Science Editors, 115
    Modern Language Association,
        113
Personal knowledge, 5, 13, 40–42,
    250
Personality, birth order and,
    179–196
Perspective, knowledge and, 5
Philosophy, bibliographic indexes,
    117
Phrase, transitional, 300
Physics, 8
    bibliographic indexes, 119
Pinker, Steven, 94–98, 106, 145
Plagiarism, 102, 111
    samples, 104–106
Poetics, 7
Points of ellipsis, 109
Political action committee, 269
Political agendas, influence on writ-
    ing, 66
Political incumbency, 267–269
Political science exam, sample es-
    say, 267–269
*Politics of Writing at the Two-Year
    College, The*, 335
Poole, Dawn M., 157–176
Portfolio, 44
    reflective, 318–323
*Poverty and Human Resources Ab-
    stracts*, 118
Predictor variable, 150
Preponderance of evidence (POE),
    210–211
Presentation, 9, 16–18, 254–292
    academic genres, 262–277
    abstract, 180, 261, 263–264
    argument, 271–275
    critical annotated bibliography,
        265–266
    essay, 17, 297–298, 327

essay exam, 266–270
lab report, 17
literature review/survey,
    110–111, 180, 182, 187–188,
    261, 269–271
scientific paper, 17
audience and, 278
dictates of genre, 257–262
in extra-curriculum, 290–292
in nursing, 282–291
understanding genre, audience,
    and purpose, 254–257
working with an audience,
    277–280
writing press release, 290–292
writing with purpose, 280–282
Present study, 180
sample, 188–189
Press release
features, 290–291
sample, 291–292
writing, 290–292
Prewriting, 43–45
Primary sources, 63, 72–75, 198
Primary traits, 231
Problem solving, in nursing, 282
Procedural, vs. personal, 13
Procedural knowledge, 57, 140
Procedural terms, 59
Professional Golfer's Association, 24
Professional writing, distribution of,
    323, 326
Profile, 321
Prompts. See Writing Prompts
Proof, academic, 272
Proposal, 321–322
PsychINFO, 118
Psychological Abstracts, 118
Psychological framework, 13
Psychology, 8
action in, 20
bibliographic indexes, 118
case study, 159, 179–196
citation in, 112
doing research in, 176–196

interview with teacher of,
    176–179
knowing-in-action in, 21–22
presentation in, 17–18
reflection in, 15–16
research in, 14, 142, 176–196
scholarship in, 12
types of questions, 9
Publication date, in citation, 112
Public consequence, of student writ-
    ing, 2
Public domain, genre in, 35
Public health, use of case study in,
    156
Public speaking, talking points and,
    324–325
Publishing, 294
Punctuation, 313
Purpose, 48
matching with audience, 285–288
reviewing, 309
selecting sources and, 74
statement of, 294
understanding, 254–257
writing with, 16–17, 19, 233,
    280–282
checklist, 281

Qualitative research, 142–144
interview method and, 145
Quantitative research, 142, 144
Questions
asking appropriate, 200–201
asking interesting, 38–40
biased, 150
to evaluate source material, 98
framing, 9–11
generative, 46
scientific, 122
survey, 150
Questionnaires
design of, 2, 151–152
research and, 140, 142
Quotations
checklist, 108–109

effective use of, 107
floating, 107
ineffective use of, 107–108
using, 101, 106–109

Racism, U.N. conference on,
    260–261
Rainforest Action Network, 137
Random sampling, 149
Rating scale, 150
Reader-based mode of writing, 231
Reader-based perspective, 303, 306
Readers
    assessing writing, 313
    drawing inferences, 213
    literature and, 13
    summarizing for, 103–104
Readership, 323. *See also* Audience
Reading
    to generate ideas, 49–54
    reflective note taking and, 75–77
    strategy, 89
Reading log, 15, 17, 54–55
Real world connections, reflection
    and, 217–218, 241–242
Reason, argument and, 272
Reasoning
    deductive, 207–208
    inductive, 207, 209
Rebuttal, 271
    sample argument, 274–275
Received knowledge, 5, 11
Reconnecting, 315–317
Recording interviews, 148
Record keeping, 20
References, 111–116, 181, 222, 270
    sample, 192, 239
    in text, 22, 101–103, 270–271
Reflecting notes, 75–77
Reflection, 9, 14–16, 206–251
    case study, 219–244
    conclusions and, 304
    deductive vs. inductive reasoning,
        207–209
    defining, 216
    drawing inferences, 39, 212–216

electronic bulletin board, 244–251
evaluation of data, 209–212
finding significance in data,
    206–207
learning, action and, 217–218
questions to ask, 208
reflective practice in education,
    216–244
writing and, 217–219
Reflection paper, 218, 240
Reflective cover letter, 319
Reflective knowledge, 58
Reflective portfolio, 318–322
Reflective thinking, 225
Refocusing, 303, 306–311
Replication, of experiment, 14, 19,
    122
Research, 9, 12–14, 140–203
    for business plan, 57
    defined, 140–144
    historical, 142, 197–198
    informed consent, 147–148
    for interview, 147
    literature survey, 270
    oral history, 196–203
    psychological, 142, 176–196
    qualitative, 142–144
    quantitative, 142, 144
    types of data, 142
    undergraduate, 140–142
Research instruments, 145–176
    case study, 156
    evaluating, 156–176
    interview method, 145–148
    observational notebook, 152–155
    psychology, 177
    surveys, 149–152
Research paper, 2
    format, 180–182
    preparing, 180
    sample, 185–196
Research subjects, 155, 160. *See also*
    Informed consent
Restructuring, 314–316
Results, in lab report, 302
Retail management, 8

Reviewer's rubric, 333
Revising, 18–20, 311–316, 324
  checklist, 331
  vs. editing, 329–330
  meaning-making and, 328–332
  overview, 311–315
  restructuring and reconnecting,
    315–317
Reynolds, Mark, 336
Rhetoric, 7, 271–272
Rural Sociology Abstracts, 118

Salutation, 257
Sampling, 183
Sandia National Laboratory, 126, 128
Sandwiching, 110
Scalia, Antonin, 25
Schnieke, A. E., 79–88
Schoën, Donald, 4
Scholarly conversation, 72
Scholarly knowledge, 11
Scholarship, 9, 11–12, 72–137
  advocacy pamphlet and, 129–137
  bibliographical indexes, 116–120
  in biology, 120–129
  citing sources, 111–116
  evaluating source materials,
    98–100
  integrating ideas with source ma-
    terial, 109–111
  selecting sources, 72–75
  summarizing, 77–98
  taking reflective notes, 75–77
  understanding contours of argu-
    ment, 88–98
  understanding format, 78–88
  understanding specialized lan-
    guage, 88
  writing with sources, 100–109
Science Citation Index, 119, 280
Sciences. *See also* Biology; Chem-
    istry; Laboratory sciences; Nat-
    ural sciences; Physics
  argumentation in, 276–277
  bibliographic indexes, 119
  inquiry in, 39

Scientific American, 126
Scientific journal
  abstracts, 263
  format, 261
Scientific paper, 17
Scientific questioning, 122
SCISEARCH, 119
Scope, evaluating Web source, 100
Secondary sources, 72–75
Secretary of Agriculture, letter to,
    255–256
Semantics, sample essay, 89–93
Seminar essay, 326–327
Sentence, transition, 300
Sentence outline, 307–308
Service learning, 217–218
Seymour, Roz, 282–285
Shakespeare, William, 49, 206
Shift report, 283–285
Shor, Ira, 244, 336
sic, 108
Singer, Isaac, 323–324, 326
Sis, Peter, 66
60 Minutes, 145
Sizer, Theodore, 243
Skocpol, Teda, 107
Social promotion, 211–212
Social psychology perspective,
    178–179
Social sciences, 7–8
  bibliographic indexes, 118
  inductive reasoning and, 209
  research in, 140
  types of questions, 9
  use of interview in, 145
Social Sciences Index, 118
"Societies as Organisms, On,"
    51–54
Sociological Abstracts, 118
Sociology, 8
  bibliographic indexes, 118
Source material
  evaluating, 98–100
  integrating with ideas, 109–111
Sources, 11, 15. *See also* Critical an-
    notated bibliography

primary, 63, 72–75, 198
referencing, 270–271
secondary, 72–75
selecting, 72–75
writing with, 100–109
Sowa, Maureen, 61–63, 67
Speakers' bureaus, 199
Speaking, talking points and, 324–325
Specialized language, 88
Spelling errors, 316–317
Spellmeyer, Kurt, 111
Sponsorship, corporate, 101
Standard and Poor's Register of Corporations, 120
Standardized testing, 211–212
Statement of reason, 180
sample, 186
Statistical evidence, 142
Stavrianos, L. S., 70
Stem-cell research, 280–281
Stevens, John Paul, 24
Stratified surveys, 149
Structure
deep, 315
restructuring, 314–316
thinking structurally, 330–332
of writing, 46
Student research, 140–142, 178
Subheadings, 302, 307
Subject matter
determining what you know, 40–42
engagement with, 39
narrowing, 68–69
Subjects, research, 155, 160. *See also* Informed consent
Subordination, 307, 315
Substantive arguments, 94
Subtopics, 45
Sulloway, Frank, 187–188
Summarizing, 77–98
checklist, 93–94
conclusions and, 304
in drawing inferences, 212–215
note taking and, 75

for readers, 103–104
understanding contours of argument, 88–98
understanding format, 78–88
understanding specialized language, 88
use of, 101
Summary of results and conclusions, 181
sample, 189–190
Summer Undergraduate Research Opportunities at The University of North Carolina at Chapel Hill, 141
Supportive detail, 296
Surface errors, 317
Surveys
cross-section surveys, 149
designing, 151–152
longitudinal, 150–151
management, 14
preparation checklist, 150
research and, 140
stratified surveys, 149
when to use, 157
Syntax, 313–314

Tables, 142, 318
Talbot, Margaret, 49–50
Talking points, 324–325
Taping interviews, 200
Tarule, Jill, 5
Taxonomy, to organize materials, 22
Technical fields, 8
"Teenage Drinking and Driving," 133–135
Terkel, Studs, 196
Terminology
procedural, 59
signifying relationship, 300–301
specialized, 261, 279
technical, 59, 88
Termites, 52–53
Text
citation styles within, 113–115

explicating, 12
reading history scholarship, 66
Theoretical perspective, research
    and, 155
Theory, in lab report, 302
Thesis, 62, 330
Thesis statement, 66, 294,
    297–299
    sample, 273
Thick description, 155, 220–221
Thinking
    conceptual, 326
    critical, 282–283
    metaphoric, 272–275, 309
    reflective, 225
    structural, 330–332
Thomas, Clarence, 25
Thomas, Lewis, 39, 51–54, 107
Thoreau, Henry David, 212,
    215–216
Time
    essay exam and use of, 266–267
    for interview, 147
    terms for, 301
Timeline, 69–70
    creating, 198–199
Time period, 100
Title page, 180, 322
    samples, 185, 224
Topic
    choosing, 180, 197
    narrowing, 68–69
Topic outline, 307–308
Topic sentences, 309
Transcripts, interview, 145, 147,
    200–201
Transitional phrases, 315–316
Transitions, 295, 299–302
Triad (trivium), 7
Triangulation, 147, 155
Tutoring
    of L2 writers, 244–249
    peer, 233, 251
    reflecting on, 219–244
    roles to avoid, 234
Twentieth Century Authors, 117

Two-Year College English, 335
Type size, 321

Undergraduate research, 140–142
Undergraduate Research Opportuni-
    ties at the University of Pitts-
    burgh, 141
Underlining, 93–94
"Under Paid Childcare Workers,"
    130–132
United Nations, 260–261
United States, protection of water
    infrastructure, 126–128
U.S. Circuit Court of Appeals, 9th, 25
U.S. Supreme Court, 24, 32
University of Pittsburgh web site,
    undergraduate research projects
    at, 141

Verb tenses, errors in, 318
Visual learners, 43
Volatile organic compounds (VOCs),
    127

Walker, Alice, 296, 315
Wall Street Journal Index, 120
Water supply, protection of,
    126–128
Watson, James D., 96
Web sites
    evaluating credibility of, 99–101
    postings, 157–175, 277
Weisberger, Ron, 216–219, 239
West, Candace, 243
West, Cornel, 111
what, asking, 45–47
when, asking, 45–47
where, asking, 45–47
who, asking, 45–47
Wilmut, Ian, 72, 78–88, 123–124
Wired magazine, 145, 299
"Women's Place in Everyday Talk,"
    excerpt, 241
Woods, Tiger, 25–26
Words and Children, excerpts,
    20–21, 89–93

Works cited, 111–116, 181, 222, 270
  sample, 192, 239
  in text, 22, 101–103, 270–271
World Wide Web
  environmental issues site, 137
  evaluating credibility of informa-
    tion found, 98–99
    checklist, 100–101
  as source of informants, 199
  undergraduate research funding
    sources, 141
Worthington, Robyn, 185–196
Writer-based mode of writing, 231
Writerly intention, error and, 318
Writing
  with consequence, 2–3, 254
  conventions of, 254
  disciplines and, 3, 7–8
  freewriting, 47–48
  integrating ideas and source mate-
    rial into, 109–111

  as learning, 327–328
  loop, 48
  participating in knowledge com-
    munities, 6–7
  as production, 294
  with purpose, 16–17, 19, 233,
    280–282
  reflection and, 217–219
  review of, 311–312
  with sources, 100–109
  as way of knowing, 3–6
  writer-based mode of, 231
Writing instruction, extracurricular, 2
Writing prompts, 56–61
  checklist, 58–59
  determining parameters, 69
  history essay, 64–65
  reflective writing, 220
  response to, 3–5

Zimmerman, Don H., 243